MEMORY, JESUS, AND THE SYNOPTIC GOSPELS

Society of Biblical Literature

Resources for Biblical Study

Tom Thatcher, New Testament Editor

Number 59

MEMORY, JESUS, AND THE SYNOPTIC GOSPELS

MEMORY, JESUS, AND THE SYNOPTIC GOSPELS

By
Robert K. McIver

Society of Biblical Literature
Atlanta

MEMORY, JESUS, AND THE SYNOPTIC GOSPELS

Copyright © 2011 by the Society of Biblical Literature

All rights reserved. No part of this work may be reproduced or transmitted in any form or by any means, electronic or mechanical, including photocopying and recording, or by means of any information storage or retrieval system, except as may be expressly permitted by the 1976 Copyright Act or in writing from the publisher. Requests for permission should be addressed in writing to the Rights and Permissions Office, Society of Biblical Literature, 825 Houston Mill Road, Atlanta, GA 30329 USA.

Library of Congress Cataloging-in-Publication Data

McIver, Robert K. (Robert Kerry), 1953–
  Memory, Jesus, and the Synoptic Gospels / by Robert K. McIver.
     p. cm. — (Society of Biblical Literature resources for biblical study ; no. 59)
  Includes bibliographical references (p.   ) and indexes.
  ISBN 978-1-58983-560-3 (pbk. : alk. paper) -- ISBN 978-1-58983-561-0 (electronic format)
  1. Bible. N.T. Gospels—Criticism, interpretation, etc. 2. Memory—Religious aspects—Christianity. 3. Jesus Christ—Historicity. I. Title.
  BS2555.52.M35 2011
  232.9'08—dc22   2011014983

Printed on acid-free, recycled paper conforming to
ANSI/NISO Z39.48-1992 (R1997) and ISO 9706:1994
standards for paper permanence.

Contents

List of Tables ix
List of Figures x
Preface xi

Introduction 1

Part 1: Personal and Collective Memory

1. Eyewitness Memory 5
   Issues Surrounding the Use of Eyewitness Testimony in
       Gospel Studies   5
   The Characteristics of Eyewitness Testimony   10
   Eyewitness Case Study 1: A Foiled Gun Shop Robbery in
       Burnaby, Vancouver   12
   Eyewitness Case Study 2: John Dean's Testimony   16

2. Transience and the Reliability of Long-Term Human Memory 21
   Seven Frailties of Human Memory   21
   Long-Term Human Memory and the Gospels   22
   Forgetting Curves   23
   Rates of Memory Loss During the First Five Years   29
   Rates of Loss for Memories up to Fifty Years Old   35
   Conclusion: Memory Stable after the First Five Years   39

3. Personal Event Memories 41
   Flashbulb Memories Perhaps Exempt from Transience   41
   The Reliability of Flashbulb Memories up to Three Years Later   44
   Flashbulb Memories as Personal Event Memories   49
   The Reliability of Personal Event Memories up to Fifty Years Later   53
   Conclusions   57

CONTENTS

4. Suggestibility and Bias 59
   Suggestibility and False Memories   60
   Hindsight and Other Memory Biases   71
   Memories as Reconstructions from Various Memory Subsystems   76

5. Collective Memory..81
   Elusive Nature and Explanatory Power of Collective Memory   82
   Experimental Evidence for Collective Memory   84
   The Influence of the Present on Collective Memory   87
   Collective Memory in Oral Societies   91
   Collective Memory Eight Decades after Halbwachs   93

Part 2: Jesus Traditions as Memory

6. Collective Memory as an Explanation of Gospel Origins...........................97
   Collective Memory and Gospel Studies   98
   Confabulation and *formgeschichtliche* Explanations of Gospel Origins   99
   Confabulations in Collective Memories   103
   Jesus as Teacher, and the Disciples as Preservers of the Jesus Traditions 110
   Kenneth Bailey's Description of Formal, Controlled Oral Traditions   115
   Collective Memory in James D. G. Dunn's *Jesus Remembered*   117
   Conclusions   120

7. Eyewitness Memory and the Gospel Traditions... 123
   Characteristics of Written Texts Derived from Eyewitness Traditions   123
   The Pericope Form and Eyewitness Traditions in the Gospels   125
   From Eyewitness Memory to Written Gospels   127
   The Apophthegmata (or Chreiai) as a Case Study of Potential
       Eyewitness Material   131

8. Memory Frailties and the Gospel Traditions.. 143
   Transience and the Gospel Traditions   143
   Personal Event Memories, the Gospel Traditions, and Transience   145
   Source Documents and the Frailty of Transience   148
   Suggestibility and the Gospel Traditions   153
   Suggestibility and the Possibility of Nonauthentic Jesus Tradition   157
   Bias and the Gospel Traditions   158
   Conclusions   160

CONTENTS

9. Collective Memory, Jesus as Teacher, and the Jesus Traditions 163
    Jesus as a Teacher   164
    Collective Memories of Jesus' Teachings and the Jesus Traditions   168
    Gospel Traditions of Jesus' Teaching: Parables   170
    Gospel Traditions of Jesus' Teaching: Aphorisms   176
    Jesus as the Origin of the Teachings Traditions   180

10. Conclusions: Memory, Jesus, and the Gospels 183

Appendix A. The Potential Pool of Eyewitnesses at the Time the Gospels
    Were Written 189
    First-Century Life Expectancy   189
    The Potential Pool of Eyewitnesses to the Life and Ministry of Jesus 202

Works Cited 211

Index of Ancient Texts and Authors 229
Index of Modern Authors 233
Subject Index 239

List of Tables

1.1. Yuille and Cutshall's Analysis of Accuracy of Eyewitness Reports	14
3.1. The Accuracy of Fifty-Year-Old Eyewitness Memories of World War II Compared to General Knowledge	55
4.1. An Example of Hindsight Bias: Mean Probabilities Assigned to Each Outcome of the War between the British and Gurkas	72
7.1. A Greek-Text Example of an Inquiry Story Apophthegm (Mark 12:13–17 // Luke 20:20–26)	136
7.2. An English-Text Example of an Inquiry Story Apophthegm (Mark 12:13–17 // Luke 20:20–26)	136
7.3. A Greek-Text Example of a Correction Story Apophthegm (Matt 8:18–22 // Luke 9:57–62)	139
7.4. An English-Text Example of a Correction Story Apophthegm (Matt 8:18–22 // Luke 9:57–62)	139
9.1. The Parable of the Sower in Matthew and Mark (Greek)	172
9.2. The Parable of the Sower in Matthew and Mark (English)	173
9.3. A Greek-Text Example of the Stability of Aphorisms in the Synoptic Gospels (Matt 7:7–11 // Luke 11:9–13)	177
9.4. An English-Text Example of the Stability of Aphorisms in the Synoptic Gospels (Matt 7:7–11 // Luke 11:9–13)	177
9.5. Greek-Text Examples of the Stability of Aphorisms in the Synoptic Gospels (Matt 5:13–16, 6:22–23 and Luke 11:33–36, 14:34–35)	178
9.6. English-Text Examples of the Stability of Aphorisms in the Synoptic Gospels (Matt 5:13–16, 6:22–23 and Luke 11:33–36, 14:34–35)	179
A1. Frier's Life Table for the Roman Empire	196
A2. Coale-Demeny South and West Models Level 3	200
A3. Surviving Eyewitnesses of Jesus at Later Time Periods	208

List of Figures

2.1. Ebbinghause percent "saving" in relearning: up to two days	24
2.2. Ebbinghaus percent "saving" in relearning: up to thirty-one days	25
2.3. Forgetting curve for lists of nouns	27
2.4. Retention curves for four-year-old autobiographical memories	32
2.5. Retention curves and retrieval cues	33
2.6. Bahrich: Spanish in permastore	36
2.7. Retention of Spanish vocabulary for periods of up to fifty years	37
4.1. Marital satisfaction over twenty years of marriage	75

Preface

While working on aspects of orality and the Synoptic Problem in 1998, it occurred to me that I should extend my reading to incorporate memory studies as they were found in the discipline of psychology. That impulse was the beginning of an intriguing and at times challenging exploration, and now, more than a decade later, this book is the eventual product. The topic of human memory and its characteristics dominates most of its pages, and although I have written on the Synoptic Problem elsewhere, in this manuscript the topic has shrunk to near invisibility. The intellectual journey that has led to this new perspective has been one of fascination and excitement, some of which I hope has remained visible, despite the constraints of formal academic writing.

Along the way a large number of individuals and institutions have been very generous with their help. I would like to express my warm thanks to the following institutions: my employing body, Avondale College and the South Pacific Division of the Seventh-day Adventist Church, for the six months' release from teaching in 1998 and a further six months in 2005 and 2010; the Avondale College Foundation and the Deutscher Akademischer Austauschdienst for their monetary underwriting of the time I spent in library research in Tübingen, Germany, in 1998 and 2010; Theologische Hochschule Friedensau for their support for several further trips to the Tübingen libraries during my twelve months' secondment between 2003 and 2004; and Avondale College Foundation for further underwriting the costs of my research leave in 2005 and 2010. Nor should I forget the various conversation partners who have helped clarify my thinking: partners such as Rainer Riesner, Armin Baum, Bernhard Oestreich, Herman Lichtenberger, Grenville Kent, and Vivienne Watts. My thanks also to Udo Schnelle, Hermann Lichtenberger and Scott Caulley,

James D. G. Dunn and Brent Holmberg, Alan Kirk and Tom Thatcher, and Risto Uro and Istvan Czachesz for invitations to explore aspects of my ideas with the Neutestamentlich Seminar at Halle University, the German-English research seminar at Universität Tübingen, the "Historical Jesus" Seminar of Studiorum Novi Testamenti Societas, the "Mapping Memory: Tradition, Texts, and Identity" Consultation at the Society of Biblical Literature meetings, and the "Mind, Society and Tradition" section of the International Meetings of the Society of Biblical Literature, respectively, as well as organizers of various ANZATS/ANZSTS and ANZABS conferences at which I have been permitted to present various aspects of my research. A special thanks to Tom Thatcher—for continual encouragement and exceptional editorial insight. Thanks are also due to my copyeditors Don Hansen, Doug Robertson, and Stella Tarakson; and to Richard Anderson, the interlibrary loans librarian of Avondale College. Most important, my warm thanks go to my family, who have followed me around the globe and who have endured a number of long separations as my research has progressed. To these and many others, I owe a deep debt of gratitude.

RKM; Martinsville, NSW 2265; December 2010

Introduction

Jesus was crucified within a few years of 31 C.E.,[1] while the appearances of the Gospels of Matthew, Mark, and Luke are usually dated somewhere between 60 and 90 C.E. (e.g., Schnelle 2002, 244, 266, 288; Kümmel 1975, 98, 120, 151, 246). These dates presuppose a period of at least thirty to sixty years between events in the life of Jesus and the time at which they were recorded in the Gospels. Thus, before it was written down, the Jesus tradition was almost certainly preserved in human memory for many years,[2] if not decades. Much can happen to traditions that are preserved in human memories for this length of time.

This simple observation has been the catalyst for much careful academic scrutiny of the character of the Gospel traditions. Although the intensity of engagement with the question varies from decade to decade, it is a theme that is constantly present in Gospel studies, and in some periods the topic has been researched with near obsessional intensity. Nor should this be surprising, given the centrality of Jesus and his teachings to Christianity. If one is to form an assessment of Jesus, then, some assessment must be made of the qualities of the available sources of information about him.

This book brings a new dimension to the ongoing discussion about the Gospel traditions. It does so by exploring many of the insights provided by the discipline of psychology. Extensive experimental investigation of human memory has been taking place for well over a century. Yet despite the awareness in Gospel studies of the importance that memory must have played in the preservation of the traditions about Jesus, the insights provided by experimental psychology have only been considered in very gen-

---

1. Dates between 26 and 36 have been suggested for the crucifixion of Jesus, and no real consensus has emerged. The options are canvassed in Riesner 1998, 35–58.
2. One cannot discount the existence of some written records earlier than the extant Gospels. Their potential contribution will be evaluated in chapter 8.

eral terms, if at all, in evaluating the Gospel traditions. The following pages will go some way to filling that lacuna.

Human memory is complex. Assessing its impact on the traditions of Jesus found within the Gospels will require the consideration of a range of different factors. Some of the topics that will appear in the following pages include: forgetting curves; long-term memory for languages and autobiographical details; flashbulb and other personal event memories; false memories; hindsight bias; the characteristics of eyewitness memory; collective memory; and confabulation. Along the way, new questions will be asked, such as: Are there personal event memories in the Gospels? How many eyewitnesses of Jesus were likely to have been alive at the time of the writing of the Gospels? What implications flow from the observation that some of the Gospel stories show characteristics that are consistent with the view that they originated from eyewitnesses? My own memories of events of thirty years ago are fragmentary at best and probably suspect, so why should the memories preserved in the Gospel accounts be any different? Are there known mechanisms for reliably preserving memories over such long periods, or must the Gospel materials be treated with the same skepticism with which other legends of distant historical figures are treated? Each of these questions will be addressed somewhere in the following pages.

The content of this book is organized in two parts. Part 1 (chs. 1–5) largely deals with what is known about individual autobiographic memories and collective memory. The first chapter introduces the characteristics of eyewitness memory. The following three chapters deal specifically with the strengths and frailties of the memory of individuals. They explore the potential impact that transience, suggestibility, and hindsight bias can have on eyewitness testimony. The final chapter in part 1 moves away from the memories of individuals to a consideration of the "memory" of groups, so-called collective memory.

Part 2 (chs. 6–10) uses the observations made in part 1 to form conclusions concerning the qualities of various kinds of tradition that can be identified in the Synoptic Gospels. It also attempts to sketch a possible model for the development and transmission of the Gospel traditions.

This, then, is a broad preview of the journey to be undertaken. As well as being largely unknown in Gospel studies, some of the experiments that will be reported are surprising and interesting in their own right and will thereby provide entertainment as well as insight along the way. The journey will begin with an examination of the characteristics of eyewitness memory (ch. 1).

Part 1
Personal and Collective Memory

1
Eyewitness Memory

Before they were written in the Gospels, the teachings and deeds of Jesus were preserved in human memory—with all its frailties—for a period that is almost certain to extend several years and could well have even been as long as thirty to sixty years. Thus, how well the Gospel traditions represent the life and teachings of Jesus depends very much on how well eyewitnesses and other transmitters of the traditions would have been able to remember them over a long period of time. Later parts of this book will explore some of the social dimensions of collective memory and the possible contribution of semiformalized mechanisms for oral transmission of tradition. Such group processes will be found to be of great significance in the picture that finally emerges. But underlying each of these group processes is the memory of individuals. It is the quality of the individual memories making up the combined group "memory" that determines the overall accuracy of the collective memory that is eventually formed. Thus, underlying every subsequent step of this investigation will be the issue of how much the frailties of human memory could have impacted the reliability of the memories of the individual eyewitnesses as they contributed to the formation and transmission of the traditions about Jesus. Thus the strengths and frailties of the memory of *individual eyewitnesses* must be addressed from the start, and they will be the focus of this and the following three chapters.

Issues Surrounding the Use of Eyewitness Testimony in Gospel Studies

Eyewitnesses are featured among the important sources of the Gospel traditions by both ancient and modern authors (e.g., Luke 1:2; 2 Pet 1:16; Bauckham 2006; Byrskog 2002, 65–94). Quite varied assessments of the qualities of the Gospel traditions have been made from this datum point.

Some argue that the contribution of eyewitness memory should be taken as evidence of the overall authenticity of the Gospel accounts, while others consider the presence of eyewitness memory should rather be taken as evidence that the Gospel traditions cannot but have significantly changed between the death of Jesus and the time the Gospels were written. The various positions taken by those who invoke the qualities of eyewitnesses in their analysis of the Gospel traditions underline the need for the careful examination of the qualities of human memory that will take place in this and subsequent chapters.

Richard Bauckham is prominent among those who use the contribution of eyewitness testimony as evidence of the trustworthiness of the Gospel traditions. At several places in *Jesus and the Eyewitnesses: The Gospel as Eyewitness Testimony*, Bauckham reacts to the model of the development of the Gospel traditions espoused by "most New Testament scholars and students," which envisages that "a long process of anonymous transmission in the communities intervened between their testimony [the testimony of the eyewitnesses to the events] and the writing of the Gospels" (Bauckham 2006, 6). He proposes a quite different model and begins building his case by considering one of the fragments that have survived from the early second-century writer Papias. In it Papias cites a very short chain of transmission as the authority for what he says: a chain that begins with some named disciples of Jesus and ends with elders and their disciples who are still living. Bauckham underlines the fact that Papias does not cite anonymous community tradition but rather cites a short chain of tradents giving authoritative accounts of what actual eyewitnesses said. As he says, "The model of traditions passing from one named individual to another—as distinct from the purely communal transmission imagined by most Gospels scholars—is in fact the model with which later-second-century Christian writers worked" (Bauckham 2006, 34–35). On this basis, and that of a careful analysis of the patterns of whether names are included in the various Gospel accounts, Bauckham concludes that:

> in the period up to the writing of the Gospels, gospel traditions were connected with named and known eyewitnesses, people who had heard the teachings of Jesus from his lips and committed it to memory, people who had witnessed the events of his ministry, death and resurrection and themselves had formulated the stories about these events that they told. These eyewitnesses did not merely set going a process of oral transmission that soon went its own way without reference to them. They

remained throughout their lifetimes the sources and, in some sense that may have varied for figures of central or more marginal significance, the authoritative guarantors of the stories they continued to tell. (Bauckham 2006, 93)

Among these witnesses, the Twelve held a special place. They were, in a sense, "the official body of eyewitnesses" (Bauckham 2006, 146), as is perhaps shown by the fact that, when choosing a replacement for Judas Iscariot, the significant criterion was that the replacement needed to have accompanied the disciples and Jesus from the baptism of John until the resurrection (Acts 1:21–22). Furthermore, as evidence of the reliability of his account, in his preface to his Gospel, Luke says his material is derived from those "who from the beginning were eyewitnesses and ministers of the word" (Luke 1:2, NRSV).[1] Bauckham also suggests that, like other ancient historians, but unlike modern historians, the Gospel writers "substantially incorporated testimony into their own writing" (Bauckham 2006, 491).

Bauckham nuances his reconstruction by recognizing the importance of community retelling of the Gospel stories and the fact that modern individualism is not to be found among early Christians. Nevertheless, he insists that, while versions of the stories of Jesus had currency in the various early Christian circles, the testimony of eyewitnesses was given priority among them.

In chapter 13 of his book, he considers the fallibility of human memory and the effect that this can have on the reliability of eyewitness testimony. After frankly acknowledging the various frailties of memory, he notes that there are some conditions that allow for the formation of reliable recollective memories and that these are the types of conditions under which the memories of Jesus were formed. For example, the Gospels recount memorable and unusual events; the events recounted were salient to the eyewitnesses in that they were of considerable personal and group significance; the eyewitnesses were emotionally involved; the stories are told with vivid imagery; they contain irrelevant detail and were frequently rehearsed (Bauckham, 2006, 341–46). In fact, the forms identified in the Gospel traditions by form critics should be considered to be like the personal story schemata noted by such psychologists as David Rubin. These schemas would have been used by the earliest narrators and polished as they frequently

---

1. καθὼς παρέδοσαν ἡμῖν οἱ ἀπ' ἀρχῆς αὐτόπται καὶ ὑπηρέται γενόμενοι τοῦ λόγου (Luke 1:2).

retold the stories. The reliability of the memories of Jesus is also enhanced by the memorization that would have taken place among the eyewitnesses of Jesus teaching, by the twelve disciples, and by other teachers within early Christianity. "Memorization," Bauckham claims, is a means of preserving the tradition "faithfully with a minimum of change" (2006, 305).

The role attributed to memory in writings of Werner Kelber forms an interesting contrast to the role it is given by Bauckham. In several places Kelber differentiates between memory processes that are based on what he describes as "cold memory" and those based on processes relating to "hot memory." Kelber characterizes as "cold memory" the suggested memory process put forward by Birger Gerhardsson, who argued that the disciples mechanistically committed the teachings of Jesus to memory, and these memories were then passively transmitted by means of continuous repetition (Kelber 2002, 61; 2005, 232). Memory, Kelber insists, does not function in this manner. "Rather, memory selects and modifies subjects and figures of the past in order to make them serviceable to the image the community wishes to cultivate of itself. Socialization and memory mutually condition each other, seeking in the last analysis preservation not of the remembered past but of group identity" (2002, 56). Such memory Kelber describes as "hot memory, propelled by active remembering and socialization" (2002, 61). Kelber criticizes any methodology that seeks for the *ipsissimum verbum*—the so-called original words of Jesus. In an oral context, a saying given in one place would not be repeated verbatim in another context. It would naturally be adjusted to take into account the new audience and situation (Kelber 2005, 236–37). Thus, Kelber concludes, there never was one original wording of a particular saying. Furthermore, any remembered saying would be adapted to the community's present needs as it was preserved. Finally, as the Evangelists dictated their Gospels, "there is a deliberate and creative imagination at work in the formation of the gospels that gives them distinct narrative profiles" (2002, 78). The Evangelists were thus engaged in an act of "creative production" (2002, 81) in which they adapted the traditions available to them to their communities' current needs as they perceived them. For Kelber, then, memory is not a mechanism for the preservation of the verbatim teachings of Jesus but rather a mechanism that is almost certain to introduce significant change into what is recorded. Even so, his approach produces a more positive view of the connection between the actual teaching and activities of Jesus and what is found within the Gospel traditions than that of John Dominic Crossan.

In his book *The Birth of Christianity*, Crossan gives considerable attention to how the teachings of Jesus may have been preserved "in the forty years that elapsed from the death of Jesus to the writing of Mark's gospel in 70 C.E." (1998, 49). He challenges suggestions that oral tradition can be invoked as a mechanism for reliably transmitting Jesus sayings and doings. As he says, "memory is creatively reproductive rather than accurately recollective" (1998, 54). Indeed, "Almost everything that common sense tells us about memory is wrong" (1998, 59). Crossan goes on to document that in human memory "fact becomes non-fact ... fiction becomes fact ... nonfact becomes fact" (1998, 60–67). Thus the very processes of oral tradition result in a mixture of authentic and nonauthentic Jesus traditions. In the light of the frailties of human memory, Crossan goes on to develop a very careful methodology that seeks to utilize only the very earliest traditions of Jesus that can be detected in such sources as Q (defined by many as the document that lies behind the material common to Matthew and Luke that is not in Mark) and the Gospel of Thomas. The result produces a substantial reduction in what Crossan considers to be genuine sayings of Jesus compared to what is found in the Synoptic Gospels. For Crossan, then, the qualities of memory are such that the oral Jesus traditions available to the Evangelists were likely to have been dramatically different from what Jesus actually did and said, and he spends considerable effort to distinguish between the original thinking that may go back to Jesus and the extraneous materials that have become deeply entwined in the Gospel traditions.

Bauckham, Kelber, and Crossan all invoke the characteristics of human memory in their evaluation of the qualities of the Gospel traditions. They may serve as illustration of much wider debates within Gospel studies. The role that should be attributed to memory is contested in many quarters, and contested strongly. Perhaps, given the importance of the Gospel materials to Christianity as a whole, this is as it should be. Behind the debate is the observation that, while human memory is generally robust, it does have some significant frailties. On top of the fact that memories of past events decline rapidly over time, even those events that involve personal trauma, human memory has been shown to be subject to suggestibility and hindsight bias. The issue of how one can account for the impact that these features of human memory have on the eyewitness accounts that have been incorporated into the Gospel traditions—taken up in part 2 of this book—is one that is of great importance to any appreciation of the Gospel materials. But before that is attempted, it is most appropriate that serious attention be given to the characteristics of human eyewitness testimony—the topic of this chapter—and the qualities of human memory that give rise to those characteristics—topics covered in chapters 2–4.

The Characteristics of Eyewitness Testimony

Eyewitness testimony is used in the modern court system as the basis for making decisions that often have considerable impact on the lives of those involved in the cases. In many jurisdictions, the outcome can even be a matter of life and death in trials deciding very serious cases such as murder. Whether a person suffers the death penalty can turn on whether or not one or another witness is believed. The credibility of the whole process often turns on the reliability of eyewitnesses. Yet because they are human, even those eyewitnesses who are sincerely trying to tell the truth will have memories that share the frailties of suggestibility, hindsight, and transience. The result can be great variety in the details of testimony given to the court. This inconsistency has been known and studied for over a century.

One of the earliest widely known books on the reliability of eyewitness testimony is the 1908 collection of essays *On the Witness Stand*, by Hugo Münsterberg. In this book Münsterberg draws attention to the wide variability that can exist in different eyewitness accounts of the same event. He cites a number of examples. In a case that turned on the time interval between the sounding of a whistle signal from the street and an explosion, one witness said the time interval was less than ten seconds, the other that it was more than a minute. Both witnesses had no reason to lie and made their statements under oath. In another case, one involving poisoning, some members of the family reported that the beverage had a disagreeable, sour taste, others that it was sweet. In a further case, one witness reported seeing a woman with a child walking along the seashore by moonlight; another claimed to have seen a man and his dog. Münsterberg even cites an example involving his own statements under oath of the circumstances of a robbery in his own home, which contained details he later discovered to be incorrect. He further reports on a meeting of a scientific association in Göttingen that was interrupted by a clown, apparently from a carnival in progress at the same time as the meetings, chased by a black man with a gun. There was a fall, a shot, and the two left. Those who were present were asked to hand in a written report that could be forwarded to the police. With the exception of the president of the association, none of the attendees knew that this was a set-up and that photographs of the event were taken. When the reports were analyzed, only six of the forty did not contain positively wrong statements. Indeed, in twenty-four of the papers, up to 10 percent of the statements were free inventions, and in 25 percent of the statements, more than 10 percent of what was said was absolutely false. Furthermore, the statements varied considerably in what information was or was not provided (Münsterberg 1908, 15–17, 39–44, 51–53).

Such is some of the variability inherent in eyewitness accounts, confirmed by all who have studied the topic. Subsequent research has identified some of the different circumstances that influence the reliability, or otherwise, of eyewitnesses. Considerable debate swirls around many of the issues identified by this research, but there is a growing consensus about several key matters. For example, in their survey of sixty-four psychologists known from their publications as experts in eyewitness testimony, most of whom had been involved in court proceedings as expert witnesses, Saul M. Kassin, V. Anne Tubb, Harmon M. Hosch and Amina Memon found that over 80 percent of them would be prepared to testify in court under oath that the following statements were correct:

- "Eyewitness testimony about an event often reflects not only what they actually saw but information they obtained later on."
- "An eyewitness's confidence is not a good predictor of his or her identification accuracy."
- "An eyewitness's testimony about an event can be affected by how the questions put to that witness are worded."
- "Eyewitnesses sometimes identify as a culprit someone they have seen in another situation or context."
- "The presence of a weapon impairs an eyewitness's ability to accurately identify the perpetrator's face." (Kassin et al 2001, 405–16; see esp. tables 1 and 5; cf. Wells et al. 2000, 582)

These observations might be compared to that made by the six psychologists who served on the U.S. Department of Justice working group that was responsible for putting together the publication, *Eyewitness Evidence: A Guide for Law Enforcement*:

> The scientific proof is compelling that eyewitnesses will make systematic errors in their reports as a function of misleading questions (or as a result

of other incorrect postevent sources of information). ... The important point is that witnesses will extract and incorporate new information after the witnessed event and then testify about that information as though they had actually witnessed it. (Wells et al. 2000, 582)[2]

Thus it is clear that memory frailties apply to eyewitness testimony as they do to all aspects of memory, which would not be so remarkable but for the importance that these frailties can have in court outcomes. However, one must not so emphasize the frailties of memory to the extent that all confidence need be lost in memories,[3] as is illustrated by the following two case studies.

Eyewitness Case Study 1: A Foiled Gun Shop Robbery in Burnaby, Vancouver

The first case study relates to a violent episode that took place in the community of Burnaby in Vancouver, Canada (Yuille and Cutshall 1986). A thief entered a gun shop, tied up the proprietor, then stole some money and a number of guns. The storeowner freed himself and went outside with the intention of noting the details of the number plate on the thief's car but found that the thief had not yet entered his vehicle. Separated by about 6 feet (1.8 m), the thief and the storeowner exchanged shots that killed the thief and wounded the storeowner, who survived. The case was ideal to study, as forensic evidence and photographs of the scene included incontrovertible knowledge concerning the physical appearance of the

---

2. Cf. the words of Elizabeth F. Loftus, "Our memories are vulnerable to 'postevent information': to details, ideas, and suggestions that come along after an event has happened. People integrate new materials into their memory, modifying what they believe they personally experienced. When people combine information gathered at the time of an actual experience with new information acquired later, they form a smooth and seamless memory and thereafter have great difficulty telling which facts come from which time" (Loftus 2002, 43).

3. The following comments about media coverage of the issues relating to eyewitness identification is true of much of the rest of eyewitness testimony as well: "Unfortunately, much of this coverage tended to send a weak and potentially misleading message, namely, that eyewitnesses are unreliable. That message misses the point of system-variable research, which is that eyewitnesses could be more reliable if the justice system adopted certain procedural improvements that the research has shown to be effective in reducing eyewitness errors" (Wells et al. 2000, 587).

thief, the guns involved, ammunition expended, and the details of the car, so that eyewitness reports could be checked against what actually happened. Furthermore, the death of the thief meant that the police file was closed, and any other investigations would not interfere with any judicial processes.

The police had originally interviewed 21 eyewitnesses, and 13 of the 15 principal eyewitnesses agreed to follow-up interviews, which took place four to five months after the incident. The follow-up interviews adopted the same pattern as the original interviews: witnesses were asked to describe the event in their own terms, then were given further questions to clarify some specific details. The follow-up interviews also included two deliberately misleading questions, as well as some questions aimed at testing the accuracy of the eyewitness memories that were irrelevant to the original police investigation (e.g., the color of the blanket used to cover the body of the dead thief). The researchers reconstructed the incident using the original police interviews and forensic evidence collected at the time (including photographs from the scene) and used their reconstruction to score both sets of eyewitness accounts for accuracy. Rather stringent guidelines were adopted for accuracy: height and age estimates had to be within plus or minus 2 (inches/years), weight within 5 pounds, and no leeway was given for the number of shots fired.

There was considerable variation in the number of details provided. The original 21 eyewitnesses provided between 17 and 95 details to the police, and the 13 principal eyewitnesses provided between 38 to 123 details in the follow-up interviews. More details were provided by the seven witnesses with a more central viewing position, although the accuracy rate remained constant between the group that was centrally positioned and those who were not in such a good position to view the event. Table 1.1 gives the range of percentage of details that were correctly reported in both interviews by individual eyewitnesses (e.g., at least one eyewitness reported as few as 40 percent of the actions correctly, at least one other eyewitness reported 98 percent of the actions correctly, and the percentage of correct actions reported by the rest of the eyewitnesses fall somewhere between these two extremes). It also presents the percentage average of the correct responses provided by the whole group of witnesses.[4]

---

4. These figures are derived from Yuille and Cutshall 1986, 295, table 3; the averages have been rounded to the nearest whole number.

Table 1.1: Yuille and Cutshall's Analysis of Accuracy of Eyewitness Reports				
Type of detail	Police interview		Research interview	
	Range	Average	Range	Average
Action	40%–98%	92%	47%–100%	82%
People descriptions	33%–100%	76%	47%–90%	73%
Object descriptions	50%–100%	89%	60%–100%	85%
Total details	59%–96%	82%	54%–95%	81%

It may be seen from the table that, just as the number of details provided by each eyewitness varied, so did his or her accuracy. Actions and objects tended to be more accurately described than people, although it must be remembered that the criteria adopted to rate accuracy for the descriptions of people were very strict. But, and this should be emphasized, while their testimony contained mistakes, their overall accuracy was greater than 80 percent, even when evaluated by rather stringent criteria.[5]

The kind of errors reported by Münsterberg were also evident in the mistakes made by this set of eyewitnesses. One eyewitness reported to the police that "about five seconds later another guy came out of the gunshop," but to the interviewers, "About two minutes later, not very long … the owner came out of the store after him…" (Yuille and Cutshall 1986, 298). One witness told the police the car was red but told the interviewers that

---

5. This accuracy rate may be compared with that of the survivors of the sinking of the *Titanic*. Of those that explicitly commented on the state of the ship as it sank, 75 percent (15 eyewitnesses out of 20) stated that it was breaking apart during the final plunge. Despite this, both the American and British board of enquiry ruled that the ship was intact as it sank. The discovery of the remains of the vessel have shown that in fact the majority eyewitness report was correct, despite the difficulty of viewing conditions (Riniolo et al. 2003, 89–95).

it was either red or blue. Another witness correctly told the police that the car was a Falcon but later told the interviewers that it was a gold Chevrolet.

None of the interviewers responded inaccurately to the misleading questions put to them by the interviewers, although three witnesses reported nonexistent events without prompting. In fact, 2.9 percent of the actions reported to the police and 3.2 percent of the actions reported to the interviewers never happened. On the other hand, there were a number of inaccuracies in the press and television reports of the event, but none of them made their way into the eyewitness accounts (Yuille and Cutshall 1986, 298–99).

Clearly, the reports of these eyewitnesses were a mixture, made up of a majority of accurate statements but with some inaccuracies intermingled. It is difficult to gainsay the following summing up of their investigation made by Yuille and Cutshall:

> We would not dispute Parker's (1980) claim that "The fact that conscientious and honest people will differ in the reporting of their observations of a crime is one of those immutable phenomenon that will exist as long as man" (p. 33). There is no doubt that witnesses do differ in their accounts: some examples were found in the present research. However, we do take issue with the essentially negative view of the eyewitness that has been consistently presented by most eyewitness researchers. … In the present research, however, a different picture emerges. Most of the witnesses in this case were highly accurate in their accounts, and this continued to be true 5 months after the event. (Yuille and Cutshall 1986, 299)[6]

In sum, then, this case study shows that human memory provides first-order faithfulness to the past, or, in other words, a good gist memory of the event. Furthermore, Yuille and Cutshall's case study allows an actual percentage for the accuracy of this "first-order" faithfulness. It is over 80 percent accurate, even when measured stringently. On the other hand, this case study reveals some of the intractability of up to 20 percent of inaccurate details. Furthermore, one inaccurate detail does not mean the

---

6. Note also the comment of Yuille and Cutshall: "Judges will sometimes dismiss the testimony of a witness because some detail has been incorrectly recalled. The present results indicate that incorrect recall of a detail such as the date of the event or the color of clothing is unrelated to the accuracy of the rest of the witness's account" (1986, 300).

rest of the testimony is discredited. Perhaps the only way to increase the accuracy of the overall judgment of the true state of affairs is that utilized by the courts—consult a number of eyewitnesses. Of course, one would try to find eyewitnesses independent of each other, as just the process of group sharing of recollections has been shown to have the capability of inducing the incorporation of inaccuracies into the memories of other eyewitnesses. So, the positive evaluation—that eyewitness memory is likely to be better than 80 percent accurate—needs to be tempered by the realization that, in group-oriented societies such as those in which the Gospels were written, it is likely to be near impossible to discern from eyewitness accounts alone which parts of the testimony are accurate and which are not.

Eyewitness Case Study 2: John Dean's Testimony

The second case study is derived from the analysis of John Dean's memory made by Ulric Neisser (Neisser 1981, 1–22). John Dean, former counsel to President Richard M. Nixon, testified before the "Watergate" committee in June 1973. He opened with a 245-page statement and was subjected to vigorous cross-examination. Subsequent to his testimony, it emerged that President Nixon had been secretly taping most of the conversations that took place in the Oval Office. Some of these were published under the title *Presidential Transcripts*, and thus Neisser was able to compare what was actually said with John Dean's memory of what was said.[7]

When questioned as to how he put together his testimony, Dean said that he had an extensive collection of newspaper clippings, and he had used them to cue his memory of the events taking place during that time period. Furthermore, he described meeting with the President of the United States as "a very momentous occasion" and not part of his regular

---

7. Since the appearance of Neisser's article, the unpublished transcript prepared for the House Judiciary Committee at the time of the Watergate Hearings has become publicly available, as have the actual tapes. According to the analysis of William Hirst and David Gluck, the transcript provided in the *Presidential Transcripts* was at times "less a verbatim reproduction than a very highly detailed summary of the conversation" and quite incomplete. Their reconstruction of the conversation between Nixon, Dean, and Haldeman that took place 15 September 1972 contained 1,109 idea units, compared to 486 idea units represented in the *Presidential Transcripts* (Hirst and Gluck 1999, 253–81).

activities. He further said that "I have an ability to recall not specific words necessarily but certainly the tenor of a conversation and the gist of a conversation" (cited in Neisser 1981, 6).

Neisser states that the assessment made of Dean's testimony by Mary McCathy has stood the test of time. She wrote that her overpowering impression was "not so much of a truthful person as of someone resolved to tell the truth about this particular set of events because his intelligence has warned him to do so" (Neisser 1981, 10). Despite this, large discrepancies are evident when Dean's nine-month-later memory of the 50-minute meeting that took place on 15 September 1972 between himself, President Nixon, and Robert Haldeman (Nixon's chief of staff) is compared with the actual transcript. Neisser compares the first few minutes of the meeting from the *Presidential Transcripts* and Dean's testimony and discovers that "hardly a word of Dean's account is true. Nixon did not say *any* of the things attributed to him here.... Nor had Dean himself said the things he later describes himself as saying" (1981, 9).

Why, then, the large discrepancies between what actually happened and what John Dean believed had happened? Neisser suggests that two things were at work in Dean's memory of this meeting. First, his account may well follow a script, an "entering-the-room script" (Neisser 1981, 9). For example, while Nixon never actually said out loud that Dean should sit, as Dean had reported, he may have indicated the chair nonverbally, and even had he not, this is something that is commonly done in many similar circumstances. But perhaps more important:

> What his [Dean's] testimony really describes is not the September 15 meeting itself but his fantasy of it: the meeting as it should have been, so to speak. In his mind Nixon *should* have been glad that the indictments stopped with Liddy, Haldeman *should* have been telling Nixon what a great job Dean was doing; most of all, praising him *should* have been the first order of business. In addition, Dean *should* have told Nixon that the cover-up might unravel, as it eventually did, instead of telling him that it was a great success. By June, this fantasy had become the way Dean remembered the meeting. (Neisser 1981, 10)

Some of what was said in meetings with Nixon and others as reported by Dean actually happened, although at times he reported that they had been said at a meeting held at a different time, a "time-slice error." Dean's memories proved to be most accurate for that part of the meeting of 21 March between Dean and the president alone, in which he went in with the purpose of informing the president that a number of his assistants had become involved in a crime ("obstruction of justice") and might eventually go to prison for it. Furthermore, it is true that he told Nixon that a number of more important aides were soon to be placed in circumstances where they would have to perjure themselves in sworn testimony, and not all could be guaranteed to do so. Dean, of course, was not so much reporting a conversation taking place at this time but was referring to a well-prepared report, given in circumstances where he did most of the talking. Interestingly enough, about an hour into the meeting, President Nixon and Dean were joined by Haldeman for a further 45 minutes. Dean apparently forgot almost everything that took place in the last 45 minutes. In other words, Dean's memories tend to emphasize his own role more than was actually the case.

In his summing up, Neisser comments that, "We are hardly surprised to find that memory is constructive, or that confident witnesses may be wrong." Yet, "his constructed memories were not altogether wrong. On the contrary, there is a sense in which he was altogether right; a level at which he was telling the truth about the Nixon White House." Dean's memories are true in general of the several repeated episodes in which he was a participant ("repisodes"). "What he says about these 'repisodes' is essentially correct, even though it is not literally faithful to any one occasion. He is not remembering the 'gist' of a single episode by itself, but the common characteristics of a whole series of events" (Neisser 1981, 19–20).[8]

Derek Edwards and Jonathan Potter have provided another assessment of John Dean's testimony where they point out some features of the

---

8. See also these assessments earlier in the article: "It is fair to say that Dean here captures the 'tenor', though not the gist, of what went on in the Oval Office that afternoon. ... His testimony had much truth it in, but not at the level of gist. It was true at a deeper level. Nixon was the kind of man Dean described, he had the knowledge Dean attributed to him, there was a cover-up. Dean remembered all of that; he just didn't recall the actual conversation he was testifying about" (Neisser 1981, 12–13). Hirst and Gluck 1999 classified the conversation that took place between the three men on 15 September into a number of subcategories. According to their count, there were "422 unique narrative tellings in the September 15 meeting. Only 65, or 15.4% surfaced in Dean's statement to Congress. ... 71% of the narrative tellings he recalled in his statement to Congress were his," compared to an actual 58 percent (Hirst and Gluck 1999, 271–72). While Dean overemphasizes the role he had in the "narrative tellings," he overemphasizes Nixon's role in statements about the future, even though Nixon had contributed more of these than the other participants.

situation in which he was testifying that mean something more is happening than just "the natural workings of memory" (Edwards and Potter 1992, 187–215). Approaching the situation in which Dean finds himself from the perspective of discourse analysis shows that Dean's testimony takes place in the context of legal testimony. It has the purpose of minimizing his own culpability and emphasizing that of Nixon's. "Rather than taking Dean's testimony as a (fairly direct) window upon his memory, ... it may be taken instead as a pragmatically designed piece of discourse. It is a series of accounts, occasioned by cross-examination, and oriented towards the avoidance and assigning of blame and mitigation" (1992, 193). Dean's claims to a good memory for gist underlies his claim that his version of events is accurate, while his denial that his memory is a tape recorder allows explanation for any inconsistencies that arise. The general vividness of the details provided, including verbatim citations, is also designed to establish the reliability of his testimony.

Edwards and Potter also point out that the special privileged status of the observer in psychological experiments regarding memory and of Neisser in the case of Dean's testimony, where the "events that really happened" are known, is virtually unknown in real-life circumstances. What happens in discourse and disputes is that different claims are being made as to "what really happened." "In effect, we are moving from a view of people struggling to remember with the aid of their mental faculties to a view of people struggling with one another in their talk and texts over the real nature of events" (Edwards and Potter 1992, 199).

The case study of John Dean's testimony before the Watergate committee provides a vivid illustration of many of the features of memory that will be canvassed in the next few chapters. His memories are most unreliable with regard to time. Dean himself says that he reconstructed the sequence of events from his collection of newspaper clippings. His actual testimony shows many "time-slice errors." In other words, he reports things that did happen but that happened on occasions other than the one that he is reporting. His memory performs best at the level of gist. In fact, it turns out to be quite unreliable at the level of detail. His testimony also reveals significant biases. In particular, he tends to overemphasize his role in what happened (egocentric bias). Most important, he is making a case justifying his own actions as far as possible and blaming others for their contributions as far as possible. He is using his memory to contest the meaning of past events in the minds of the wider community.

Taken together, the two case studies—the robbery of the gun store in Burnaby, Vancouver, and John Dean's testimony before Congress—reveal many of the basic characteristics of eyewitness memory. It is generally trustworthy, but the level of accuracy varies from individual to individual. Eyewitness testimony, then, is almost certainly a mixture of correct and incorrect items. But where an eyewitness is not intentionally lying, there is a general, if not specific, reliability about his or her testimony. Such is the character of eyewitness testimony, given the frailties of human memory. One might therefore conclude that the eyewitness memories that contributed to the formation of the Jesus traditions would share similar characteristics. In other words, they would be rather more malleable than might have been suggested by Richard Bauckham but would have a much wider correspondence to the actual teachings of Jesus and events from his ministry than would be allowed by the reconstruction of John Dominic Crossan. What is clear, though, is that a close investigation of the frailties and strengths of human memory is a necessary prerequisite to understanding further the qualities of the eyewitness testimony that formed the bases of the Gospel traditions.

2

Transience and the Reliability of Long-Term Human Memory

Seven Frailties of Human Memory

Human memory is based on incredibly complex and robust processes that enable individuals naturally to perform feats that are still beyond the abilities of computers and robots. Memory systems play a crucial role in allowing humans to learn from experience and work together in social groups, as they adapt to and prosper in any number of varied circumstances and environments. Yet the very adaptability of human memory is associated with a number of phenomena that are described in this and subsequent chapters as frailties, but which Daniel Schacter has provocatively termed "sins." In his book *The Seven Sins of Memory*, Schacter lists the "sins" of transience, absent-mindedness, blocking, misattribution, suggestibility, bias, and persistence (Schacter 2001, 1–11 and *passim*). As the "sins" of transience, suggestibility, and bias have the greatest potential to impact eyewitness memories of events, they will receive the most attention in the following pages.

Human memory is, for the most part, transient. That is, most things that happen are forgotten. Yet, amidst all the many things that are forgotten, some events form long-lasting memories. Somehow, most of what is most important for making sense of things is remembered, and the transience of most memories means that the significant ones that remain are readily accessible. The frailty of transience thus turns out to be one of the important strengths of memory.

The frailties of bias and suggestibility are a consequence of the fact that human memories are largely reconstructions formed from a very complex set of memory subsystems. Current circumstances naturally influence how memories of previous events are reconstructed and give rise to hindsight bias. Likewise, the input of others often forms part of the data set used to reconstruct memories of events. Generally such suggestibility is useful, as one individual is less likely to have a better recollection of what happened than the combined memory of a group. However, this process does allow false memories to be incorporated into the reconstruction, and, under many circumstances, humans can have difficulty in determining which parts of their memory were incorporated from other sources.

Examples of the frailties of transience, hindsight bias, and suggestibility can all be found in eyewitness testimony. Still, it is important not to overstate the impact of these frailties. Yuille and Cutshall's study cited in the previous chapter has revealed that details offered by eyewitnesses are likely to be 80 percent accurate. One could wish that they were 100 percent accurate or that it was easy to detect the inaccurate 20 percent (it isn't), yet it should not be overlooked that eyewitness testimony is generally accurate, at least in the absence of deliberate attempts to deceive.[1]

The "sins" or frailties of memory—particularly those of transience, suggestibility, and bias—have the potential to impact the Gospel traditions and should be explored further. The frailty of transience will be the topic of this and the next chapter, while suggestibility and bias will be considered in chapter 4.

Long-Term Human Memory and the Gospels

The life, teachings, death, and resurrection of Jesus stand at the center of Christianity. Yet, as James Dunn observes, "What we actually have in the earliest retellings of what is now the Synoptic tradition, then, are the memories of the first disciples—not Jesus himself, but the remembered Jesus" (Dunn 2003b, 130–31). What is known of Jesus, then, is mediated by long-term human memories. This observation has the effect of placing fallible human memory at the center of any inquiry into the historical Jesus.

Others besides Dunn have stressed the importance of human memory to a discussion of the historical Jesus. Some have even revealed an aware-

---

1. As Daniel Schacter observes: "Although this volume is concerned primarily with understanding distortion, it must be emphasized again that memory is quite accurate in many situations. ... Therefore, the key issue is not whether memory is 'mostly accurate' or 'mostly distorted'; rather, the challenge is to specify the conditions under which accuracy and distortion are most likely to be observed" (Schacter 1995, 25).

ness of the experimental work on human memory that has taken place in the discipline of psychology. Yet, aside from the occasional use of Frederic Bartlett's book *Remembering: A Study in Experimental and Social Psychology*, first published in 1932 (Bartlett 1961), almost nothing has been made of this resource by those working in biblical studies. This chapter, and several of the following chapters, will attempt to fill this lacuna.

Initially, the huge volume of published research reporting human memory experiments seems not only daunting but also largely irrelevant to questions relating to the issue of how well the traditions of Jesus may have been remembered. Most psychological experiments on memory focus on periods of seconds and minutes, rather than periods as long as the thirty to sixty years that most likely intervened between the crucifixion-resurrection and the writing of the Gospels. Furthermore, the stimulus materials usually used in psychological experiments are quite different from the materials found in the Synoptic Gospels. Despite this, some experiments occasionally surface with results that are pertinent to the way the Jesus traditions may have been remembered, and many of these will be reported in this and later chapters.

The experiments reported in this chapter all deal in some way with the memory frailty of transience. Moreover, when their results are graphed, nearly all of them produce forgetting curves that have a similar appearance, despite the fact that the time scales involved range from seconds to years. What will emerge is that, although human memory consists of many different types of subsystems, most of them follow a similar pattern of transience (or forgetting). This is true for some types of memories that last only a few seconds and for other types of memories that last up to five years. Toward the end of the chapter it will be discovered that memories become stable after about five years and persist at least for a further twenty years.

Forgetting Curves

The experimental investigation of the performance of human memory is generally traced back to the work of Hermann Ebbinghaus, published in 1885.[2] His experimental investigations into the way in which information

---

2. Herman Ebbinghaus, *Über das Gedächtnis* (Leipzig: Duncker & Humblot, 1885); translated into English by 1913 and published as Ebbinghaus 1964.

is forgotten revealed the characteristic forgetting curve found in so many subsequent experiments.

In his efforts to establish stable experimental conditions that would allow him to make reliable measurements of the characteristics of memory, Ebbinghaus developed a technique based on the learning of lists of three-letter nonsense syllables.[3] His definition of memorization and forgetting is as follows: he considered a list to be successfully memorized after two completely correct repetitions. He used the time taken to relearn a list (after the lapse of time) as a measure of the amount of a list that was not forgotten. In other words, he argued that it should take him less time to relearn a list that had been previously learned and that the difference between the original time it took to learn the list and the time taken to relearn the list was an indication of what he had retained of the list.

Ebbinghaus discovered that much of each memorized list was very quickly forgotten but that the rate of loss slowed over time. For example, after 20 minutes, there was a 58 percent saving in the time taken to rememorize a previously memorized list of thirteen nonsense syllables; 44 percent two hours later, 36 percent nine hours later, 34 percent one day later, 28 percent two days later, 25 percent six days later (144 hours), and

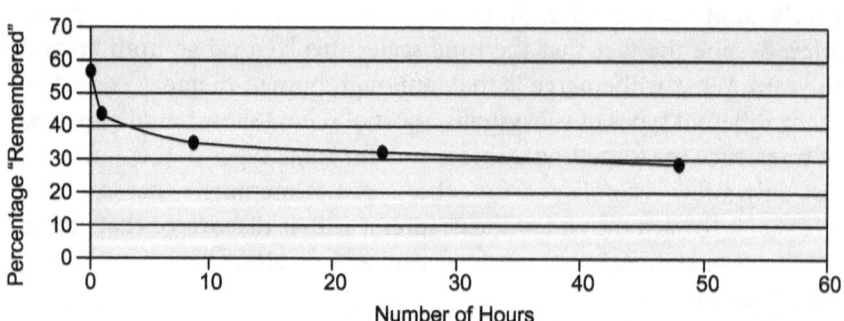

Figure 2.1. Ebbinghause percent "saving" in relearning: up to two days

---

3. Ebbinghaus created a pool of 2,300 syllables that had no meaning to him, beginning with one of the letters b, d, f, g, h, j, k, l, m, n, p, r, s, ß, t, w; with one of the vowels a, e, i, o, u, ä, ö, ü, au, ei, eu as the central letter, and ending with f, k, l, m, n, p, r, s, ß, t, ch, sch, confessing that "a German tongue even after several years practice in foreign languages does not quite accustom itself to the correct pronunciation of the mediae at the end" (Ebbinghaus 1964, 22 n. 1).

TRANSIENCE AND THE RELIABILITY OF LONG-TERM MEMORY 25

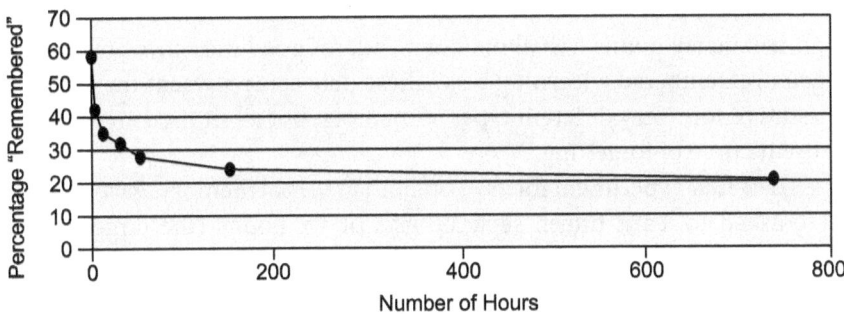

Figure 2.2. Ebbinghause percent "saving" in relearning: up to thirty-one days

21 percent thirty-one days later (744 hours). When graphed, his "forgetting curve" looks like that found in figures 2.1 and 2.2.[4]

The memory tasks encountered in real life rarely involve remembering nonsense syllables. Furthermore, nonsense syllables are completely absent from the traditions found in the Synoptic Gospels. Thus, if it were not for the fact that many types of memory exhibit a very similar pattern of transience, the experiments of Ebbinghaus would be irrelevant to this study. It turns out, however, that what happens in human memory for the first three to six years after significant events is modeled rather well by Ebbinghausian curves of forgetting. Evidence for this assertion will be provided in three steps, each describing experiments spanning increasing time periods, culminating in a group of experiments that investigate long-term memories that are up to fifty years old. The first step, though, will be the description of a series of experiments that show that forgetting curves are regular enough to be modeled by mathematical equations. Like the majority of experiments found suitable for laboratory investigation, the types of memory tested in the three experiments conducted by John T. Wixted and Ebbe B. Ebbesen are of short duration (1991, 409–15).

Wixted and Ebbesen set out to determine which family of mathematical equations best modeled forgetting curves. They did so by the use of four data sets, the first being that which Ebbinghaus reported from his investigation of his memory of nonsense syllables. The other three sets were derived from experiments deliberately chosen to represent differ-

---

4. While Ebbinghaus does provide some graphs, the data giving the results of the experiment just described is only provided in a tabular form (see Ebbinghaus 1964, 76). These data were graphed to produce figures 2.1 and 2.2.

ent kinds of memory. Wixted and Ebbesen measured memory for lists of high-frequency nouns, visual memory, and, for good measure, how well a pigeon remembered a learning task. These data sets represent the characteristics of four very different types of memory, but all showed an Ebbinghausian curve of forgetting.

Their first experiment focused on human verbal memory. Participants were asked to learn fifteen separate lists of six nouns (the target lists). These lists were formed by randomly drawing from a previously identified list of 540 high-frequency nouns. Each target list was presented to the participants on a computer monitor at a rate of two words per second. The complete list was then left for a further 1 second (the low degree of learning condition) or 5 seconds (the high degree of learning condition). Participants were asked to read the words in the target list aloud as they appeared and during their extra learning time. They were then distracted for varying intervals of time (2.5, 5, 10, 20, and 40 seconds, respectively). The distraction task was presented on a computer monitor in the same manner as the original tasks. In it, participants were asked to read words from one or more distracter lists (depending on the length of the distraction interval). The distracter lists consisted of five nouns and adjectives drawn randomly from a pool of six hundred words, separate from that used to derive the target lists. After a set of question marks appeared on the monitor, the subjects were allowed 60 seconds in which to write down the original target list in any order (free recall).

The proportion of words recalled after varying amounts of distraction is shown in figure 2.3, which reproduces figure 1 from the original article by Wixted and Ebbesen (1991, 411). It shows the same kind of pattern evident in the data from Ebbinghaus: there is an initial sharp drop in what is remembered, but the rate of loss slows over time.

In their second experiment, Wixted and Ebbesen tested memory for faces. The experimental subjects were divided into four groups and were each initially shown forty color slides of male faces. They returned after 1 hour, 1 day, 1 week, or 2 weeks, depending on their group, then shown eighty slides of male faces, forty of which they had already seen in the first session. They were asked to respond to each slide by simply responding "yes" or "no" to indicate if they had seen the face before. A "forgetting curve" was discovered very similar to that found in their experiment 1: the longer the interval, the more was forgotten; the rate of initial forgetting was high but declined over time. In the third experiment, Wixted and Ebbesen tested the memories of pigeons for either a red circle or a green

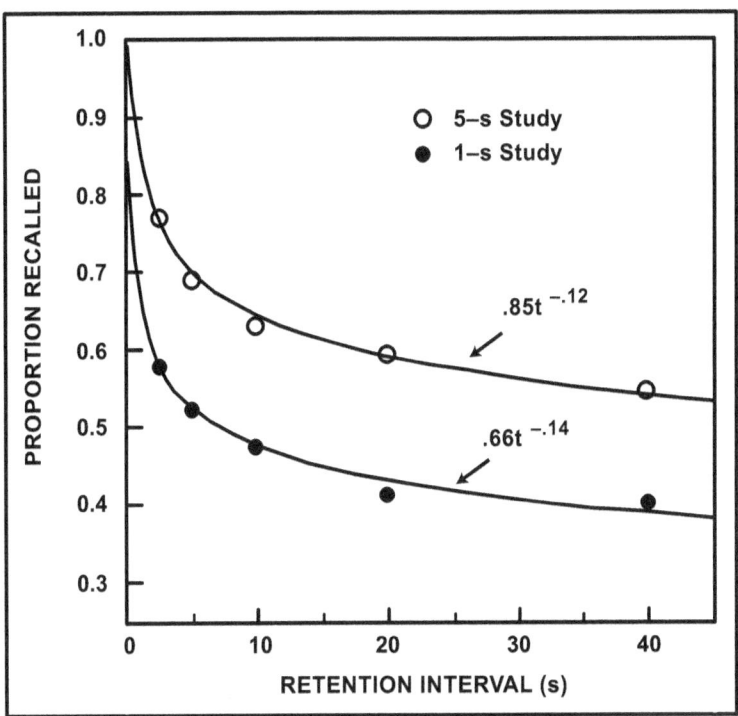

Figure 2.3. Forgetting curve for lists of nouns, showing the "proportion of words recalled for the high (5-s) and low (1-s) degree of learning conditions as a function of retention interval. The solid curves represent the best-fitting power functions (Wixted and Ebbesen 1991, fig. 1).

square over periods of 0.5, 1, 2, or 6 seconds. Experimentally naïve white Carneaux pigeons were placed in a conditioning box with three response windows, which could show either a red circle or green square. They were shown either a red circle or a green square in the center window, and after one of the learning intervals, a red circle and a green square appeared at one or other of the side windows. Pigeons were rewarded with food pellets if they pecked at the side window that was showing the same image that they had recently seen in the middle window. When plotted, the data associated with pigeon memory also showed an Ebbinghausian forgetting curve.

The three data sets from the experiments all showed a similar type of forgetting curve, despite the fact that they were gathered by testing quite different aspects of memory. Wixted and Ebbesen then used these three data sets and the "memory saving" data from Ebbinghaus to determine whether they could be described by one type of mathematical formula common to them all. Ebbinghaus himself had suggested that a logarithmic function best fitt his data,[5] but in their review of literature on previous experiments Wixted and Ebbesen discovered that other functions had also been suggested as possibilities.[6] After doing their analysis, they concluded that in fact a power curve ($y = ax^{-b}$) is a better fit for their data, although a logarithmic curve is almost as good.[7]

---

5. Ebbinghaus even went as far as to identify the actual mathematical function as: $b = 184/((\log t)^{1.25} + 184)$, where b is the saving of work evident in relearning, t is the time in minutes counting from one minute before the end of the learning (Ebbinghaus 1964, 77).

6. For example, Wayne A. Wickelgren suggests that "exponential decay functions provide a good fit for certain retention data at delays under 10 or 20 sec" but that "[e]mpirical strength retention functions for a variety of materials under a variety of conditions can be well fit by some type of power function at delays from 10 or 20 sec to at least 2 years" (Wickelgren 1974, 776). He suggests that, "where encoding is primarily in a ... semantic memory system, the form of the retention function appears to be some type of power function" (1974, 776). Harry P. Bahrick reports an exponential forgetting curve for periods of up to 6 years for most features of Spanish when it is learned as a second language in school or university but is not used thereafter (Bahrick 1984, 21).

7. Clearly the forgetting curve is curvilinear (i.e., curved, not straight), but even so Wixted and Ebbeson first tested their data against a downward sloping straight line for goodness of fit as a kind of worst case scenario with which to compare the success or otherwise of other types of mathematical function. Many things in nature, including the decay of nuclear materials, follow a exponential curve, and so this was tested next, along with a hyperbolic, and exponential/power, a logarithmic, and a power curve. They then performed a least-squares regression analysis to discover what percentage of the variation in the data each of these functions explained. Their results are as follows (the higher the number the better the "fit"; 100 is a perfect "fit"):

Percentage of Variance in Amount Remembered as a Function of Time Which Are Accounted for by Different Mathematical Formulas (after Wixted and Ebbesen 1991, table 2)					
Function	Word Recall		Face Recognition	DMTS [pigeon memory]	Ebbinghaus
	1 sec	5 sec			
Linear: $y = a-bx$	74.4	77.5	64.5	78.6	44.8

Rates of Memory Loss during the First Five Years

The exact mathematical formula that best fits a forgetting curve is probably not an essential datum for the purposes of this book. What makes the previous experiments worth reporting, though, is that they represent the large number of experiments that have revealed that forgetting curves are very regular for many types of memory. The results of such experiments are so regular, in fact, that they can be represented by smooth lines on graphs and described quite accurately with mathematical equations. If this were also true of the kinds of memories that ended up in the Synoptic Gospels, then it may prove possible to estimate how much of their initial memories of Jesus may have been retained by the eyewitnesses over the thirty to sixty years envisaged between the crucifixion-resurrection and the writing of

Exponential: $y = ae^{-bx}$	78.1	80.2	67.6	90.2	48.8
Hyperbolic: $y = 1/(a-bx)$	82.7	83.2	70.7	98.2	58.4
Exponential-Power: $y = ae^{-2bx}$	90.9	91.7	83.4	96.0	73.8
Logarithmic: $y = a-b\log(x)$	96.8	97.8	97.0	92.5	94.6
Power: $y = ax^{-b}$	98.0	98.9	98.7	99.1	97.8
Note: in the sample formulae: x is the independent variable (time, in this case), a and b are constants for each specific set of data (but have different values in the different data sets), and y is an estimate of the amount remembered.					

As can be seen, the power curve is by far the best "fit" of all the different possibilities tested. In a later article, Wixted and Ebbesen respond to various criticisms of their methodology and again conclude that power curves fit the forgetting curve better than any other (Wixted and Ebbesen 1997, 731–39). This is their position also in Wixted's 2004 article (Wixted 2004, 235–69, esp. 243). Power curves also fit other aspects of human memory and learning. Allen Newell and Paul S. Rosenbloom find that power curves are a better fit than exponential or hyperbolic curves for a wide range of skill acquisition tasks where time of performance changes according to the amount of practice (Newell and Rosenbloom 1981, 1–55).

the Gospels. That is the issue, of course. Compared to periods of thirty to sixty years, the retention period of the kind of memories considered by Ebbinghaus, Wixted, and Ebbeson are risible: they range from seconds to days, not years. Nor have the materials used as stimuli in the various experiments reported so far resembled what is found within the Synoptic Gospels. The results of longer-term experiments are needed to determine whether long-term memories also follow an Ebbinghausian forgetting curve. Such experiments are difficult to mount, and they present methodological challenges. As a consequence, few are conducted. Among them, though, the five-year experiment on autobiographical memory by Willem A. Wagenaar provides data that will prove helpful to several aspects of our investigation (1986, 225–52).[8] Wagenaar's experiment shows that autobiographical memory does, in fact, generally follow an Ebbinghausian forgetting curve over a five-year period. It also provides insights about which aspects of life events are best remembered.

Wagenaar used himself as his experimental subject. For a period of six years, at the end of each day he filled out at least one, sometimes two preprinted forms headed with a random number. On each form he recorded one event, which judged on the basis of the categories *who, what, where,* and *when* were "at the time of recording, unique and fully distinguishable from all other things that happened before" (Wagenaar 1986, 229). As well as noting *who, what, where,* and *when,* Wagenaar gave an assessment of salience (was this an event that happened on average once per day, once per week, ... once per 15 years, once per lifetime), emotional involvement, and pleasantness (ranging from extremely unpleasant to extremely pleasant). Furthermore, to ensure that he was not just reconstructing his later memory on the basis of similar events, he noted down a critical detail in the form of a cue question, as well as its answer. In his article he gives a sample of a filled-in form, which has the following information: *random number*: 3329; *who*: Leonardo da Vinci; *what*: I went to see his "last supper"; *where*: in a church in Milano; *when*: Saturday, September 10, 1983; *salience*: 1/month; *involvement*: nothing; *pleasantness*: pleasant; *critical detail*: question: who were with me?; answer: Beth Loftus and Jim Reason.

---

8. Wagenaar was able to benefit from earlier studies, such as Linton 1975, 376–404; 1978, 69–76; and White 1982, 171–83. Linton's study of her own autobiographical memory extended over six years, while that of White extended for seventeen months.

In this manner Wagenaar accumulated approximately 400 events per year, a total of 1,605 events in the main study, 400 in the pretest period, and 397 in the post-test period. One of his colleagues turned the forms recording these events into question booklets. The first page gave one cue. For example, if presented with the answer to the cue *who?*, Wagenaar attempted to write down the remaining information (*what*, *where*, and *when*, then answer the critical question). If this was the cue given for the sample given above, the cue would be "Leonardo da Vinci," and Wagenaar would attempt to write: *what*: I went to see his "last supper"; *where*: in a church in Milano; *when*: Saturday, September 10, 1983. If he could not do this, he turned to the second page, which gave two cues. The third page had three cues. The critical question was on the last page. The cues *who*, *what*, *where*, and *when* can be combined twenty-four different ways in order of presentation (e.g., the cues could have been presented: when?, who?, where? ... or what?, where?, who? ..., etc.), and each event was randomly assigned one of these twenty-four orders of the presentation of cues, so that each sequence was represented equally in the booklets.

There were three phases in the experiment: a one-year pretest, the four-year main experiment, and a one-year post-test. The booklets were sorted according to their random numbers at the end of each test period and used by Wagenaar to test his memory at the end of the one-year pretest, the four-year main experiment, and the one-year post-test. He says, "Unexpectedly, the recall appeared to be somewhat torturous. Most of the events were quite trivial by the time of recall, and I needed much motivation to search my memory for trivia. It was hardly possible to recall more than five events on a day, which explains why the recall period of the main experiment itself lasted a full year" (Wagenaar 1986, 231–32). This had the fortuitous result that the main experiment extended over five years. The pre- and post-tests were to ensure that his memory performance did not either decline with age or become more proficient with practice over the time period.[9]

---

9. After noting that the pre- and post-tests showed that the process of recalling many events did not improve the ability to recall, Wagenaar suggests that either the two factors of memory decline with age and greater proficiency with practice did not play a role in this type of memory for his age group (he was 37–43 years old during the six-year time period of the experiment) or that the two factors canceled each other out.

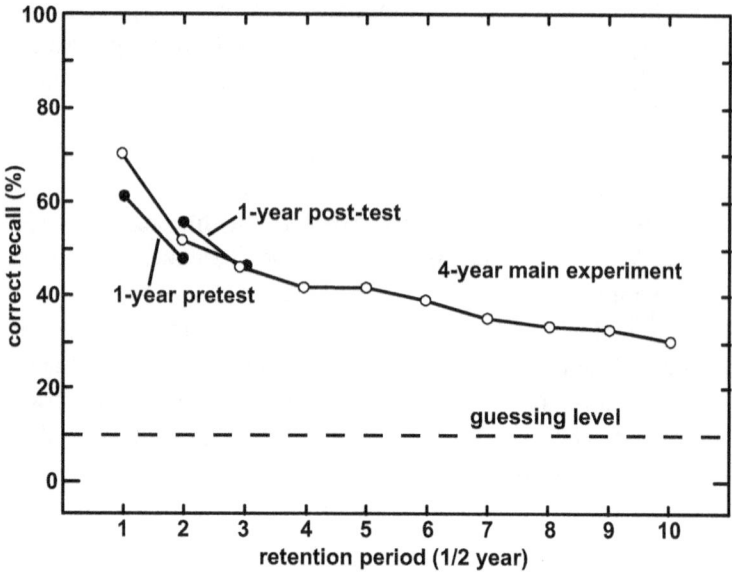

Figure 2.4. Retention curves for four-year-old autobiographical memories (Wagenaar 1986, fig. 2).

The graph in figure 2.4 of the percentage of correct things recalled shows a typical Ebbinghausian forgetting curve. There was an initial loss of details, but the rate of loss declined over time.[10]

In another graph, Wagenaar gives the details of how much was recalled with only one cue, how much with two cues, and how much with three cues. This is reproduced in figure 2.5.

After six months, Wagenaar was able to remember about half of the events with only one cue, but this dropped to be less than 20 percent after five years. The "critical details" questions were recorded to give a reasonably definitive way of testing whether he in fact was remembering a specific event or reconstructing the event from general memories, and this curve is shown with a solid black line in figure 5, correctly so, as it is probably the most important of them. It shows that, given the cues *who*, *what*, *where*, and *when*, Wagenaar was able to remember accurately more than 90 percent of the events up to six months later, although this had fallen

---

10. The retention curve is described by a simple power curve, $y = 0.54x^{-0.36}$ ($r = .99$) (so Wagenaar 1986, 233).

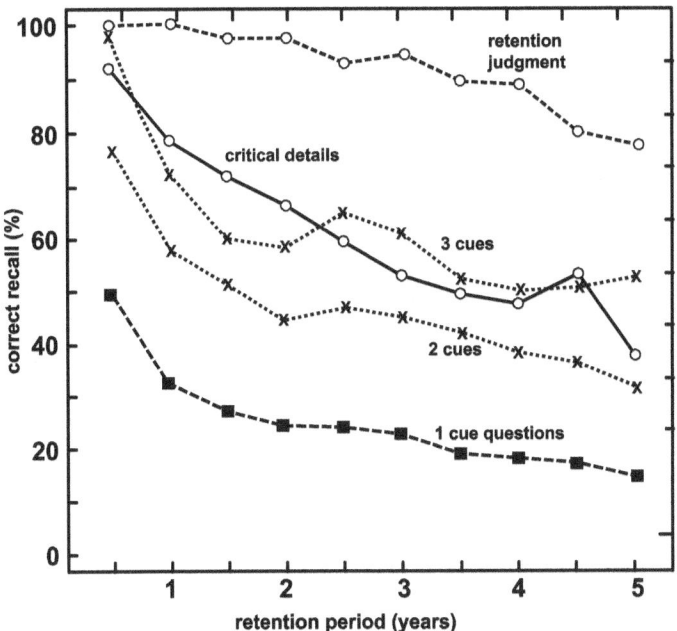

Figure 2.5. Retention curves and retrieval cues (Wagenaar 1986, fig. 3).

to around 40 percent after five years. Given what else is known about the performance of memories and the everyday nature of most of these events, this is an impressive result indeed.

Wagenaar's data also gives evidence that an event was more likely to be remembered if it was of greater salience, emotional involvement,[11] or more pleasant. Interestingly enough, unpleasant events were not remembered any better than events of neutral pleasantness.[12] He also notes that

---

11. A number of experiments have demonstrated that "memory for emotional events tends to be greater than that for neutral events." See the literature cited in Hulse et al. 2007, 73–90 (the quotation is taken from 73); and in Otani et al. 2007, 23–42.

12. In his experiment on his own autobiographic memory (White 1982), Richard White used a much looser criterion for determining whether or not he remembered an event than Wagenaar. On the first occasion of testing his memory, White looked at the short description of the event and self-graded whether or not he could remember it on a scale of 1–5; on the last he did this again, but this time after reading the full description. Wagenaar's provision of a critical detail that could be tested avoids the problem of false recognition that White's data may be subject to. On the other

the order in which the cues were presented yielded differences almost as great as the time elapsed since the event. By far the best single cue was the category *what*; "*when* was almost useless" (Wagenaar 1986, 241).[13]

The research of Wagenaar and others into their own autobiographic memories of episodes in their life—their so-called episodic memory—has revealed that episodic memories also follow an Ebbinghausian-like curve of forgetting, at least for periods of up to five years.[14] As many of the traditions found in the Synoptic Gospels that could have originated from the memories of eyewitnesses would be classified as episodic memory, this research result is of great potential importance. On the other hand, while these experiments have taken place over quite long time periods, they still fall far short of the thirty to sixty years that the Jesus traditions are likely to have been retained in human memory. What is needed are reports of experiments that study memories for periods longer than thirty years. Despite the difficulty of developing a suitable methodology, such experi-

---

hand, many of White's results are similar to those of Wagenaar. His ability to date an event was generally very poor; he tended to remember events that were infrequent occurrences, that were more vivid, and that were emotionally intense. On the other hand, "perceived importance and association with knowledge was not related to recall, nor is any physical sensation other than sight" (White 1982, 176). He observed, "it is not surprising to find high recall of events labeled ridiculous, enlivening, humiliating, frivolous, exhilarating, enraging, astonishing, ludicrous, amusing, elating or funny, but one might also have anticipated the same relation for unpleasant, cheering, revealing, irritating, regrettable, harrowing, exciting, poignant, bitter, embarrassing, or distressing. There is some hint here of suppression of unpleasant memories" (176). The tendency to remember more pleasant memories may explain why the involuntary autobiographical memories of the elderly tend to have more positive content than those of younger volunteers (Schlagman, Schulz, and Kvavilashvili 2006, 161–75).

13. There is some evidence that space (where) and time (when) are encoded differently in memory (see, e.g., van Asselen, Van der Lubbe, and Postma 2006, 232–40). Wagenaar criticizes Linton's research on her own autobiographical memory because her testing of memory was based around the cue "when?" (see Linton 1978, 72), the cue least likely to recall memories. Wagenaar's own criterion for a correct answer to the cue "when?" was a date within one week of the true date.

14. Compare the graphs of memory of news events over periods of up to two years found in Meeter, Murre, and Janssen 2005, 793–810, esp. figs. 2, 4, and 5, which have the typical form of an Ebbinghausian forgetting curve. These graphs have nonzero asymptotes; in other words, most news events were forgotten fairly quickly, but the rate of forgetting slowed over time, and some news events appeared to be permanent memories. This feature of long-term memory will also be noted later in this chapter.

ments have been contrived, and they reveal that the shape of the forgetting curve changes for memories between five and twenty-five years of age.

Rates of Loss for Memories up to Fifty Years Old

One of the best-known studies of memories that extend for over fifty years is the research conducted by Harry P. Bahrick into the retained knowledge of Spanish that had been learned as a second language in high school or college but never used thereafter.[15] Such research confronts considerable methodological challenges, not least among which are the accurate assessments of the level of original knowledge and individual differences in performance. Nor is it very easy to form a reliable assessment of subsequent usage (rehearsal) of that knowledge. Bahrick addressed these concerns in several ways. Initial learning was assessed on the basis of the number of courses in Spanish taken[16] and the grade awarded in the last class taken. It was possible to allow for variations in individual performance by involving a large number of participants in the study.

Bahrick's Spanish language study involved 773 participants. Of these, 146 were studying Spanish at the time of testing, 587 had previously studied Spanish between one and fifty years prior to testing. A control group of forty had not formally studied Spanish at all, half of whom were of an age group equivalent to those currently in college, with the other half aged between forty-one and sixty-two. Although data was gathered by means of questionnaires on how much use had been made of the language since it was initially learned, an analysis of the performance showed that subjects had used their Spanish so little that "no significant rehearsal effects" were observed (Bahrick 1984, 2).

As might be expected on the basis of the research reported in the previous section, Bahrick's data reveals an Ebbinghausian-like forgetting curve for the first three to six years, depending on the type of knowledge. Unexpectedly, however, what is retained in memory after that initial period of forgetting stays in "permastore" for the next twenty or so years with undetectable loss. As Bahrick puts it, "There is a period from approximately 5 to

---

15. Bahrick 1984, 1–29; see also 2000, 247–362, where he outlines not only his own research on the maintenance of long-term knowledge but other relevant research.
16. One year of high school Spanish was equated to one term or semester course at college, although previous high school Spanish was not taken into account where such students also studied at college.

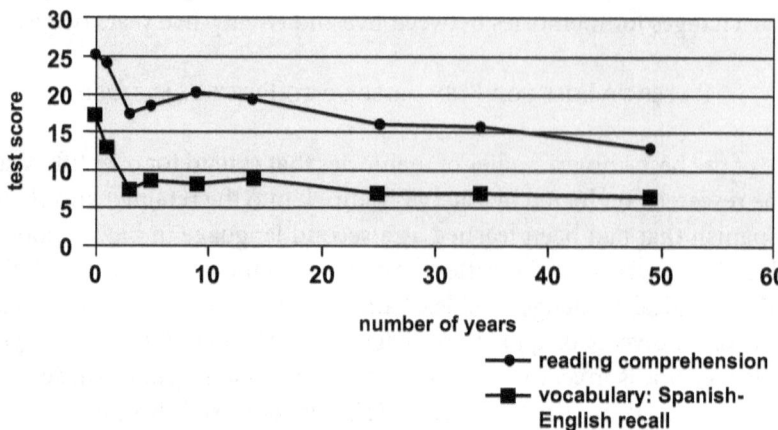

Figure 2.6. Bahrich: Spanish in permastore

25 years after training during which no responses appear to be lost" (Bahrick 1984, 22–23). This period of constant memory is observable particularly in the graph tracing vocabulary recall in figure 2.6, which shows test scores for both reading comprehension and Spanish-English vocabulary.[17]

Bahrick also found that the quality of the initial learning was very important for the long-term survival of the information. Not unexpectedly, the better the initial learning, the more that survived the initial period of loss, and the better the long-term results. Bahrick's graph, reproduced in figure 2.7, shows vocabulary results for three levels of training.[18] Those with the least exposure and mastery of the language lost so much during the initial period that nothing was left after five years. But those who had had the best initial exposure and mastery of the language retained about half of their original knowledge up to the period in which it had consolidated. It then remained available for a further twenty years, after which there was further gradual decline.

Some of the other research into very long-term memory supports the results reported by Bahrick. One such example showing that the rate of

---

17. The graph in figure 2.5 is constructed out of statistics from table 5, Bahrick 1984, 12. Figure 2.6, a graph taken from Bahrick, gives similar information but uses a logarithmic scale, which turns the curvilinear initial loss of information into a straight line.

18. The graph is scanned from Bahrick 2000, 349 fig. 22.1; the original graph is found in Bahrick 1984, 16.

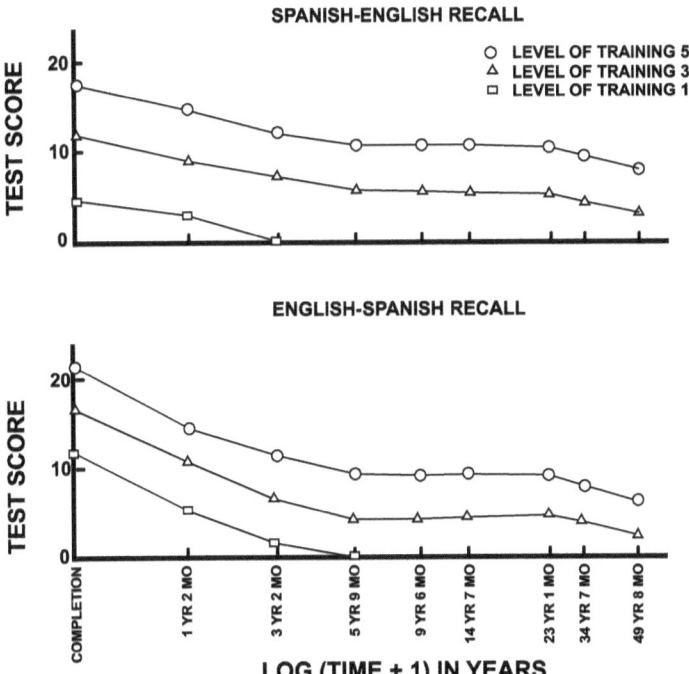

Figure 2.7. Retention of Spanish vocabulary for periods of up to fifty years (Bahrick 2000, fig. 22.1)

memory loss approaches zero after three to four years is research conducted by Martin A. Conway, Gillian Cohen, and Nicola Stanhope in their investigation into what was retained of an Open-University course on Cognitive Psychology over a period of up to twelve years (Conway, Cohen, and Stanhope 1991, 395–409). The 373 former students who participated in their study represented about 40 percent of those who had taken the specific subject in the previous twelve years, with between eighteen and forty-eight students responding for any given year. They discovered that "retention rapidly declines over the first 36 to 48 months of retention and then levels out and stays at the same level throughout the remaining 8 years. It is also clear ... that the decline in retention is more rapid for names than concepts" (1991, 400).

Not all research into very long-term memory has shown these kinds of forgetting curves. For example, H. P. Bahrick, P. O. Bahrick, and R. P. Wittlinger discovered that a different pattern existed for how well 392 high school graduates remembered names and faces for periods of up to fifty years (Bahrick, Bahrick, and Wittlinger 1975, 54–75). Although those tested on graduation could only recall about 15 percent of the names of their classmates when asked to sit down and write as many of them as they could remember in 8 minutes, they showed a much higher recognition rate for visual information, which is retained virtually unimpaired for at least thirty-five years. Among others, they were given the following tests: Could they identify ten of their fellow students' names that appeared on ten separate cards, each of which had four other names taken at random from a phone book in addition to the target name? Could they identify ten pictures of their fellow students that appeared on ten cards, each of which had four other similar pictures taken from yearbooks from the same time period? Could they match the picture with the name given at the top of the card when it appeared with four other pictures taken from the same yearbook? And, could they match a name to the single picture on the card, given four other names from the same class? Soon after graduation, all of these tasks were performed with approximately 90 percent accuracy, and this ability remained at about the same level for at least thirty-five years for those that involved picture recognition and matching. Even name recognition remained at a high level, declining from 91 percent to 77 percent. It was only with the fifty-year cohort that inaccuracies began to appear, and accuracies between 60 percent and 80 percent were discovered for the various tasks for this group.[19] Thus, the process of forgetting visual information appears to have different parameters from that of forgetting verbal information, an observation of potentially great importance in the upcoming discussion of flashbulb memories.

Nor would an account of long-term memory be complete without reference to studies that reveal that some aspects of autobiographical memory do not show good reliability over the long-term. One such study compared the memories of sixty-seven males first interviewed in the first month of their freshman year in high school in 1962, with their adult memories of that time in 1997, some thirty-five years later. Subjects were initially

---

19. See figure 1 and table 4 in Bahrick, Bahrick, and Wittlinger 1975, 66, 62, as well as the discussion of results on 65–69. Tertiary teachers such as myself may be reassured to discover that such long-term memories of names and faces were only true of the students in the classes. "Later study shows that the accuracy of recognizing the names and faces of former students by the college instructors declines with the logarithm of time. The decline begins very soon after exposure, and relatively little information survives beyond 8 years" (Bahrick 1984, 23).

chosen because they had average academic records, and no indication was given from either the school or their parents that they were other than mentally healthy. In lengthy interviews conducted in 1962 and between 1991 and 1997, the participants were asked a number of questions, such as their mother's best/worst trait, whether their parents worked together on projects, whether girls liked them (as teenagers), what activities they enjoyed most (as teenagers), and so forth. The researchers found large differences between what was reported in 1962 and what was remembered as an adult.

> For example, 28% of the teenage boys said that they did not like high school and homework. During adulthood, however, 58% said they remembered not liking school and homework. Similarly, in high school 24% said that they most enjoyed relationships with their peers. In adulthood, 52% thought that they had most enjoyed relationships with peers. Eighty-two percent of the boys reported that they were disciplined with physical punishment, whereas only 33% of men stated that they had received such punishment. (Offer et al. 2000, 737)

In fact, the researchers discovered that the relationship between what teenagers reported in 1962 and their memories thirty-five years or so after the event was no better than chance (Offer et al. 2000, 737). Research reported in later chapters will provide evidence that human memory can remember some significant autobiographical events from the distant past, but the study of Offer et al. shows that caution needs to be exercised lest a too-optimistic view of the capabilities of human memory be adopted.

Conclusion: Memory Stable after the First Five Years

Each of the experiments on human memory reported so far has underlined the fact that human memories are indeed transient. Moreover, most reveal that the macro-effects of this transience are largely predictable. Many of the different kinds of memory have been shown to exhibit a similar pattern of retention and loss (the forgetting curve). The characteristic forgetting curve found by Ebbinghaus in his study of memory of nonsense syllables has also been found in most types of verbal memory, in aspects of visual memory, and in a wide variety of other types of memory. When it is possible to accurately measure these rates of forgetting under laboratory conditions, the results become predictable enough to be represented by curves on a graph. It is even possible to provide mathematical equations for such curves.

Several results stand out as of particular relevance for this investigation into the impact that the frailties of human memory may have had on the traditions in the Synoptic Gospels. First, it is noteworthy that memories of life episodes—episodic memory—appear to follow an Ebbinghausian forgetting curve for at least five years. Second, none of the experiments reported have explicitly studied episodic memory for longer than five years. Yet because episodic memories share the Ebbinghausian forgetting curve characteristic of so many different types of memory, and because the results of Bahrick's experiments on the very long-term memory of Spanish learned as a second language exhibit such a curve for the first three to six years, there appears every likelihood that very long-term episodic memory shares a similar long-term forgetting curve to that of the long-term memory of an unused second language. In other words, episodic memory that survives for the first five years after an event is likely to be very stable for the next twenty years or more, after which time a further slow decline takes place. It may even be estimated that between 30 and 50 percent of significant material is likely to survive long enough to become a near-permanent part of long-term memory.[20] Third, time references are the weakest component of episodic memory.

However, the results of experiments into very long-term memory do not all conform to the uniform picture of memory transience just presented. In particular, not all of them have shown an Ebbinghausian forgetting curve. This is particularly true of the long-term memory of the faces of classmates. Perhaps some kinds of visual memory and other memories attached to strong sensory inputs are exempt from the frailty of transience. Indeed, such has been argued in the case of so-called flashbulb memories, a topic considered in the next chapter.

---

20. A fact reported in their survey of fifty-six articles reporting ninety-six separate experiments in long-term retention of memory by George B. Semb and John A. Ellis 1994.

3
Personal Event Memories

Many of the events described in the Gospels are of such a nature that they would have had a significant emotional and sensory impact on participants and eyewitnesses. In the results of experiments looking at long-term human memories described in the previous chapter, there were hints that emotional and sensory memories may be less susceptible to the frailty of transience than other types of memory. For example, the long-term memory for the faces of school and university classmates provided one example of the remarkable persistence of a certain type of visual memory. This suggests the possibility that participants and eyewitnesses to some of the dramatic events in the ministry of Jesus may have developed special kinds of memories of them. The present chapter will examine claims that memories of events with significant emotional and sensory impact are, in fact, immune to the normal processes of forgetting.

Flashbulb Memories Perhaps Exempt from Transience

Some memories may be exempt from the frailty of transience described in the previous chapter. At least, that was a possibility raised in a 1977 article by Roger Brown and James Kulik, in which they introduced a new term into the academic literature on human memory research: the flashbulb memory (Brown and Kulik 1977, 73–99). In their seminal article, Brown and Kulik argue that events such as the assassination of John F. Kennedy, which combine surprise with a high level of consequentiality and emotional arousal, are recorded in the human memory in a manner not dissimilar to a flash photograph. They suggest the term "flashbulb memory" is an ideal descriptor of something that combines surprise, indiscriminate illumination, and brevity, although, as they hasten to point out, an actual photograph provides a largely indiscriminate record of everything within view, while flashbulb memories do not.

In their investigation of this phenomenon, Brown and Kulik examined the memories that eighty students held of ten significant events. The list of events included the assassination of John F. Kennedy, as well as an unspecified "personal, unexpected shock, such as the death of a friend or relative, serious accident, diagnosis of a deadly disease, etc." As the two researchers analyzed the student's self-reported memories of the ten events, they found that the descriptions of those events that they deemed to have formed a flashbulb memory consistently include many of the following six items of information: the "Place" in which the news was heard, "the 'Ongoing Event' that was interrupted by the news, the 'Informant' who brought ... the news, the 'Affect in Others' upon hearing the news, as well as 'Own Affect' and finally some immediate 'Aftermath'" (Brown and Kulik 1977, 80). These six they termed "abstract canonical categories." In addition, they discovered that many accounts of flashbulb memory events included some highly idiosyncratic information, which seems to have been included almost by accident, such as the articles of clothing worn at the time, memories of fragments of the conversation that took place, or what the weather conditions were like.

The reported study included forty white students and forty black students. It was discovered that the black students were much more likely to form a flashbulb memory of the death of Malcolm X and Martin Luther King than the white students. Brown and Kulik concluded that this is evidence that personal consequentiality is important in the formation of flashbulb memories. Interestingly enough, the assassination of John F. Kennedy formed a flashbulb memory for seventy-nine of the eighty students in the study, despite the fact that twenty-four of them were between seven and eleven years old at the time of the event. This memory came a close second in the amount of elaboration in the memory to the category "a personal, unexpected shock." "On the evidence, John Kennedy rated as a memory of almost everyone's immediate family" (Brown and Kulik 1977, 87).

As a result of their analysis, Brown and Kulik postulated that, "a FB [flashbulb] memory [is] fixed for a very long time, and conceivably permanently, varying in complexity with consequentiality but, once created, always there, and in need of no further strengthening" (Brown and Kulick 1977, 85). This memory, they suggested, is not preserved in a narrative or verbal form but in other forms, such as images. Thus, any subsequent narrative description of the events is reconstructed using the flashbulb memory, and frequent rehearsal results in a coherent narrative.

Brown and Kulik's paper also considered the survival value of a flashbulb memory mechanism. While they had defined a flashbulb memory strictly in terms of reported events, not eyewitness events,[1] they explain the mechanism in terms of the survival value of an accurate recording of startling events—including the concomitant circumstances. For "primitive man," the ability to know not just that a new and dangerous predator was in the environment but where, when, and what else was happening at the time would provide a distinctive survival advantage. Thus, Brown and Kulik explained the mechanism more in terms of an eyewitness of an event rather than of someone learning of an event by hearsay.

Are flashbulb memories especially privileged, so that they are "always there, unchanging as the slumbering Rhinegold, and serving by means of rehearsal to generate some variety of accounts," as suggested by Brown and Kulik (1977, 86)? On this matter there is a growing body of experimental evidence that gives important clues as to the long-term reliability of flashbulb memories.

---

1. "Remember that it is not memory for the central newsworthy event that constitutes a FB memory, but rather memory for the *circumstances* in which one first heard the news" (Brown and Kulik 1977, 95). Some later research has shown that this observation may need to be nuanced somewhat. For example, Steen F. Larsen's experiment on his own autobiographical memory showed that, while the attendant circumstances are preserved in a flashbulb event, it is the memory of the event itself that is best preserved. At the end of each day for a period of months, Larsen made notes about two events during the day: one an event from his personal life, the other a news item. It so happened that several news items in this period were of a nature that would be expected to form flashbulb memories: the prime minister of Denmark was assassinated (Larsen is a Dane); the Chernobyl nuclear power station experienced a meltdown; and the space shuttle Challenger exploded on launch. On testing, Larsen found that, while the memories for the central elements of these momentous events were higher than for ordinary news, "the more intuitively impressive and emotionally involving the events are, the more memory of the event seemed to increase at the expense of memory of the context; that is, they behaved exactly opposite to what is expected from flashbulbs" (Larsen 1992, 53). Larsen did experience a number of events where the memory of the context was much greater than the memory of the event itself: events such as watching the semifinal game between Brazil and France in World Cup soccer and the newspaper report of a man beaten to death by three youngsters in a nearby small town (Larsen 1992, 32–64).

The Reliability of Flashbulb Memories up to Three Years Later

Forgetting curves are ubiquitous in memory studies. Thus Brown and Kulik's paper suggesting a new type of memory immune from transience was greeted with great interest, and it has subsequently generated a significant body of research. Naturally, this research has had to be opportunistic. After all, events such as the moment one hears about the death of a close friend are like most other events that might form flashbulb memories: they are very personal and do not generate memories in enough individuals to form a suitable sample to study. What makes the assassination of John F. Kennedy the prototypical flashbulb memory event is that Kennedy had such a national and international standing that his unexpected death had a strong emotional impact on millions. Consequently, psychologists have usually studied the reliability and stability of flashbulb memories of events of national and international importance, events such as the start of the bombing of Iraq, the O. J. Simpson trial verdict, the death of Princess Diana, the resignation of Margaret Thatcher, the loss of the space shuttle Challenger, and the terrorist destruction of the twin towers in New York on 9/11. Clearly, many of these will have had greater emotional impact or have been of more personal significance to some people than others. One would expect that the death of Diana, Princess of Wales, would have had more emotional impact than the resignation of Margaret Thatcher, for example, although the latter did form flashbulb memories for some. Not surprisingly, both of these events were more likely to form flashbulb memories for U.K. nationals than for non-U.K. nationals (Conway 1995, 55, fig 3.5).[2] Of the events listed, though, perhaps that of 9/11 may have

---

2. One might compare the results of the study by Lia Kvavilashvili, Jennifer Mirani, Simone Schlagman, and Diana E. Kornbrot, who compared the events of 9/11 with memories of the death of Diana, Princess of Wales, reasoning that this might overcome, to some extent, the problem of high drop-out rates when following the same group of participants of a number of years. They discovered that Italian participants had higher flashbulb memories scores for 9/11 than for the death of Princess Diana but that "British participants' 51-month old memories of the death of Princess Diana were as detailed, specific and vivid as the 2/3 and 10/11-days old memories of September 11," although they hasten to point out that their methodology did not make any claim about whether or not these vivid details were "partially or even completely wrong" (Kvavilashvili et al. 2003, 1030). Antonietta Curci and Olivier Luminet also report a cross-national difference in the specificity of flashbulb memory (the autobiographical component) and event memory (the nonautobiographical component) between U.S.

had the widest impact. The event was unexpected and disquieting. Thus one would expect most of those who heard about it to form a flashbulb memory. These memories would be reinforced by the frequent repetition of the dramatic and disturbing images of the event shown by most television stations worldwide.

On 12 September 2001, within one day of the dramatic events of 9/11, Jennifer M. Talarico and David C. Rubin arranged for fifty-four students at Duke University to note both their memory of first hearing about the terrorist attacks and their memory of a recent everyday event. They were randomly allocated to one of three groups, which were respectively tested at intervals roughly equivalent on a logarithmic scale:[3] at 7 days, 42 days (6 weeks), or 224 days (32 weeks, or just short of 8 months) later. Each group was retested once. Their memories were cued for the 9/11 event with the words "How you first heard about the news of the attacks on America on Tuesday, September 11, 2001" and for the personal memories by a short description provided by the participant at the time of the first testing. It was discovered that *both* the flashbulb memory and the everyday memory show a similar logarithmic decline in consistent details and a similar increase in the number of inconsistent memories. In fact, the real difference between the two groups of memories was in the confidence that the participants felt in their memories of 9/11 when compared to an everyday memory. As Talarico and Rubin conclude: "Our most consistent finding is that a flashbulb event reliably enhances memory characteristics such as vividness and confidence. The true 'mystery,' then, is not why flashbulb memories are so accurate for so long, as Brown and Kulik (1977) thought, but why people are so confident for so long on the accuracy of their flashbulb memories" (Talarico and Rubin 2003, 460).[4]

---

respondents and those of other nationals, all differences being statistically significant but being greater for event memory and greatest for those between those from the U.S. and Romania (the other countries with respondents in the survey included Belgium, Italy, the Netherlands, and Japan) (Curci and Luminet 2006, 329–44).

3. According to the discussion in the previous chapter on "forgetting curves," the process of forgetting follows most closely a power function, although a logarithmic function comes close. Thus time intervals based on a logarithmic progression make sense in the context of this experiment.

4. Other researchers have formed a more positive assessment on the reliability and durability of flashbulb memories of the 9/11 attacks. For example, Curci and Luminet suggest that the "results from the present study seem to give support to the idea of flashbulb memories as a special class of memories, which persist unchanged

Other researchers have published results that tend to support this assessment of flashbulb memories. Within twenty-four hours of the 1986 Challenger disaster, for example, Ulric Neisser and Nicole Harsch obtained questionnaire responses from 106 students at Emory University enrolled in Psychology 101. The questionnaire first elicited a free recall account of how the participants had heard about the disaster and then, on the next page, asked questions based on Brown and Kulik's "canonical categories." Two and a half years later, a group of forty-four students, which consisted of most of the original group who were still enrolled at Emory, took part in a follow-up study in which they answered the same questionnaire, with some additional questions, such as their confidence in their recall (ranging from 1 "just guessing" to 5 "absolutely certain), and whether or not they had ever filled out a questionnaire on the Challenger disaster before (75 percent answered no!). Curiously, even though thirteen of the respondents were "absolutely sure" of their memories and a further seventeen rated their confidence at 4 or above, only three of the subjects were accurate in all major details in their recall, and eleven (25 percent) of them gave completely different accounts. For example, participant "RT" initially reported hearing about the disaster in the following manner:

> I was in my religion class and some people walked in and started talking about [it]. I didn't know any details except that it had exploded and the school teacher's students had all been watching which I thought was so sad. Then after class I went to my room and watched the TV program talking about it and I got all the details from that. (Neisser and Harsch 1992, 9)

Two and a half years later, RT's memories of hearing the news is as follows:

> When I first heard about the explosion I was sitting in my freshman dorm room with my roommate and we were watching TV. It came on

---

and consistent over time" (Curci and Luminet 2006, 342). Lauren R. Shapiro agrees, stating, "In the current research, the durability of flashbulb memory was clearly demonstrated by the participants who remembered detailed information about their location, activity, and source of their reception context of September 11th, even after 2 years. Respondents provide essentially or exactly the same detailed information for the three major attributes at each retention interval between the event and the assessment, despite differences in the amount of overt rehearsal (i.e., surveys) they had between assessments" (Shapiro 2006, 145).

a news flash and we were both totally shocked. I was really upset and I went upstairs to talk to a friend of mine and then I called my parents. (Neisser and Harsch 1992, 9)

In many accounts in the two-and-a-half-year follow-up that showed marked differences between the follow-up survey and the original, there was a tendency to give television as the source of information, whereas in the initial survey the information had been said to originate in some interaction with fellow students or friends. Neisser and Harsch suggest that these different accounts might in fact be memories of events that actually happened. The frequent and graphic reshowing of the explosion would have formed very strong images, and the participants might have made a "time-slice error."[5] That is, they might be remembering a slightly later event, although some of the differences between responses cannot be accounted for in this manner. Many of the other accounts fell somewhere between the extremes of totally consistent and quite different, some elements being repeated without change and others quite differently.

What is particularly interesting, though, are the follow-up interviews that took place six months later with forty of the forty-four participants, in which the experimenters attempted to discover whether it was possible to elicit the earlier memories. Even when confronted with the original handwritten account, "No one who had given an incorrect account in the interview even pretended that they now recalled what was stated on the original record. ... As far as we can tell, the original memories are just gone" (Neisser and Harsch 1992, 25–26). On the other hand, there was a very high degree of consistency in the accounts taken at two and a half years and three years (Neisser and Harsch 1992, 21).[6]

---

5. Time-slice errors are known from other research (e.g., Brewer 1988, 21–90, esp. 58–59, 79–80). Ira E. Hyman Jr. has provided what he describes as a preliminary list of memory errors, of which time-slice error is but one of eight: gist description, intrusions, inferences, misinformation effect, source and reality monitory errors, time slice errors, and other errors. These he broadly categorizes under schema-based reconstructions and source-monitoring failures (Hyman 1999, 230–35).

6. One might compare these results with those obtained by H. Schmolck, E. A. Buffalo, and L. R. Squire in their investigation of the consistency of the memory of the O. J. Simpson trial verdict of sixty-three students of the University of California, San Diego, over the periods three days and fifteen and thirty-two months after the event. Most students had detailed memories that could be classified as flashbulb memories, yet when objectively tested, these memories showed a distinct decline in accuracy.

This last observation, that flashbulb memories become stable after a certain time period, was used by Robert G. Winningham, Ira E. Hyman Jr., and Dale L. Dinnel to explain the various assessments of the consistency of flashbulb memories in their meta-analysis of six previous research reports. In these reports, the consistency ratings of flashbulb memories ranged from 18 percent to 99 percent, a truly remarkable range. A number of factors were suggested to be of importance in accounting for this variation in consistency. Perhaps, they suggest, not all events studied as flashbulb memory events have the "consequentiality and emotionality needed to form flashbulb memories in a Brown and Kulik sense." But the crucial factor may well be the time lapse between the event and the initial collection of memories of the event. A longer delay between the event and the collecting of indexing memories leads to a higher consistency of these memories. Perhaps these types of memories become more consistent after an initial period of consolidation (Winningham, Hyman, and Dinnel 2000, 215). Emauele Coluccia, Carmela Bianco, and Marie A. Brandimonte did find some consolidation of event memories (nonautobiographical memories) of the 9/11 attacks but not of flashbulb (autobiographical) memories associated with that event. Curiously enough, they also discovered that the "confidence on autobiographical components of a FBM is unrelated to consistency of recall. On the contrary, the more people are confident in their event memory, the less they are consistent. … Surprisingly, a negative correlation emerges between veridicality [historical accuracy] and event consistency ($n = 452$, $r = -.32$, $p < .001$), which means that the less the information is veridical, the more consistent it is" (Coluccia, Bianco, and Brandimonte 2006, 465). The inconsistency in veridical information was often the result of omission of elements of previous descriptions or the introduction of new elements.

Such studies as have been just described allow a relatively well-informed assessment of flashbulb memories. They have confirmed much of what was initially postulated by Brown and Kulik. Hearing startling news that is of such personal consequence that it arouses a strong emotional response does indeed form a special type of memory, aptly described as a flashbulb

---

"After 15 months, 50% of the recollections were highly accurate, and only 11% contained major errors or distortions. After 32 months, only 29% of the recollections were highly accurate, and more than 40% contained major distortions." Moreover, "individuals were frequently as confident of their inaccurate recollections as they were of the accurate recollections" (Schmolck, Buffalo, and Squire 2000, 39 and 44)

memory. Such memories encompass a brief time period and are accompanied by a vivid memory of details of what was happening at the time, as well as a strong memory of the emotional response to the news. Those recounting such memories consider them to be highly accurate, probably on the basis of their vividness. It is here, though, that further research has refined Brown and Kulik's initial suggestion that such memories were in fact very accurate and long-lived. While vivid and long-lived, flashbulb memories have been discovered to be no more accurate than memories of more mundane events, despite the fact that the one possessing such a memory is convinced of its veracity.

Flashbulb Memories as Personal Event Memories

David Pillemer has argued that flashbulb memories are but a subset of a wider type of memory that he calls "personal event memories." Pillemer begins his book *Momentous Events, Vivid Memories* (1998) with a number of examples of memories of momentous events. A soldier in World War II describes in vivid detail an incident in the war that he had been lucky to survive. A Jewish survivor of the same war remembers the circumstances in which he last saw his mother as she was taken away to a concentration camp. Somebody else remembers hearing about the assassination of President Lincoln, and a woman remembers the circumstances in which she accepted a marriage proposal. All of these events were remembered in vivid detail, including details of concomitant circumstances, and share many of the characteristics of flashbulb memories. Pillemer suggests that these might all be termed "personal event memories" and develops the following criteria by which they may be recognized. An event is a personal event memory if:

- "The memory represents a *specific* event that took place at a particular time and place, rather than a general event or an extended series of related happenings."

- "The memory contains a *detailed* account of the rememberer's *own personal circumstances* at the time of the event."

- "The verbal narrative account of the event is accompanied by *sensory images*, including visual, auditory, olfactory images or bodily sensations, that contribute to the feeling of 'reexperiencing' or 'reliving.'"

- "Memory details and sensory images correspond to a particular *moment* or moments of phenomenal experience."

- "The rememberer *believes* that the memory is a truthful representation of what transpired." (Pillemer 1998, 50–51)

For Pillemer, memories of personal trauma, flashbulb memories, memories of critical incidents, and moments of insight are but varieties of personal event memories (1998, 30–49).[7] They all involve something so significant to the individual concerned that they leave a strong emotional and sensory memory. Indeed, this is the crucial thing: the experience of the momentous event is remembered in terms of what is seen, heard, and felt. On the other hand, these experiences are usually shared with others in terms of a narrative account of the event. Pillemer finds much explanatory power in the fact that verbal and narrative memory appears to be a different system from memory of emotional and sensory information. Given the importance of the differences between memory systems that will emerge later in our investigation, Pillemer's references to and uses of the differences between some of the subsystems of memory are worthy of further exploration.

As evidence for the distinction between narrative memory and sensory memory, Pillemer discusses the phenomenon of infantile amnesia. A number of studies have convincingly demonstrated that most adults cannot remember any event, such as the birth of a sibling, that took place earlier than when they were aged three.[8] Memories of specific events occur-

---

7. One might compare the grouping of eyewitness memory, flashbulb memories, and memory for traumatic events by Jonathan W. Schooler and Eric Eich (2000, 379–92).

8. "On average, adults do not recall events in their lives before about the age of 3½ years" (Pressley and Schneider 1997, 8). In their analysis of the earliest memories of 467 undergraduate students, Darryl Bruce et al. discovered that their earliest childhood memories were very fragmentary, and in this sample the median age at which such memories could be dated was 3.29 years of age (Bruce et al. 2005, 567–76). Cf. the more nuanced result in Ros A. Crawley and Madeline J. Eacott: "The commonly cited age for the offset of childhood amnesia is around 3:6.... Nonetheless, our study indicates that memories from before the age of 3:6 are quite common ... and also that memories from the ages of 2:4–3:5 do not differ qualitatively from those recalled from the ages of 3:6–5:5" (Crawley and Eacott 2006, 291). A result more similar to that of Bruce et al. was found by investigations of the youngest age from which adults can remember a childhood dream (in Fiske and Pillemer 2006, 57–67).

ring when the individual was older increase in number with age, although more comprehensive childhood memories are only available from middle childhood. Yet a number of studies have also demonstrated that children between zero and twenty-four months do indeed have memories and that these memories are persistent.[9] Several explanations have been put forward to explain these apparent discrepancies, many of which revolve around the fact that language skills are insufficient to develop narrative memory before the age of two or three.[10] Thus, while children less than two or three years of age remember actions and emotions, there is no corresponding narrative memory, and thus the memories are unavailable to their adult selves.[11]

Pillemer uses the fact that narrative memory is different from visual and emotional memory to explain some post-trauma experiences of trauma victims, especially those that experience post-traumatic stress syndrome. A particularly disturbing feature of post-traumatic stress syndrome is that images and emotions associated with the trauma intrude unexpectedly into the present consciousness, often so vividly that the trauma is re-experienced, sometimes at quite inappropriate times. Treatment of post traumatic stress syndrome varies, and is frequently challenging. It often involves developing a detailed narrative description of the event, with an

---

9. See, for example, the graph at Rovee-Collier and Gerhardstein 1997, 18, which shows a three-month-old retaining a memory for up to a week, a nine-month old retaining a memory for up to six weeks, and an eighteen-month-old retaining a memory up to twelve weeks. See also Rovee-Collier and Hayne 2000, 267–82; Bauer et al. 2000.

10. "Which aspects of early mental development are directly implicated in childhood amnesia? Hypothesized psychological factors include language development (Nelson, 1993; Terr, 1998), socially induced changed in the categories of thought (Neisser, 1967; Schachtel, 1947), developmental changes in cognitive processing and understanding (White and Pillemer 1979; Pillemer and White, 1989; Pillemer et al., 1994), developmental changes in perception (Hayne and Rovee-Collier, 1995), development of an interpersonal and autobiographic self (Fivush, 1988; Nelson, 1993); and development of a representational theory of mind (Perner and Ruffman, 1995)" (Pillemer 1998, 113).

11. Stephen J. Ceci's observation that "a developmental-cognitive principle states that the cognitive status of the organism at time 1 sets the conditions for memory recovery at time 2. A similar cognitive mechanism must be available at time 2 in order to make contact with the trace as it was originally encoded. ... If the adult mind is organized differently from a 2-year-old's mind, then there is scant evidence that the former can gain access to the cognitive products of the latter" (Ceci 1995, 95–96), adds yet another dimension to the issue of infantile amnesia.

aim to integrating the images and a narrative, thereby bringing both types of memory into greater correspondence (Pillemer 1998, 162–70).[12] This is a process that usually takes place naturally. Sensory and emotional memories exist for all of the events of personal significance that fit Pillemer's definition, although for most of them there is an easy relationship between the sensory memory and the narrative memory. One curious feature of descriptions of events for which there is strong sensory memory, though, is the tendency for the short period of such events for which sensory memories exist (the "flash") to be described using the present tense, even if the rest of the narrative is expressed in the past tense.

In a chapter entitled "Memory Directives," Pillemer explores a number of categories of personal event memories that provide guidelines for current and future behavior and that offer interesting parallels to some of the materials in the Gospels. The first of these involves memorable messages that have made a significant impact on a person's life. He cites several examples. In one, a Jewish father explains to his seven-year-old son, "the spoken word is the Jew's weapon. We can't really be soldiers; we must always rely on the spoken word." In another example, a Harvard undergraduate student uncertain of which career to choose is told, "Try medicine, why don't you. Lots to keep you busy, and lots to make you think. The great thing is— you get to forget yourself a lot of the time." A Jewish expert in faulty eyewitness identification experiencing internal conflict when asked to help defend an accused war criminal was told by a friend, "Do you know what Emerson said about consistency? A foolish consistency is the hobgoblin of little minds" (Pillemer 1998, 65–68). Sentences from parents, teachers, and close friends can be vividly remembered and used to give guidance to current and future behavior.[13] Pillemer describes an inspiring example as a

---

12. Cf. the words of Dorthe Berntsen and Dorthe K. Thomsen: "Intrusive memories are generally viewed as an important signpost of posttraumatic stress reactions … [and] reflect an inability to integrate a stressful experience into the overall knowledge base of the person, leading to a fluctuation between intrusions and attempts at avoiding reminders of the event" (2005, 245; cf. Krystal, Southwick, and Charney1995, 150–72, esp. 162–63).

13. Mark L. Knapp, Cynthia Stohl, and Kathleen K. Reardon gathered examples of significant messages that had had a significant impact on the lives of the 227 students, faculty, and acquaintances they interviewed. Such messages were communicated orally in a single sentence, directed specifically at the individual who remembered them, 75 percent of them contained an (often implicit) injunction or command, 70 percent of informants considered they remembered the precise words used, 72 per-

symbolic message. Others point back to an event that started a significant trend in their lives: examples include the four- or five-year-old Einstein's fascination with a magnet or Dorothy Reed Mendenhall's experience in her first lecture on general biology that this is what she had been waiting for all these years. Some events act as anchoring events—they give encouragement to continue at times of doubt. Some events form turning points in people's lives.

What can be said about the reliability of personal event memories? One might argue that what has been discovered to be true of one type of personal event memory—flashbulb memories—is highly likely to be true of other types of personal event memories. This argument has an inherent plausibility. After all, the distinctive features of flashbulb memories—their short time frame, their vivid details, and their emotional content—are true of all the various kinds of memories considered by Pillemer to be examples of personal event memories.

On the other hand, it would be desirable to confirm this by considering evidence that might exist for the reliability of other types of personal event memories, particularly those associated with the memories of eyewitnesses, and particularly eyewitness memories of events from thirty to sixty years earlier. Such studies are rare because of the difficulties of developing an adequate experimental methodology. Yet it has proven possible to formulate several methodologies that have enabled the study of the fifty-year-old memories of eyewitnesses to events associated with the Second World War.

The Reliability of Personal Event Memories up to Fifty Years Later

All of the experiments reported thus far in this chapter have investigated memories that are only three years old or less, which is but a small fraction of time compared to the probable period between the events of the life and death of Jesus and their recording. Dorthe Berntsen and Dorthe K. Thomsen, on the other hand, found a way to study eyewitness personal event memories more than sixty years old (Bernsten and Thomsen 2005, 242–57). They did so by comparing the memories of two groups: the first consisted of 145 older Danes between seventy-two and eighty-nine years

---

cent of the content was action oriented, and 97 percent of the messages came from a person of same or higher status (e.g., boss, parent, college professor) (Knapp, Stohl, and Reardon 1981, 4–31).

of age; the second were a group of sixty-five faculty members, staff, and psychology majors from Aarhus University, aged between twenty and sixty years of age, who were either not born or were less than two years old at the end of the Second World War. The events studied were the German invasion of Denmark, which had taken place early in the morning of 9 April 1940, and the BBC broadcast at 8:35 PM, 4 May 1945, announcing the surrender of the German troops in Holland, northwest Germany, and Denmark. These two events should have been known to those in both groups, especially the events of the liberation. Those who had not personally lived through the experience would have learned about it in school and been reminded by the frequent public commemorations of the liberation.

Several items of information were gathered from both groups about the two events, including the day of the week, the time of day, and weather conditions. In addition, the older group were initially given a task of free recall. They were asked where they were and what were they doing at the time of the two events and to describe the context in which they learned the news in the greatest possible detail. They were also asked about their most positive and most negative memory of the war, whether they had dreams or intrusive memories of the events of the war, and whether they try to avoid thinking about one or more of the four events (i.e., the invasion, their positive and negative memory, and the liberation).

All of the older group (the "war" group) had lived through the experiences, and 95 percent had memories of the two public events that Berntsen and Thomsen considered as fulfilling Brown and Kulik's criterion for a flashbulb memory. In the light of what has been said earlier, however, it is probably better to describe them as personal event memories, as these were not memories of reports of the events, but memories of actual experiences of the events. Be that as it may, the open-ended description given by 95 percent of the "war" group contained one, and usually more, of Brown and Kulik's "abstract canonical categories," and most contained idiosyncratic details. It is evident from the data presented in Table 3.1 that some of these memories also contained information that is more detailed and more accurate than the memories of the control group.[14]

The differences between the two groups are remarkable and statistically significant: 69 percent (i.e., 100 individuals) of those who experi-

---

14. Table 3.1 was constructed on the basis of tables 2, 4, and 5 of Berntsen and Thomsen 2005, 248–49.

Table 3.1. The Accuracy of Fifty-Year-Old Eyewitness Memories of World-War II Compared to General Knowledge: Percentage Results for Questions Regarding Weather, Which Day, and Exact Time of Capitulation

	Weather for Invasion		Weather for Liberation		Day of Invasion		Day of Liberation		Exact time Capitulation	
	War	Control	War	Control	War	Control	War	Control	War	Control
No answer	16	80	14	86	63	89	64	86	13	55
Wrong	7.5	4.5	8	3	1	3	7	6	39	34
Close	7.5	11	11	6	8	3	6	5	32	11
Correct	69	4.5	67	5	28	5	23	3	16	0

All figures are expressed as percentages (n = 145 for war group; 65 for control group)

enced the invasion remembered the weather on the day correctly, whereas only 4.5 percent (3) of the control group did so; 28 percent (40) of those who experienced the invasion remembered the exact day of the week correctly, compared to only 5 percent (3) of the control group; and 16 percent (23) of those who experienced the liberation remembered the time of the capitulation announcement to within 5 minutes, which none of the control group were able to do. Interestingly enough, if those who experienced the events made a mistake on the weather, they tended to bias the weather on the day of the invasion negatively and the day of liberation positively.

Here, then, is strong evidence that personal event memories can persist over very long periods and carry with them accurate information about details of the events. Naturally, not every memory contains all of the events—after all, over 60 percent of those who experienced it could not remember on which day of the week the invasion or the liberation took place, and some of those who thought they knew got the answer wrong. But of those who answered, by far the greatest number knew the correct response, and in a manner dramatically different from others who had been exposed repeatedly to the same information but who had not experienced the event.

A similar assessment of the general reliability of long-term personal event memories is made by Willem A. Wagenaar and Jop Groeneweg on the basis of their research into the records of police interviews of the Dutch survivors of a World War II concentration camp (Wagenaar and Groeneweg 1990, 77–87). Camp Erika, set up as a Dutch prison for convicted criminals, was run under the kind of German rule common in concentration camps throughout Europe in World War II, including the appointment of some prisoners as Kapos, who had the explicit task of terrorizing their fellow prisoners. Immediately after Camp Erika was closed in 1943, the Dutch police started interviewing survivors, a process that continued until 1948. Forty years later, between 1984 and 1987, the Dutch police took statements from seventy-two witnesses while investigating the case of one of the notorious Kapos, Marinus De Rijke. De Rijke had also featured in the interviews of a total of twenty-two witnesses between 1943 and 1948. A total of fifteen witnesses gave testimonies in both time periods, and it was possible to compare what they said in depositions given some forty years apart.

Wagenaar and Groeneweg report that "[t]he most striking aspect of the testimonies is that the witnesses agreed about the basic facts" (1990, 80), although omissions and actual errors increased with time. For example, in interviews given between 1943 and 1948, of those who volunteered the information, nine ex-inmates gave their date of entry into the camp correct to one month, and two gave it incorrectly. Between 1984 and 1988, of those who volunteered the information, eight gave the correct date, but eleven did not. Thirty-eight witnesses reported that they had been maltreated or tortured by De Rijke. Surprisingly, three of these thirty-eight had forgotten his name after forty years, nor did such maltreatment and torture promote the recognition of his picture. Indeed, by this time some witnesses had not only forgotten some of the dreadful incidents that they had seen, but one of them did not even remember his own extensive maltreatment by De Rijke reported by other witnesses. Yet even after forty years, almost all of the witnesses remembered Camp Erika vividly, and their reports have an overall remarkable consistency. A good number had accurate recall of details: "Seventeen out of 30 witnesses remembered their date of arrival in the camp; 16 out of 30 witnesses remembered their full registration number" (Wagenaar and Groeneweg 1990, 84).

Another study, this one of forty-three veterans of the 6 June 1944 invasion of France using interviews undertaken in 1994, fifty years after the event, showed that all had very vivid memories of that day. As one said, "When you think about it, you think it was just yesterday. It's so clear in my mind. I'll never forget" (Harvey, Stein, and Scott 1995, 316). These memories include vivid sensory memories, such as the smell of the surf and sea as one of the participants crawled inch by inch toward land. Twenty of the forty-three said that they had experienced sporadic nightmares and daytime flashbacks associated with their combat experience, and thirty of them mentioned bouts of depression associated with thinking about the events. The experimental protocol did not enable the testing of the accuracy of such memories, but it did reveal that those veterans who were able to talk through their experience with others also reported that they were coping better with their memories than those who had not had such an opportunity. This finding is consistent with what is reported above from Pillemer's observations on the therapeutic advantage of integrating the sensory memories of traumatic events into narrative.

Conclusions

The fifty-year-old personal event memories of World War II survivors, then, appear to be consistent with what is known about the reliability of flashbulb memories. This observation gives weight to the supposition that what is known about the characteristics of flashbulb memories is likely to be true also of other types of personal event memories. That is important to this study, because flashbulb memories have received the greatest scrutiny among the various types of personal event memories identified by Pillemer,[15] and consequently more is known about their reliability. Thus, the results of such investigations give the best currently available insight into the general reliability of memories that include vivid recollection of sensory images. What, then, should be concluded about their potential

---

15. This is not to say that the accuracy of other types of personal event memory is never discussed. For example, in the field of post-traumatic stress disorder, Krystal, Southwick, and Charney do give some of the mechanisms whereby PTSD patients can have distorted memories for their underlying trauma: "While some flashbacks are accurate depictions of a traumatic situation, others have unreal or distorted quality, similar to dreams" (1995, 156). "People in a stressful situation show good recall of the central event, but confabulate about motives and reactions of participants in the event" (1995, 158). They point to the moment of encoding and suggest that "it is possible that during traumatization, there is a shift away from verbal encoding towards encoding in emotional, pictorial, auditory, and other sensory-based memory systems. ... Dissociative states at the time of the trauma may also result in the encoding of bizarre or distorted traumatic memories" (1995, 158). Repetitive rehearsal may also change both the content and meaning of encoded memories.

reliability? As Daniel Reisberg and Friederike Heuer comment: "It is not clear, however, what to make of findings like these. Should we be impressed by the high levels of retention in these studies? Or should we instead focus on the substantial numbers of errors, often large errors?" (1992, 165).

In other words, the assessment of such memories comes down to what is considered to be reliable. Should one demand that flashbulb and other personal event memories retain 100 percent of information with 100 percent accuracy? If this is the demand, then such memories clearly fall short. But compared to many other types of memory, flashbulb and other personal event memories are long-lived and have the ability to retain many details with great accuracy.[16] It is an impressive feat of memory to remember the exact time of day, the day of the week, and the weather of events that happened fifty years before, as did many of those who experienced the liberation of Denmark. Not all details are remembered, and not with 100 percent accuracy. What is retained, though, is sufficient to contain the gist of the event.[17] Thus, one is safe in concluding that personal event memories are more long-lived than other types of memory and can be relied on to conserve the general gist of the event, even if some of the details might be lost or even wrong. This is similar to the assessment of personal event memories made by Pillemer: "memories of personal life episodes are generally true to the original experience, although specific details may be omitted or misremembered, and substantial distortions occasionally do occur" (1998, 59).

Such are some of the conclusions that can be drawn from a study of the memory frailty of transience, and all of these observations will prove important in later chapters. Two other frailties that have a great potential to impact eyewitness testimony—suggestibility and hindsight bias—will form the subject matter of the next chapter.

---

16. Compare Martin Conway's assessment of flashbulb memories: "The evidence for the existence of highly detailed, vivid and durable memories, FMs [flashbulb memories], is both extensive and compelling. The studies reviewed in Chapter 3 found FMs to be basically accurate and the finding considered in Chapter 4 strongly implicated the role of affect in the formation of FMs. Other findings, however, identified personal importance as the more critical factor in FM encoding" (Conway 1995, 109).

17. "The gist of the emotional event (i.e., the sum of the central aspects of the event) is well retained in memory over longer retention intervals, whereas a considerable loss is seen for peripheral aspects, or details surrounding the emotion-eliciting event" (Christianson 1992, 196).

4
Suggestibility and Bias

The memory frailty of transience has a more benign effect on eyewitness memory than both suggestibility and hindsight bias. After all, while forgetting some aspects of an event may give a lop-sided account of it, at least what remains can be considered reliable. By way of contrast, suggestibility has the potential to introduce false memories into accounts under certain conditions. Moreover, these false memories often have little or nothing to differentiate them from those elements of memory that are factually based. Thus they can introduce an element of error that is virtually impossible to eliminate. Consequently, the memory frailty of suggestibility has the potential to introduce a near-irrevocable distortion of the past, something that is also true of hindsight bias. While it is sometimes possible to take account of hindsight bias in attempting historical reconstructions, it can have such a powerful influence that it acts as a well-nigh impenetrable barrier between the present and the past.

Several mechanisms have been discovered that consistently generate false memories. These include memorizing lists of words that have a strong association with another word not on the list, providing potentially misleading visual evidence, leading questions, and, most important for this study, a process described as social contagion. The process of social contagion is one in which plausible but false memories contributed by others in a group can be seamlessly incorporated into an individual's memory.

The second frailty considered, that of memory bias, can be detected in a number of different circumstances. Detailed information will be provided about two experiments, the first involving likely outcomes of little-known historical events, the second involving a twenty-year study of married women's feelings about their marriage. Together with others that are cited, these two experiments provide evidence for the reality of some of the various types of memory bias.

The chapter will conclude by suggesting that the two frailties of suggestibility and hindsight bias should be seen as part of a wider body of evidence that human memory is actually reconstructed from a variety of subsystems. It will be further argued that they should be considered as positive aspects of the adaptability of human memory. Furthermore, it will be argued that the nature of suggestibility and hindsight bias, even though they have the potential to impact negatively the reliability of the memory of eyewitnesses, is not such that eyewitness memory becomes totally suspect. In fact, most ways to induce false memories rely on the fact that they are plausibly consistent with what actually happened. At a level deeper than the specific details (which may include incorrect information), there is a basic congruence between what an eyewitness remembers and what actually happened.

Suggestibility and False Memories

It has been shown that false memories are induced by a number of different circumstances. These will be described one after another in the following pages.

The Deese, Roediger, and McDermott False Memory Procedure (DRM)

Memorizing various lists of words has long been a staple of experimental research into memory. Naturally so, as such a task induces a number of errors and other results that can be usefully studied in a short time frame, and the task of learning lists is amenable to varied experimental manipulations. Little wonder, then, that when Henry Roediger III and K. B. McDermott used the results of an earlier experiment of J. Deese to develop a procedure that reliably induced a false memory into memorized lists of words, this procedure was widely adopted by other researchers who used it to investigate the variety of conditions under which false memories can be generated.

Deese had asked research participants to learn a list of words, such as "bed, pillows, rest, sheets." When asked to reproduce the list, participants would often include the word "sleep," a word that was not in the original list (Deese 1959, 17–22). Building on Deese's earlier work, Henry Roediger III and K. B. McDermott developed a series of lists of fifteen words that are the strongest associate to a missing word. Such a list might be "bed, rest, awake, tired, dream, wake, snooze, blanket, doze, slumber, snore, nap, peace, yawn, drowsy," all strong associates of the word "sleep" (Roediger and McDermott 1995, 803–14).[1] These lists consistently create false memories of the missing word, and their use in experiments has become known as the Deese, Roediger, and McDermott false memory procedure (often abbreviated to DRM procedure). The DRM procedure has generated a considerable body of subsequent research.[2] Two characteristic results are found under a wide variety of experimental conditions. When asked to reproduce a DRM list from memory, experimental participants produce the critical nonpresented item with the same probability as an item appearing in the middle of the list. When asked to recognize words that were in the list, "Recognition of the critical lures typically equals or exceeds recognition of the studied words" (Roediger et al. 2001, 386).

Several explanations have been put forward to explain the phenomena of false memories elicited by the DRM procedure. Roediger himself argues that the best explanation of his results is that of "spreading activation." "The mind is an exquisitely tuned device for holding associative information. ... Activation of a concept in episodic or semantic memory is believed to spread among neighboring concepts, partially arousing them." According to Roediger, spreading activation explains both the generation of false memories using the DRM procedure and also the phenomenon of semantic priming whereby the speed of retrieval of a word from memory (e.g., "doctor") is increased if it has been preceded by an associatively related word (e.g., "nurse"). All of the words in the DRM list partially activate the missing word, and thus it is presented to memory along with the others on recall (Roediger, Balota, and Watson 2001, 95).

Another explanation of how false memories are generated by the DRM procedure is the dual-process theory, or fuzzy-trace theory (e.g., Brainerd and Reyna 1998, 484–89). Among the many complex subsystems of memory appear to be one subsystem devoted to remembering the exact words used in a conversation (verbatim memory) and another devoted to storing the overall meaning of the words used (gist memory). According

---

1. See also the analysis of fifty-five fifteen-word lists with their associated critical items, together with figures for backward associative strength and forward associative strengths, in Roediger et al. 2001, 385–407, esp. 399–407. Suitable lists using German words may be found in Brueckner and Moritz 2009, 276.

2. See, e.g., the many different variables that have been tested by a DRM procedure given in Seamon et al. 2003, 445.

to fuzzy-trace theory, both verbatim and gist (fuzzy-trace) memory operate in parallel rather than in serial, as is usually thought. In other words, gist memory is not derived from the verbatim memory but is formed at the same time. This is evidenced by the fact that, "Adults begin to store the meaning content of a target event within 30–50 milliseconds after onset, long before targets' surface forms can be fully processed" (Brainerd 2005, 220). In a DRM task, both verbatim and gist memories would converge to produce correct responses, but false memories would come from the gist memory. As verbatim memories decay much faster than gist memories, fuzzy-trace theory predicts that over time the number of correct responses would decline, but the number of false memories of the critical lures would remain constant for a longer period. Experiments conducted by C. J. Brainerd, D. G. Payne, Ron Wright, and V. F. Reyna confirm that this is in fact the case (Brainerd et al. 2003, 445–67; see also Brainerd et al. 2008, 1048–51):[3] paradoxically, the so called "true" memories decline over time at a much faster rate than the "false" memories generated by the DRM procedure.

An experiment using thirty English-French bilingual students of the University of Alberta reported by Roberto Cabeza and E. Roger Lennartson provides further support for a fuzzy-trace explanation of DRM results. For the experiment, thirty lists were translated into French, and students were given fifteen seconds to study each list, some in English, some in French. They were then given a test list of sixty words, half in each language: twenty were new, twenty were list items, and twenty were critical lures. Students were asked to identify words that were on their studied lists, and in exactly the same language. As is consistent with other research, this task produced a considerable number of false memories of the critical lures, and the results were very similar for lists in both languages. But what was of greater significance to the researchers was that proportionately more of these critical lures were remembered if the list

---

3. A similar result was reported by Kathleen B. McDermott (McDermott 1996, 212–30); and David G. Payne, Claude J. Elie, Jason M. Blackwell and Jeffrey S. Neuschatz (Payne et al. 1996, 261–85). McDermott notes: "An interaction occurred between accurate and false recall as a function of retention interval: after a one-day delay, false recall levels rose, whereas accurate recall decreased" (p. 212), although this was but one of a number of changes observed by McDermott, who finished the article by observing, "Resolution of when the various patterns are observed must await future research" (McDermott 1996, 228).

was given in a language other than that used for the lure. They explain their results in terms of fuzzy-trace theory. Within-language assessment would draw largely on verbatim memory traces, although gist memory would play a part in producing the critical lures. Across-language, though, gist memory would predominate and therefore produce a greater number of falsely remembered critical lures (Cabeza and Lennartson 2005, 1–5).[4] The results of other experiments using a DRM task, while ruling out other theories put forward to explain the phenomena of the false memories, are consistent with either the spreading activation theory or fuzzy-trace theory (Seamon et al. 2003, 455; cf. the words of Roediger et al. 2001, 395: "Both theories can explain many empirical results").

Imagination of Events, Doctored Photos, and Plausible Early Memories

DRM procedures are not the only means by which false memories have been elicited in experimental conditions. Ayanna K. Thomas and Elizabeth F. Loftus, for example, were able to generate false memories by the imagination of events that had not happened, even bizarre events (Thomas and Loftus 2002, 423–31). On the first day of their experiment, participants were asked to perform or imagine thirty-six tasks (out of a possible fifty-four critical events). These tasks included a number of familiar items, such

---

4. Subjects were asked to mark as "old" test words which had appeared in the earlier lists in exactly the same language. The following is a reproduction of table 1 (p. 3) in Cabeza and Lennartson 2005. It shows that, tested in French, the across-language number of critical lures "remembered" is greater than the actual list items!

Proportion of "old" responses as a function of item task and the match-mismatch between language at study and at test		
	Tested in English	Tested in French
Within Language		
List items	.69	.59
Critical lures	.41	.40
Across Language		
List items	.32	.32
Critical lures	.25	.39
New Items	.18	.24

as "sign your name on the paper with the pen," "stir the water with the spoon," and a number of bizarre items, such as "sit on the dice" and "print WORD with nail polish on the napkin." Twenty-four hours later, the participants returned and imagined eighteen of the fifty-four critical actions once and a further eighteen five times. These thirty-six items included some of the actions performed and imagined on the first day, but some new ones as well. Two weeks later, participants were tested. After multiple imaginings, participants falsely reported that they had performed new bizarre actions 14 percent of the time. As might be expected, they falsely reported that they had performed familiar actions more often (24 percent of the time).

Kimberly A. Wade, Maryanne Garry, J. Don Read, and D. Stephen Lindsay used doctored photos to induce false memories (Wade et al. 1992, 597–603). Twenty adult confederates of the researchers each recruited a family member who had not taken a hot-air balloon ride and provided a selection of photographs in which the family member was four to six years old. Three true photos of moderately significant events such as family vacations were digitized, and part of a picture of the subject with one or more family members was cut and pasted into a photograph of a balloon ride. Subjects were interviewed three times over a period of seven to sixteen days. They first told all they could remember of the events associated with the photos. For those they could not remember, which usually included the balloon-ride photo, they were told that one of the purposes of the study was to assess the efficacy of different memory retrieval techniques, and they were asked to mentally go back to the scene and imagine themselves in it. At the end of the third interview, subjects were told one of the photos was fake and asked to determine which one it was. At the first and last interviews confidence ratings were obtained. Of the sixty true events, subjects remembered 93 percent at interview one and 97 percent at interview three. Of the false events, one subject reported a clear memory at interview one, and six reported partial memories. At the end of three sessions, ten of the twenty subjects (50 percent) recalled the false balloon ride "either partially or clearly, claiming to recall at least some details of a hot air balloon ride during childhood," and "most of the details reported were not explicitly depicted in the photograph" (Wade et al., 1992, 601–2).

Asking participants to remember plausible childhood events that never happened is another experimental method that has shown that it is possible to implant false memories of entire events. Elizabeth F. Loftus and Jacqueline E. Pickrell recruited twenty-four participants and close family members as a confederate (usually a parent). They used the confederate to determine three true memories from the childhood of the subject and details that would make plausible the reconstruction of an event that did not happen (e.g., being lost in a mall). Subjects were first given four short paragraph descriptions of the one invented and three true events from their childhood, then asked to write down their own memories of the four events. They were also given two follow-up interviews. The twenty-four subjects remembered forty-nine of the seventy-two true events (68 percent), and in the initial response and subsequent two interviews, between six (25 percent) and seven (29 percent) of the subjects "remembered" the false event (Loftus and Pickrell 1995, 720–25). These rates are not as high as that discovered using doctored photos as a source of false memories, and Wade et al. suggest that this is because "photographs are a denser representation of perceptual details" (1992, 602).[5]

Elizabeth F. Loftus, Julie Feldman, and Richard Dashiell provide the following assessment of research into inducing false memories conducted by Loftus and others:

> What do we now know as a result of hundreds of studies of misinformation, spanning two decades and most of the world's continents? That misinformation can lead people to have false memories that they appear to believe in as much as some of their genuine memories. That misinformation can lead to small changes in memory (hammers become screwdrivers) or large changes in memory (barns that didn't exist, or hospitals that were never visited). (Loftus, Feldman, and Dashiell 1995, 65)

Inducing False Memories with Leading Questions

Even asking a question a certain way has the ability to introduce false memories in the right conditions. Hans F. M. Crombag, Willem A. Wagenaar, and Peter J. van Koppen found "that it was relatively easy in a real life situation to make reasonable intelligent adults believe that they have witnessed something they actually have not seen themselves" (1996, 95). On 4 Octo-

---

5. Ira E. Hyman Jr. also reports being able to induce false childhood memories by first suggesting an event took place, then tracing what happened to that "memory" over several interviews. "After a few interviews, however, between 15% and 25% of the students not only claimed the event happened but actually provided memories of the experience that included details we never suggested." On the other hand, asking the participants to form a mental image of the false event "led more than 40% of the students to create a false memory after three interviews" (Hyman 1999, 236–37).

ber 1992, an El Al cargo plane lost both starboard engines and crashed into an apartment building in Amsterdam, killing all four crew members and thirty-nine people in the building. Naturally, this event attracted considerable media attention in Holland, but as no film footage existed of the plane crashing into the apartment building, all TV reports were either reconstructions or given against later footage. In one of their experiments, Crombag, Wagenaar, and van Koppen gave a questionnaire to ninety-three law students from the University of Nijmegen. The questionnaire began with an introduction that stressed that the task was an illustration of memory failure. The first six questions were labeled "biographical questions" and included questions such as: (1) What is your age? (2) What is your gender? (3) Were you in the country when it happened? (4) Have you seen the TV film showing the plane crashing? The six biographical questions were followed by three "memory" questions asking for further details. A clear majority of respondents—66 percent—said that they had seen the nonexistent TV film of the plane crashing, and many of those who answered no to this question still answered the subsequent questions asking for details relating to the footage. The experimenters concluded, "people often mistake post-event information, either from hearsay or from their own visualization, for firsthand knowledge. This is particularly easy when, as in our studies, the event is of a highly dramatic nature, which almost by necessity evokes strong and detailed visual imagery" (Crombag, Wagenaar, and van Koppen 1996, 103).

Other experiments confirm the power of misleading questions to elicit false memories. Quin M. Chrobac and Maria S. Zaragoza used as a stimulus an 18-minute clip from a movie. Participants were then asked a series of questions, some of which were based on assumed action that was completely different from that shown in the film clip. Although participants strongly resisted having to answer these questions, and after one week still clearly stated that the questions did not correspond to what they had seen in the movie clip, after eight weeks 50 percent freely reported the false reconstruction of events as having taken place (Chrobak and Zaragoza 2008). Other researchers also found that misleading questions produced false memories. They investigated the effect of positive and negative emotional content of visual scenes and discovered that negative emotion significantly "heightens suggestibility in the presence of major misinformation" (Porter et al. 2010, 55).

Maria S. Zaragoza and Karen J. Mitchell documented that increasing the number of times a question is asked with a certain item of misinformation also increases the likelihood that it will be incorporated into a person's memory. Subjects were shown 5 minutes of a police training video depicting a home burglary by two youths and a car chase by police. They then filled out a questionnaire that had some questions that presupposed the existence of objects or events that were not in the video. The subjects were questioned about the twelve scenes in the video three times successively, each time about a slightly different aspect of the scene. Subjects received misleading questions about four of the scenes, some once, some three times. The more times a subject heard a misleading question (they either heard them zero, one, or three times), the more likely they were "to (a) claim with high confidence that they remembered the suggested events from the video (Experiment 1) and (b) claim that they consciously recollected witnessing the suggested events (Experiment 2)" (Zaragoza and Mitchell 1996, 298). Henry L. Roediger III, J. Derek Jacoby, and Kathleen B. McDermott also recorded a similar result. Their experimental subjects saw slides depicting a crime and read a narrative containing misleading information about the items on the slides. This generated "robust misinformation effects," and those who recalled wrong detail on their first test given in the session in which they viewed the slides were much more likely to do so again. The researchers concluded:

> The general point is that when a person is queried about memory for a distant event, recall is almost certain to be influenced not only by what transpired during the event in question, but by all the previous recollections of that event. The information retrieved from the most recent account of the event may be a more powerful determinant of the current recollection than the original event itself. (Roediger, Jacoby, and McDermott 1996, 316)

Carol L. Baym and Brian De Gonsalves generated false memories by first providing participants with short photographic sequences of common events and subsequently providing written statements about those events that contained errors. One day later, when given a surprise test, participants reported information that had been in the written statements but that was contradictory to what was portrayed in the sequence of photographs (Baym and Gonsalves 2010).

Steven Rose, a neuroscientist who works on memory at the level of biochemistry and neurological structures, also highlights the importance of not just the initial memory but of all subsequent retrievals of that memory. He reaches the following conclusion from a consideration of biological processes that take place at the level of a cell:

> Indeed there is good evidence that the act of recall, retrieval, evokes a further biochemical cascade, analogous to, through not identical with, that occurring during initial learning. The act of recall remakes a memory, so that the next time one remembers it one is not remembering the initial event but the remade memory of the last time it was invoked. Hence memories become transformed over time. ... What they [memories] absolutely are not is "stored" in the brain in the way that a computer stores a file. Biological memories are living meaning, not dead information. (Rose 2005, 161–62)

In his two book-length surveys of the physiology, biochemistry, and other aspects of memory, Rose continuously emphasizes the dynamic nature of the human brain and therefore of human memory.[6] Nothing is static. The organism is continually adjusting to changes in blood supply, emotions, outside stimuli, and so forth. Chemical and neurological traces are being made and broken continually.[7] Memories are dynamically stored. Furthermore, he suggests that each memory is reconstructed from different stores of the various types of memory. It is such mechanisms that may well allow for the intrusion and incorporation of false memories.

The Social Contagion of Memory

Given that early Christians lived in a strongly group-oriented society, the series of experiments that showed that social interaction has a very strong influence on inducing false memories may be of great significance to this

---

    6. E.g.: "Memory ... [is] an emergent property of the brain as a dynamic system rather than a fixed and localized engram [memory trace]. ... memory—declarative memory, that is—is not some passive inscription of data on a wax tablet or silicon chips of the brain, but an active process. ... whilst the 'system' that comprises the tape recorder and its tape is fixed and inanimate—dead—the essential feature of live biological systems is that they develop and change with time" (Rose 2003, 318–22). "The brain, like all features of living systems, is both being and becoming, its apparent stability a stability of process, not of fixed architecture. Today's brain is not yesterday's and will not be tomorrow's" (Rose 2005, 147). See also the comment at Rose 2005, 62: "All of life is about *being* and *becoming*; being one thing, and simultaneously transforming oneself into something different. It is really like ... rebuilding an aeroplane in mid-flight. And we all do it, throughout our lives—not just babies but adults, not just humans but mice and fruitflies and oak trees and mushrooms."
    7. R. Douglas Fields explains some of the complex relationships between signaling molecules and the formation of synaptic connections in Fields 2005, 59–65.

study. Henry L. Roediger III, Michelle L. Meade, and Erik T. Bergman showed that the amount of false memories can be dramatically increased by suggestions from others and have labeled this effect the social contagion of memory (Roediger, Meade, and Bergman 2001, 365–71; Meade and Roediger 2002, 995–1009). In one series of experiments, they showed participants six slides, verbally labeled "the toolbox scene," "the bathroom scene," "the kitchen scene," "the bedroom scene," "the closet scene," and "the desk scene." In the original experiment, participants were paired with one other individual whom they were given to understand was a fellow student undertaking the same experiment but who was actually a confederate of the experimenter. After viewing the six slides, then completing a filler task, the participant and confederate alternated in suggesting items that had been in each of the scenes. The confederate introduced a high-expectancy contagion item on the fourth "turn" that had not actually appeared in the original slide and a low-expectancy contagion item on the sixth "turn." Each then went into another room. Every 2 minutes thereafter, participants were given a sheet of paper identified at the top with one of the scenes and asked to write down as many of the items they remembered seeing in the relevant slide. As might be expected, even without the "help" of the confederate, a number of items were falsely remembered that might be expected to fit the scene (e.g., a toaster was often recalled among the items in the kitchen scene, but it was not present in the relevant slide). In the control group where the confederate only reported items actually in the slide, high-expectation items were falsely recalled in 11 percent of the trials of those who saw the slides for 15 seconds. This percentage, though, increased to 41 percent due to the influence of the "social contagion" of the confederate suggesting something not actually present in the original slide (Roediger, Meade, and Bergman 2001, 367 fig. 1).[8] "Social contagion" was found to be a relatively robust effect. Even a warning that some of the answers given by the confederate were wrong, as was done in a follow-up experiment, did not eliminate

---

8. In a later experiment, Meade and Roediger report a higher rate of "natural" false memories: "One interesting feature of the present experiments is the relatively high rates of false recall and false recognition in the control condition, especially for the expected or typical items. For example, averaging across the two presentation durations of Experiment 2, subjects recalled the expected or typical items as having been in the scene on 22% of the trials in the control condition" (Meade and Roediger 2002, 1007).

the false memories, although the warning reduced the errors somewhat (Meade and Roediger 2002).[9] Other experiments have shown that the social contagion effect in eliciting false memories for what is viewed in a video is greater for peripheral features of the witnessed event, and less—but not zero—for events and items central to the story viewed (Dalton and Daneman 2006, 486–501).

Roediger points out that, while they have labeled the effect "social contagion," the pooling of memories usually has a beneficial effect in real life. "If one person has poor memory for a jointly witnessed event and another person reports detailed memories, it would be adaptive for the first person to incorporate the newly learned details into memory of the event" (Roediger, Meade, and Bergman 2001, 370). Indeed, experimenters have found that groups remember more details of random lists of words, random pictures, or details from a narrative than any one individual in the group, although, interestingly enough, the group remembers fewer details than the nominal group (of pooled individual responses) (Weldon and Bellinger 1997, 1160–75; Basden et al. 1997, 1176–89; cf. Maki, Weigold, and Arellano 2008, 598–603).[10]

---

9. Barbara H. Basden, Matthew B. Reysen, and David R. Basden (2002, 211–31) were able to increase the rate of false memories using DRM lists by using a computer to insert "false memories" into a situation where four subjects working on computers in the same room thought they were working together in a four-person collaborative group. Also using a computer to simulate responses of others, Andrew L. Betz, John J. Skowronski, and Thomas M. Ostrom (1996, 113–40) were able to persuade statistically significant numbers of first-year college students to change their answer to a factual multichoice question that related to an passage of prose, even when warned that some of the second-hand information on other student answers was bogus.

10. Using a variation of the Deese-Roediger-McDermott procedure, Masanobu Takahashi (2007, 1–13) discovered that collaborative remembering reduces both the number of correct and incorrect words remembered. Ruth Maki, Arne Weigold, and Abigail Arellano (2008), also using a form of the Deese-Roediger-McDermott procedure, found that nominal groups provided more correct and incorrect responses than individuals but that collaborative groups produced more correct responses and the same number of incorrect responses as individuals. The popularly written book by James Suroweicki, *The Wisdom of Crowds* (2004), documents some remarkable occurrences where many individuals working independently from very limited knowledge were able to give very accurate judgments and predictions.

Hindsight and Other Memory Biases

Like the frailty of suggestibility, the memory frailty of hindsight bias has the potential significantly to impact the reliability of the Gospel accounts. Hindsight bias is, in fact, but one of several biases that have been identified in memory processes. In his chapter entitled "The Sin of Bias," Daniel Schacter lists five major types of memory bias:

> Consistency and change biases show how our theories about ourselves can lead us to reconstruct the past as overly similar to, or different from, the present. Hindsight biases reveal that recollections of past events are filtered by current knowledge. Egocentric biases illustrate the powerful role of the self in orchestrating perceptions and memories of reality. And stereotypical biases demonstrate how generic memories shape interpretation of the world, even when we are unaware of their existence or influence. (Schacter 2001, 139)

All of these biases are of potential relevance to how the reliability or otherwise of memory should be used to gauge the reliability of the traditions in the Gospels, but perhaps the most important for this investigation is that of hindsight bias.[11] As Schacter has so succinctly expressed it, hindsight bias is that process by which memories of past events are influenced by present circumstances and knowledge. A number of studies have provided relatively good information on how much impact hindsight bias has on human memory.

The seminal study in hindsight bias was reported by Baruch Fischhoff (1975, 288–99; cf. 2007, 10–13). Fischhoff based the stimuli used in his experiment on historical events that could potentially have produced several different outcomes at the time they occurred and that were unlikely to be known by the participants in the study. One such event used in the study was the war between the Gurkas of Nepal and the British in the early nineteenth century. Four possible outcomes were suggested: (1) British victory; (2) Gurka Victory; (3) military stalemate with no peace settlement; and (4) military stalemate with peace settlement. For this experiment, one hundred subjects were randomly assigned to five groups

---

11. Consistency and change bias will be illustrated later in this chapter in the study of marital satisfaction, while egocentric bias was a theme that emerged in the discussion of John Dean's memory found in chapter 1.

of twenty. They all read the same prose description of the background of the event, and each group was then asked to assess the probability of each of the possible four outcomes (as a percentage) when considered at the moment the war started. The first group was only given the background paragraph and no further information about the outcome. The other four groups had one further sentence added to the background information that stated that the outcome was one of the four possible outcomes (one group was told that the result was a Gurka victory, another that the result was a stalemate with no peace, etc.). In other words, one of the groups was told what really happened historically, and three of the other groups were given false information about the historical outcome. The results that relate to the Gurka war are given in table 4.1 (Fischhoff 1975, 291 table 1).

Table 4.1. An Example of Hindsight Bias: Mean Probabilities Assigned to Each Outcome of the War between the British and Gurkas

Outcome Provided	Antecedent Probability of Outcome (Expressed as a Percentage)			
	A (British victory)	B (Gurka victory)	C (stalemate/no peace)	D (stalemate/peace)
None:	33.8	21.3	32.3	12.3
A (British victory)	57.2	14.3	15.3	13.4
B (Gurka victory)	30.3	38.4	20.4	10.5
C (stalemate/no peace)	25.7	17.0	48.0	9.9
D (stalemate/peace)	33.0	15.8	24.3	27.0

As can be observed from the table, the group that had no information about the outcome of the war thought that a British victory or a stalemate with no peace were the likeliest outcomes (they had been assigned probabilities of 34 and 32 percent). The Gurka victory was seen as less likely (21 percent), and a stalemate that resulted in a peace accord the most unlikely (12 percent). These figures are dramatically different from those where the participants had been told the outcome of the war. Knowing that the British had won the war increased the probability assessment of that outcome from 34 percent to 57 percent, with the rest of the outcomes assessed as much less likely. The effect is less dramatic if the participants had been told that the Gurkas had won the war but still evident. With the hindsight from that particular information, a 38 percent probability was assigned to that outcome, although a 30 percent probability was still assigned to the possibility of a British victory. With those who had been told that the outcome was a stalemate that resulted in a peace accord, participants still thought that a British victory was a more likely outcome, although there is a significant increase between the 27 percent likelihood assigned by this group compared to the 12 percent likelihood from the group that did not know the outcome. Very similar results were gained from the three other scenarios that were presented to a further 267 participants. Fischhoff did further experiments with the same basic testing material, but under conditions that would reveal whether or not it is possible for a participant to ignore the hindsight bias when informed of its existence. On the basis of these experiments, Fischhoff concluded: "Finding out that an outcome has occurred increases its perceived likelihood. Judges are, however, unaware of the effect that outcome knowledge has on their perceptions" (1975, 297).

Hindsight bias has also been discovered in a wide variety of other circumstances. It affects the post-sporting-event memory of pre-sporting-event expectations (Bonds-Raacke et al. 2001, 349–52; Roese and Maniar 1997, 1245–53); the memory of expectations that the Y2K issue would actually cause the computer problems moving between 1999 and 2000 that had been predicted throughout the years leading up to 1 January 2000 (Pease et al. 2003, 397–98); determining which of two people in a video clip were likely to be having an affair or have committed suicide (Bradfield and Wells 2005, 120–30); the visual identification of blurred faces (Harley, Carlsen, and Loftus 2004, 960–68); gustatory judgments (Pohl et al. 2003, 107–15); the memory of emotions (Levine and Safer 2002, 169–73); couples remembering relationship events the previous week (Halford, Keefer, and Osgarby 2002, 759–73); the memory of expected outcomes from the introduction of the Euro (Hölzl, Kirchler, and Rodler 2002, 437–43); perceptions of business ethics (Sligo and Stirton 1998, 111–24); potential juror's judgments (Smith and Greene 2005, 32–47; Lowe and Reckers 1994, 401–26); decision-making processes (Louie, Rajan, and Sibley 2007, 32–47); as well as a wide range of other phenomena.

Evidence appears plentiful, then, for the existence of hindsight bias. Consistency and change bias may be illustrated from the results of a twenty-year longitudinal study of married women's feelings about their marriage (Karney and Coombs 2000, 959–70). In 1969–1970, 175 women married to medical trainees were approached to participate in a longitudinal study of marital adjustment, and followed up after ten (time two) and then twenty (time three) years. Benjamin Karney and Robert Coombs looked for memory bias in the reports of the 131 of them who were still married to the same partner and willing to participate further in the study after ten years, and the 98 of them still married to the same partner after twenty years. At each of time one, two, and three, the women responded to nine items (e.g., "How happy are you with your marriage?"; "How many interests do you and your husband share in common?"; "How often do you think about divorce?"). These items were rated on a four-point Likert scale and combined to give a marital satisfaction rating. At times two and three, the women were also asked to answer the same questions about their relationship as they remembered it ten years earlier. There was a slight but statistically significant correlation between the marital satisfaction scores reported at time one and the memory of that satisfaction at time two, which suggested to Karney and Coombs "that recollections of the early years of the marriage were informed by the perceived quality of the relationship at that time." Yet the reporting does show a pattern of memory bias, clearly visible in the graph in figure 4.1.

Figure 4.1 reveals that, while some individual women reported increasing marital satisfaction over the twenty years, marital satisfaction declined when the women were considered as a group. Worthy of particular note are the womens' reports at time two (ten years after the initial survey), when they reported their remembered satisfaction levels of the period ten years earlier as much lower than they had actually reported them at that earlier time. Indeed, they reported their satisfaction levels had been lower then than they currently were at time two. Twenty years after the initial survey, the women reported that ten years earlier their marital satisfaction at time two had been about the same as it was at time three. Karney and Coombs suggest that this reflects two different models by which married women

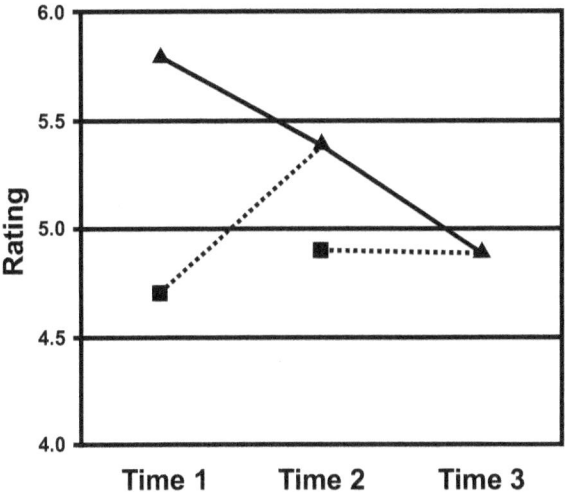

Figure 4.1. Observed and perceived marital satisfaction over twenty years of marriage. Note: solid line represents actual trend of marital satisfactory; dotted lines represent perceived trend of marital satisfaction (Karney and Coombs 2000, fig. 1)

reconstructed their past memories of marital satisfaction. In the first ten or so years of marriage (over half the wives had been married for less than three years at time one), the women used a model of improvement to describe their marriage (i.e., a change bias), so they (incorrectly) reported that their marital satisfaction had been improving between time one and time two. For the next ten or so years of marriage, the women used the model of consistency (a consistency bias), so they reported (also incorrectly) that their current marital satisfaction at time three was the same as it was at time two.

As with other memory frailties, while hindsight and other memory biases can at times be problematical, they usually have a positive influence on the individual's ability to cope with and adapt to changing circumstances. Ulrich Hoffrage, Ralph Hertwig, and Gerd Gigerenzer (2000, 566–81), for example, suggest that hindsight bias is a by-product of the adaptive process of the updating of knowledge after feedback, part of the reconstructive process of memory.[12] In other words, hindsight bias

---

12. Lioba Werth and Fritz Strack (2003, 411–19) also suggest that hindsight bias grows out of an individual's use of feelings and experience to reconstruct (infer) one's prior judgments.

is further evidence that memories are adaptive and that they are reconstructed.

Memories as Reconstructions from Various Memory Subsystems

Several lines of research have shown that human memory resides in a number of different subsystems,[13] each of which has different qualities of persistence and reliability. Visual memory is distinct from verbal memory and has different short-term and long-term capacity limits, as well as different rates of decay. Verbal memory itself is made up of different components. There are other memory subsystems for memories of life incidents (episodic memory), general knowledge (semantic memory), and motor skills (procedural memory) (Schacter, Wagner, and Buckner 2000, 627–43; cf. Tulving 1972, 381–403; 1983; and especially 2001, 17–34).[14] There is even a separate memory subsystem for recognizing faces (Hill and Schneider 2006, 667–68). The types of memory problems associated

---

13. The brain subsystems associated with memory are but a small subset of its collection of specialized areas. Something of the overall complexity of the brain can be discerned in the following summary by Nicole M. Hill and Walter Schneider: "The brain has many domain specific representational areas connected in a quasi-hierarchical fashion. There are an estimated 500–1000 specialized processing regions (Worden & Schneider, 1995). A complex process, such as visual processing, occurs in over thirty distinguishable processing regions (Felleman & Van Essen, 1991), including those for detecting lines, colors, shapes, structure (e.g., houses, faces), motion, and special relationships. ... Information is coded in the pattern of activity, with any one region encoding many exemplars and types of stimuli ... These representations areas include input (visual, audition, somatsensory, gustatory) and output motor areas" (Hill and Schneider 2006, 656).

14. In distinguishing episodic, procedural, and semantic memory, Tulving distinguished autonoetic (self-knowing), anoetic (not knowing), and noetic (knowing) memories. In "Origin of Autonoesis in Episodic Memory" (Tulving 2001), Tulving describes how his ideas have developed over time and recounts at length the case of K.C. as evidence for a separate memory system for episodic memory. K.C. experienced a motorcycle accident that left him with brain damage of a very unusual type. K.C. still has almost all the mental capabilities of a healthy adult, but while he knows factual knowledge about himself, such as his date of birth, the address of his home, and the like, he has absolutely no memory of events that happened to him; not even the accidental death of his brother, or a fight in a pub that resulted in a broken arm. In sum, while the rest of K.C.'s memory faculty appears to be intact, he lacks an episodic memory.

with different types of brain lesions, and experiments involving functional magnetic resonance imaging (fMRI) and positron emission tomography (PET) scans of brains doing different types of memory tests, have shown that a number of different parts of the brain are involved in these various types of memory. For example, memories of rewards, punishments, and stimulus-reinforcer associations are found in the orbitofrontal cortex and amygdala, the temporal cortical visual area is involved in learning invariant representations of objects, the hippocampus is implicated in episodic memory (Rolls 2000, 599–30),[15] and so on. Even language ability itself is distributed in different areas: "Broca's area is necessary for the production of syntax, [and] grammatical formations involving verbs, ... whilst Wernick's area is relevant for semantics, the meaning of words, especially nouns" (Rose 2005, 129).[16] Perhaps the most remarkable and least understood aspect of memory is how these various subcomponents are first activated during the time a memory is being formed, and later, on retrieval, how memories are seamlessly reconstructed from their various components (Fodor 2000, 71–80). In the case of memory, the whole is indeed greater than the sum of its parts.

That memory functions are distributed and that memories are, in fact, reconstructed from their various components has proved to be a powerful explanatory tool. As Daniel Schacter says of hindsight bias:

> we do not record our experiences the way a camera records them. Our memories work differently. We extract key elements from our experiences and store them. We then recreate or reconstruct our experiences

---

15. Cf. the rather more complex picture of the different parts of the brain implicated in various memory tasks in Markowitsch 2000, 465–84. Petersen et al. 2000, 397–404, gives further information on the parts of the brain involved with the processing of language. The role of the hippocampus and amygdala in the formation of long-term memories has been long known, thanks to intensive study of the patient HM, who in 1953 had large regions of these parts of his brain removed in an effort to control serious epileptic fits. The operation was successful in controlling HM's fitting, did nothing to damage already existing long-term episodic memories, nor did the patient lose short-term memory. He could even learn new skills (procedural memory). Yet he could not form any new long-term episodic memories. He did not recognize long-term neighbors nor recognize the route over which he goes every day to work and could not even describe what he does for employment when asked to do so the next day (Rose 2003, 143–47).

16. For further information on Broca's area, see Schubotz and Fiebach 2006, 461–63, as well as the other articles on pp. 464–658 of this special issue of *Cortex*.

rather than retrieve copies of them. Sometimes, in the process of reconstructing we add on feelings, beliefs, or even knowledge we obtained after the experience. In other words, we bias our memories of the past by attributing to them emotions or knowledge we acquired after the event. (Schacter 2001, 9)[17]

Similar conclusions are expressed by several of those working in the area of false memories, whose research has been reported earlier in this chapter. For example, in their reports of the generation of false memories of words not presented in a list, Henry Roediger III and his co-writers state, "In some sense, all recollection, even immediate recall and recognition of lists of words, is reconstructive" (Roediger et al., 2001, 386). Commenting on their ability to generate false memories of childhood events using "doctored" photographs, Kimberly Wade and her co-writers say, "The results of our clause analysis fit with the view, endorsed by most contemporary memory theorists, that remembering is a constructive activity. ... the act of remembering past experience involves generating thoughts, images, and feelings from multiple sources (such as distributed memory records, inferences, expectations, etc.) and attributing those thoughts, images, and feelings to a particular past episode" (Wade et al. 1992, 602).[18] From his work in engendering false autobiographical memories, Ira Hyman Jr. also concludes that "memory is not like a videotape. Instead people combine schematic knowledge from various sources with personal experiences and current demands to construct a memory. ... All memories are constructions" (Hyman 1999, 239). Martin Conway explains autobiographical memories as "transitory mental representations constructed by a centrally mediated complex retrieval process" (Conway 1997, 23). Guiliana Mazzoni

---

17. Cf. Schacter's earlier comments: "The implications of research on multiple forms of memory for distortion-related issues are severalfold. ... Third, the idea that storage and retrieval of explicit memories involving binding together different kinds of information from diverse cortical sites provides a biological basis for the notion that retrieval of a memory is a complex construction involving many different sources of information—not a simple playback of a stored image" (Schacter 1995, 19).

18. The experiment concerned is reported earlier in the chapter, although the reference to "clause analysis" needs further explanation. The subjects' memory reports were divided into clauses, and each clause was analyzed to see whether or not the information could have been derived from viewing the photograph. The researchers concluded "that perceptual details in the photographs (true and false) played a limited role in determining the context of subjects' memory reports" (Wade et al. 1992, 601).

and Manila Vannucci go so far as to explain not just false autobiographical memories by the fact that memories need to be reconstructed; they also suggest that hindsight bias is to be attributed to the same process (Mazzoni and Vannucci 2007, 214–15). In sum, memories should not be compared to the playback of a videotape, nor should they be called "memory texts."[19] They are reconstructions.

That memory functions are distributed in different subsystems, and that these subsystems exist in different parts of the human brain, gives memory a great resilience. Parts of the memory system can sustain damage without bringing the whole system to a catastrophic halt.[20] In fact, the human brain is flexible enough to compensate for certain types of damage with little loss of overall functionality. Furthermore, the frailties of suggestibility and hindsight have been shown, in fact, to be part of the extraordinary flexibility of humans to adapt to new circumstances. One should not overstate the frailties of human memory by overemphasizing those circumstances for which it is ill-suited and in which it gives false results. As James Lampinen and Timothy Odegard say, the human memory does *not* act

> as a video-recorder, faithfully recording all events in detail for mental examination into perpetuity.... memory serves survival functions that do not typically require verbatim-level recall of details (Reyna and Brainerd, 1995). However, memory is also not wanton in the way in which it stores and recovers past events. Memories are sometimes inaccurate, but provide a good first approximation of the events that make up our personal past. This first-order faithfulness also tells us something important about memory. Errors in memory are errors that "make sense" in terms of constructing a more or less accurate rendition of the gist of past events

---

19. James Fentress and Chris Wickham (1992, 1–8) criticize the usage of the terminology "spoken text" and "memory text" as it is found in much work on oral history and ethno-history, in part on the grounds that memories are reconstructions.

20. Stephen Rose describes his surprise when, after using a variety of approaches to determine the position in a chicken brain where one might find the memory of the unpleasant taste of methylanthranilate on a bead that the chicken had pecked, he discovered that causing a lesion in that part of the brain did not cause the chicken to forget what it had learned. Further experimentation showed that chickens stored the color of the bead in a different place than its shape. Thus, even with one part of the brain destroyed, the chicken could still avoid going back to the unpleasant-tasting bead. One had to destroy two parts of the chicken brain to cause it to forget the bad-tasting bead (Rose 2003, 313–28).

> ... Memory, like vision, fails to provide an entirely *faithful record* of our historical past. That much is clear. However, as with vision, memory provides a constrained interpretation of our past based on ambiguous fragmentary evidence, but does so in a way that makes sense in terms of the world we live in and our own personal experiences with it. ... A quality control memory system fills in gaps with schemas and post-event information because such information is reliable more often than it is not. (Lampinen and Odegard 2006, 649–50)[21]

The relevance of these remarks to the investigation of the reliability of any eyewitness memory that underlies the traditions found in the Synoptic Gospels scarcely needs comment. Despite the frailties of suggestibility and hindsight bias, one might expect such memories to have what Lampinen and Odegard describe as "first-order faithfulness." It may not be possible to give an a priori guarantee for the exact accuracy of all the details of such memories, but they would have preserved the gist of the situations described. These preliminary conclusions about the memory of individual humans are consistent with what has been discovered of eyewitness memory in chapter 1. Yet what has been discovered about individual memory must now be supplemented with what is known about the collective memory of groups.

---

21. This editorial surveys past research on the mechanisms that memory uses to reject false memories with relatively high success, and much of issue 6 of *Memory* 14 is devoted to the theme.

5
Collective Memory

Since the publication of books such as *The New Testament World: Insights from Cultural Anthropology* by Bruce Malina, New Testament scholarship has been increasingly aware of the group-oriented nature of the first-century Mediterranean cultures in which Christianity began. As Malina says, "the primary emphasis in the culture we are considering is on dyadic personality, on the individual as embedded in the group, on behavior as determined by significant others" (Malina 1981, 59–60).[1] Thus, even if each of the Gospels was primarily written by one individual, one cannot ignore the group or groups in which the writer of the Gospels was embedded. Nor can one ignore the influence of the community in the initial shaping and preserving of the traditions about Jesus in early Christianity. It is therefore important to consider the group processes by which common traditions are formed, processes that in their turn may have influenced the selection from those traditions made by one or more individuals working on a Gospel. These matters will dominate this chapter.

The current chapter will move beyond the qualities of the memory of individuals as they have been identified using the results of experimental psychology that has dominated the previous four chapters. It will consider the importance of group processes. In particular, it will explore the usefulness and limitations of a concept first developed by sociologists and taken

---

1. Malina uses the term "dyadic" personality in contrast to "individualistic" personality. Western society values the individual, and much Western literature explores the internal psychology of the individual. By way of contrast, writings that survive from the first century do not deal with the internal psychology of individuals. Malina argues that this was because first-century Mediterranean societies were honor-based; thus a person's value and worth was evaluated in terms of others' perceptions, and personal weaknesses and doubts were usually deliberately concealed from the larger group.

up with enthusiasm by historians—the concept of collective memory. It will answer the questions: What is meant by the term collective memory, and which of its characteristics may be of importance in the development of the traditions found within the Synoptic Gospels? As the chapter develops, reference will be made to population surveys that have shown that the different age groups within American society do remember different clusters of past events. Such studies reveal that the various demographic groups within that society do have defining sets of memories in common that mark them off from other groups and shape their attitudes and collective identity. Other evidence that will be cited comes from the academic discipline of history. Historians provide many case studies to illustrate not only the concept of collective memory but also its characteristics. Perhaps the most important of these characteristics for the present study is the influence that the present circumstances of the group have in shaping their collective memories. These will be discovered to be influential not just in determining which memories are featured in community discourse but also how they are shaped to the purposes of the present. Other evidence from the observations of anthropologists will reveal that this feature of collective memory has an even greater impact in oral societies than it does in literate societies such as that of North America.

Elusive Nature and Explanatory Power of Collective Memory

Collective memory is an elusive concept that suggests that groups and nations have sets of common memories that contribute to the group's self-understanding and identity.[2] Naturally, these memories have no independent existence outside the memories of individuals, be they in the group or not. Nevertheless, such memories are "collective" in the sense that they are common to all the individuals that form the group. These collective

---

2. While he was not the first to use the expression—that honor goes to Hugo von Hofmannsthal, who used it in 1902 (Olick and Robbins 1998, 106)—most modern uses of the concept of collective memory can be traced back to the French sociologist Maurice Halbwachs, who began to use the term in 1925. Read today, Halbwachs is a fascinating mixture of very useful insights and rather idiosyncratic arguments (e.g., Halbwachs 1992), and assessments of Halbwachs's writings on the topic range from an enthusiastic, if selective, account of those parts of his general theory subsequently found to have been useful (e.g., Hutton 1993, 73–90) to a discrediting of his work by a hostile concentration of those parts of his arguments that few take seriously (e.g., Gedi and Elam 1996, 30–50).

memories can also represent the esoteric knowledge that provides the theoretical basis for the professional conduct of groups such as judges, doctors, and priests.

In recent decades, the concept of "collective memory" has been discovered to have a great explanatory power. It is used to analyze a wide variety of phenomena: the "community memory" of a group of technicians servicing photocopiers (Orr 1990, 169–89), biodiversity in historic kitchen gardens (Jordan 2010), fears about central government-sponsored attacks on personal fertility among the Bamileke in Cameroon (Feldman-Sevelsberg, Ndonko, and Yang 2005, 10–28), the effect of memories of the Greensboro massacre on American race relations (Cunningham, Nugent, and Sloddin 2010, 1517–42), Holocaust consciousness in Israel or Poland (Hasian 2004, 136–56; Brog 2003, 65–99; Irwin-Zarecka 1994), the transition from dictatorship to democracy in Spain or Chile (Aguilar and Humlebaek 2002, 121–64; Lira 1997, 223–35), the Mafia (Fentress and Wickham 1992, 173–99), war memorials in World War I (Laqueur 1994; Piehler 1994), the formation of the national identities of Britain, Germany, France, and the United States (Lebovics 1994; Bodnar 1992; Kammen 1991), and Israelite religion as revealed by the Old Testament (Smith 2002, 631–51)—these are but some of the many phenomena that have been examined from the perspective of collective memory. Related concepts, such as institutional memory and public opinion, are entrenched in the language of a wide variety of disciplines, from business studies to politics.[3] Some academic disciplines, such as that of historical studies, have taken to the concept with particular enthusiasm. Noa Gedi and Yigal Elam observe without pleasure: "Today it is almost impossible to read a text in history that does not mention the term 'collective memory' or its complementary counterpart 'narrative'" (Gedi and Elam 1996, 30). In sum, the concept of collective memory has become nearly ubiquitous. In the words of Alon Confino, "The beauty of memory is that it is imprecise enough to be appropriated

---

3. Samuel Byrskog notes that "[t]here is a confusing variety of terminology. The literature uses 'family memory', 'local memory', 'popular memory', 'public memory', 'relational memory', 'cultural memory', etc. These expressions sometimes carry different connotations, but are also often employed synonymously" (Byrskog 2006, 321–22). Byrskog goes on to make a helpful distinction between "social memory"—the act of recollecting in a group—and "collective memory"—that which is retained in the collective memory of a community by "mnemonic socialization."

by unexpected hands, to connect apparently unrelated topics, to explain anew old problems" (1997, 1403).

Yet the very ambiguity that gives the term its power is, at the same time, what makes collective memory such a difficult concept to work with. As Wulf Kansteiner so pertinently observes:

> Students of collective memory are indeed pursuing a slippery phenomenon. Collective memory is not history, though it is sometimes made from similar material. It is a collective phenomenon but it only manifests itself in the actions and statements of individuals. It can take hold of historically and socially remote events but it often privileges the interests of the contemporary. It is as much a result of conscious manipulation as unconscious absorption and it is always mediated. And it can only be observed in roundabout ways, more through its effects than its characteristics. In essence, collective memory studies represent a new approach to "that most elusive of phenomena, 'popular consciousness.'" (Kansteiner, 2002, 180)

What, among this plethora of evidence and usage, is of most direct relevance to the study of the historical Jesus? As the concept is so "slippery," this chapter will need to examine whether or not there is experimental and case-study support for it, before considering how a contemporary concept of collective memory might be expressed. It will then be in a position to explore some of the relevance of the concept to Gospel studies and to the historical Jesus. Is there, then, any experimental or other evidence that might reveal both the existence of collective memory and its nature?

Experimental Evidence for Collective Memory

The concept of collective memory has, in fact, received experimental support. For example, in 1985, as part of a wider survey, Howard Schuman and Jacqueline Scott asked a national probability sample of 1,410 Americans the open-ended question: "There have been a lot of national and world events and changes over the past 50 years—say, from about 1930 right up until today. Would you mention one or two such events or changes that seem to you to have been *especially* important. There aren't any right or wrong answers to the question—just whatever *national or world events or changes* over the last 50 years that come to mind as important to you." As might be expected, there were a considerable number of answers, which led Schuman and Scott to comment: "Such responses serve as a reminder that a random sample of Americans yields a vast variety of memories and concerns, and that the last 50 years is viewed by members of the population in many diverse ways" (Schuman and Scott 1989, 363 and 364). Despite this variety, twelve topics stood out. One or more of the following were mentioned by 82 percent of the 1,253 respondents who answered the question (numbers in parentheses represent the total number of mentions): World War II (367), the Vietnam war (276), space exploration (159), Kennedy assassination (111), civil rights (107), the threat of nuclear war (98), communication/transportation (77), the depression (70), computers (49), terrorism (43), moral decline (41), and women's rights (37).[4] Schuman and Scott also note that the age of a respondent was a very important factor in whether or not an event was considered to be of great significance. For example, World War II was thought very important by some from all age groups, but it was mentioned by those that lived through the experience at twice the rate of those who had not. The difference is even more marked for those mentioning the Vietnam War and John F. Kennedy's death. Those in the age brackets that experienced a particular event mentioned it much more frequently than those who did not.[5] In fact, Schuman and Scott discovered that events that were experienced in late adolescence and early

---

4. Nearly the same open-ended question was asked of a probability sample of 600 British respondents by Jacqueline Scott and Lilian Zac in 1990. In that sample, the two stand-out responses were World War II (45%; n=251; cf. the 29% of Americans who had responded with Word War II in 1985) and the events in Europe including the fall of the Berlin Wall (30%; n=160). Other responses included space exploration (9%; n=48), Gulf crisis (6.5%), national health service (6%), Falklands war (5%), transport and communication (4.5%), common market/monetary union (4%), environment (4%), Thatcher (3.5%) (Scott & Zac 1993:315–31, esp. tables 1 & 2). A similar open-ended question was also asked in the 1993 General Social Survey of 1,606 Americans carefully chosen to represent all regions, age groups, etc. Five responses stood out in 1993: the end of communism, World War II, Space Exploration, JFK assassination, and the Vietnam war. (Griffin 2004, 547, Figure 1).

5. Interestingly enough, the age-relatedness of the responses to the Vietnam war only showed up among white respondents. Black respondents showed an age-related response about civil rights, and women an age-related response to woman's rights, something that was not evident in other groups. Griffin 2004, 544–57, reanalyzes the 1985 data in terms of current residential address and compares data from the 1993 General Social Survey, which provided information on where the respondents were living when they were sixteen years of age, and discovered that there was an age-related difference to those that included civil rights in their responses among whites who were or had been living in the southern states most affected by the civil rights

twenties were much more likely to be remembered by each age cohort.[6] Two of the twelve most commonly mentioned events, though, did not show this age-relatedness: the exploration of space, and the introduction of computers.

Participants were next asked, "What was it about ____ that makes it seem especially important to you?" The responses related to John F. Kennedy's death often had the characteristics of a flashbulb memory, and those of the age cohort that experienced World War II tended to answer in terms of their military involvement or how the war affected them personally. As Schuman and Scott comment, if one wishes to describe the fact that a large part of the population might remember a particular event as a form of collective memory, "it may be a rather superficial form, especially when on closer examination the memories turn out to be quite personal and particular." Yet the "Vietnam" cohort showed a different type of collective memory. They tended to describe the importance of Vietnam as a time of distrust and division, while their comments on World War II often reflected the idea that it was a "good war," a war in which an evil that might have changed the whole world was defeated. "This is collective memory in the more general sense" (Schuman and Scott 1989, 378–79).

In 1997 Howard Schuman, Robert Belli, and Katherine Bischoping published the results of a 1993 survey that approached the matter of the generational basis of historical knowledge using a different methodology (Schuman, Belli, and Bischoping 1997, 47–77). In this national phone-interview survey of 2,382 Americans, rather than being asked open-ended questions, participants were asked about their knowledge of eleven dateable events. Midway through the interview, the surveyors asked the following question: "The next section concerns a few words and names from the past that come up now and then, but that many people have forgotten. Could you tell me which ones you have heard of at all, and, if you have, what they refer to in just a few words?" The results show sev-

---

movement. Those who were aged between fifteen and nineteen in 1965 were much more likely to include civil rights in their responses.

6. In his widely cited article, "The Problem of Generations," Karl Mannheim notes that biology only creates the possibility of a generational style. What is needed in its formation are "Crucial group experiences" that act as "crystallizing agents" (Mannheim 1970, 402). The research of Schuman and Scott shows that these "crystallizing agents" are more effective when they occur when a generation is in their late teens or early twenties.

eral different types of patterns of remembrance across the various age groups. The oldest event tested, "WPA," referred to a work program for the unemployed set up by Franklin D. Roosevelt in 1935 under the New Deal and administered by the Work Projects Administration (WPA). At its peak in 1938 it employed 8.5 million, but once ended, it was not celebrated with any anniversary, neither has it been the subject of a major movie. As might be expected, this event was remembered well by most of those in the oldest group in the sample, and there was a constant decline in memory of the event with each younger group. Interestingly enough, age was a much stronger predictor that the WPA would be remembered than was education. On the other hand, knowledge of the Tet Offensive and Mylai (both events from the Vietnam War) and Woodstock showed a strong cohort effect. It was remembered significantly better by those who had been in their late teens and early twenties at the time. A third category of events was remembered by all age groups. These included Rosa Parks (associated with civil rights),[7] the Holocaust, Christa McAuliffe (who died in the Challenger explosion), and Watergate.

From these and other studies, it might be concluded that there is some experimental evidence for the proposition that various groups have distinctive sets of memories, collective memories, if you will.[8]

The Influence of the Present on Collective Memory

When he put forward his ideas about collective memory, Maurice Halbwachs emphasized that, although collective memories are rooted in the past, it is the present that is decisive: "social beliefs, whatever their origin, have a double character. They are collective traditions or recollections, but they are also ideas or conventions that result from a knowledge of the present. ... From this it follows that social thought is essentially a memory and that its entire content consists only of collective recollections or remembrances. But it also follows that, among them, only those recollections subsist that in every period of society, working within its pres-

---

7. Rosa Parks was remembered significantly better by African Americans in the sample.
8. "Belonging to the same generation, according to Karl Mannheim, endows members with a common location in the social and historical process, limiting them to a specific range of experience and predisposing them to characteristic modes of thinking and feeling" (Schwartz 2008, 9).

ent-day frameworks, can reconstruct" (Halbwachs 1992, 88–89). In other words, collective memories are determined by the needs and interests of the present as much as they are by the past. Furthermore, those working with the concept of collective memory note that memories of the past are often used in identity formation. The amount of evidence that illustrates the influence of the present on collective memory is impressive.[9] Take, for example, the first-century Jewish group who committed suicide at Masada rather than become Roman slaves. According to Josephus, who provides the only written account of the events, this group was made up of *sicarii* who were notorious for their use of assassination as a political tool and who spent most of their time during the Jewish Revolt killing other Jews rather than fighting the Romans. Forced out of Jerusalem, these particular *sicarii* moved to their earlier acquired base at Masada. They gained provisions to support themselves by raiding nearby villages. In one notable raid on Ein Gedi, they killed over seven hundred of the villagers and forced the others to flee. By this account, admittedly by one hostile to them, the group appears to provide poor role models. Yet for twentieth-century Zionists, particularly Shmaria Guttman, they become archetypical Jewish resistance fighters who would rather die than give up their freedom. For many years the slogan "Masada shall not fall again" was used to galvanize Jewish nationalism. Aspects of the information provided by Josephus that are inconsistent with this view have been ignored in materials as diverse as history textbooks and tourist guides. For example, the group are usually described as zealots, a term more suitable for nationalist freedom fighters, not *sicarii*; further, the less savory aspects of their raiding of local villages is ignored entirely. In sum, the need for good role models for Jewish resistance fighters in the early to mid-twentieth century among Zionists has powerfully influenced the collective memory of those who committed suicide in first-century Masada (Ben-Yehuda 1996).[10]

---

9. "Memory selects and distorts in the service of present interests [a process Schudson describes as "Instrumentalization"]. ... Examples of instrumentalization are legion. Indeed, the problem may be to find cases of cultural memory that cannot be readily understood as the triumph of present interests over truth" (Schudson 1995, 351).

10. As Ben-Yehuda says: "Thus, the myth was born. In effect, it was Shmaria Guttman who *created* much of the mythical narrative. How was this done? Simply, by emphasizing some aspects of the original Masada narrative, by repressing others, and by giving the whole new mythical construction an interpretation of heroism" (Ben-

Another case study, Barry Schwartz's investigation into the collective memories concerning Abraham Lincoln, shows how the present influences collective memories, as well as the limitations of this process (Schwartz 1990, 81–107; 1996, 908–27; 2000; 2008). When he died in 1865, Lincoln was not a particularly popular president, and his assassination did not change that fact in the collective memory of the nation just recovering from civil war. The Reverend Hepworth summed up the tone of many sermons and orations about Lincoln that were given shortly after his death when he suggested "that Lincoln dead may yet do more for America than Lincoln living" (Schwartz 1990, 84). His assassination was widely represented as God's will. "God 'permitted' the murder because He needed a stronger man to effect the righteous punishment of the Confederacy" (1990, 84). Lincoln had been too conciliatory and too compassionate. Even speeches given in Congress show that both sides of politics shared the view that Lincoln's role in history had been modest. However, at a later time the same qualities that appealed so little to his contemporaries elevated Lincoln to the same status as George Washington, perhaps greater.[11] In fact, comparing the number of articles about Lincoln and Washington in the periodical literature, and the number of times their names were invoked in newspapers such as the *New York Times* and the *New York Age*, as well as in speeches in Congress, allows this emergence of Lincoln as a cultural icon of collective memory to be dated rather precisely to the period of 1908 to 1909. The latter year, 1909, was the centennial year of Lincoln's birth. As much as anything else, the communal processes of remembering Lincoln at that time led to his establishment in communal memory that has since continued. His impressive, larger-than life statue in the heart of Washington has only confirmed his stature among subsequent generations.

What made Lincoln so attractive as a national icon in 1908–1909? It was a time when the nation was changing. It was looking outwards. Its

---

Yehuda 1996, 76). Note also Ben-Yehuda's analysis of the portrayal of Masada in history textbooks in Ben-Yehuda 1996, 163–78.

11. Throughout the nineteenth century, George Washington had been attributed the paramount role in the nation's representation of itself, and he had a prominence that greatly overshadowed all others, especially Lincoln. One can also see the influence of the present on the collective memory of Washington. Barry Schwartz has also shown how the collective memory of George Washington changed after 1865 from a man of remoteness, gentility, and flawless virtue to an ordinary, imperfect man with whom the common people could identify (Schwartz 1991, 221–36).

quick success for little cost in the Spanish-American war in 1898 had led to a confident, outward-looking nationalism. It was the progressive era in which federal power grew. Antitrust legislation, the pure food and drug law, child and sweatshop labor laws, federal workmen's compensation, and the progressive income tax were all reforms to protect free enterprise and property. Unrestricted immigration and a climate of aspiration made Lincoln's qualities as a nation-builder through consensus, conciliation, and compassion particularly evocative. "Had Lincoln's assumed character and achievements not echoed the concerns of a new society—a stronger and more democratic society—he would have never been recalled so vividly" (Schwartz 2000, 297).

While he fitted the ideology of the new times, there were still aspects of Lincoln that became either deemphasized or conveniently ignored. His jokes and stories, collected and published in his lifetime, were discarded, along with some of his more troubling comments on racial relations. Yet, Schwartz insists, one must "appreciate the limits of Lincoln's reconstructability." "'To make a good symbol to help us think and feel,'" we must start "'with an actual personality which more or less meets this need,' and we improve it by omitting the inessential and adding 'whatever is necessary to round out the ideal'. … The 'actual personality' that we start with … limits the range of things the collective memory can do. … From the initial conception of Lincoln as a man of the people we know that later generations subtracted little; they only superimposed new traits" (Schwartz 1990, 104; citing the words of Charles Horton Cooley).[12] Indeed, "The remaking of

---

12. In her article "The Historic, the Legendary, and the Incredible: Invented Tradition and Collective Memory in Israel," Yael Zerubavel traces the "rise and fall" of the place of Yoseph Trumpeldor amongst the "heroes" of the national state of Israel and notes a similar connection between historical reality and the ability to build credible "legends." Trumpeldor was a one-armed, ex-Russian soldier who died on 1 March 1920 while helping to defend the Jewish settlement of Tel Hai. "As with other historical heroes, Trumpeldor's life and character lent themselves to the formation of his 'legendary' image. … [yet, on the other hand], the social construction of a new 'legend' reveals a highly selective attitude towards tradition" (Zerubavel 1994, 108, 110). Curiously enough, there appears to be good historical evidence that Trumpeldor's last words were indeed, "It is good to die for the country," although among many modern Israelis they have been discredited as a Russian curse that was misunderstood by a Hebrew-speaker. As Zerubavel comments, "That the subtext of the dialogue on the authenticity of the Tel Hai commemorative narrative is not its historical validity is quite clear" (Zerubavel 1994, 116). In the matter of his last words, historical

Abraham Lincoln, although based on some invention and much exaggeration, is nonetheless constrained by the historical record" (Schwartz 2008, 234). The place attributed to Abraham Lincoln in American public life and culture illustrates "collective memory's change and continuity" (Schwartz 2000, 302). One cannot say that memories of the past are immune from the influence of present ideals and beliefs, nor can one say that collective memory is so malleable as to totally distort the past.[13] In other words, while the exigencies of the present have a powerful influence on collective memories, there are limits to how much such memories can be changed.

Collective Memory in Oral Societies

If the needs of the present play an important part in the collective memories of modern Western societies such as America and Israel, they play an even more important role in oral societies and take relatively distinctive forms in them. As Jack Goody and Ian Watt point out of such societies, "the whole content of social tradition, apart from the material inheritances, is held in memory. ... What the individual remembers tends to be what is of critical importance to his experience of the main social relationships" (Goody and Watt 1968, 30). Thus, in an oral culture, what is remembered corresponds in a large manner to what is relevant to the present. This means that in oral cultures "the individual has little perception of the past except in terms of the present." Oral cultures experience "structural amnesia." What is not relevant to the present does not come to memory and is not passed on.

Goody and Watt give some case studies that illustrate structural amnesia. The Tiv people of Nigeria, for example, place a great deal of impor-

---

fact appears to be on the side of the "legend," although collective memory thinks otherwise.

13. In discussing where "collective memory's change and continuity inheres [in] the broader question of how culture's need for stability and revision reconcile themselves to one and another and to society..." Schwartz highlights two erroneous evaluations of how much change is possible in the collective memories that contribute to the symbolic code that undergirds a society: "Emphasizing its revisions and discontinuities, constructionists Bodnar, Alonzo, and Hobsbawm make this code seem more precarious than it actually is. Stressing the continuities of collective memory, essentialists like Durkheim and Shils—who believe in society as an entity *sui generis* (self-generating and self-maintaining)—underestimate the extent to which the code adapts to society's changing needs and tendencies" (Schwarz 2000, 302).

tance on genealogies, which go back about twelve generations, and refer to them as precedents to solve many different types of disputes. Because of their frequent mention in court cases, early British administrators carefully recorded the long lists of names. Forty years later, anthropologists noted the differences between the then current genealogies and those written down by the British. The forty-year-later genealogies were still about twelve generations deep—there had been a telescoping of some of the generations to accommodate important personages from the previous forty years into the genealogy. Further, whereas an important ancestor had previously had seven sons, in the later genealogy he had five—the change reflecting the loss of power of two of the major subdivisions of the tribe. Thus the genealogies had apparently "automatically adjusted to existing social relations" in the intervening forty years.

Goody and Watt also note that writing not only allows more individual introspection, but it also allows the avoidance of some forms of cultural tradition. In an oral society, on the other hand, because cultural traditions were communally expressed, there was much greater homogeneity in the cultural experience of the members of that society than would be true in today's literate Western cultures (Goody and Watt 1968, 34–35, 60).

Walter J. Ong notes further characteristics of the type of materials held in collective memory in oral cultures that grow out of the necessity that they contain material that must be remembered.

> Sustained thought in an oral culture is tied to communication. But even with a listener to stimulate and ground your thought, the bits and pieces of your thought cannot be preserved in jotted notes. How could you ever call back to mind what you had so laboriously worked out? The answer is: Think memorable thoughts. ... you have to do your thinking in mnemonic patterns, shaped for ready oral recurrence. Your thought must come into being in heavily rhythmic, balanced patterns, in repetitions or antitheses, in alliterations and assonances, in epithetic and other formulary expressions, in standard thematic settings ... in proverbs..., or in other mnemonic form. Serious thought is intertwined with memory systems. (Ong 1982, 34)

The stories told in oral cultures are memorable. They are full of larger-than-life figures, stock characters, heroic deeds, and violent passions. They describe actions rather than motives, and ideas are illustrated by means of concrete examples rather than abstract notions. Epithets are common (brave warriors, beautiful princesses, sturdy oaks), and repetition and redundancy abound. All of these arise out of the need to make stories and ideas memorable and entertaining to those who must follow the story or argument by listening only (Ong 1982, 36–57). Ong also notes some of the ways in which oral cultures structure some materials designed to be memorized.

Naturally, not all the collective memories in an oral culture would show these kinds of characteristics, but they can usually be observed in the stories of the founding families, in the stories of past heroes, and in the patchwork of behavioral principles handed down from one generation to the next. In other words, they are found in precisely those memories most important for the formation of group identity.

Of course, the world from which the Gospels emerged was neither a purely oral world nor a literary world in the sense of modern Western cultures. It was a scribal culture. But the observation that a greater reliance on the mechanisms of oral transmission leads to a heightening of the influence that the present can have on collective memories is of real relevance to the topic of this chapter—which is to define the characteristics of collective memory. It appears that the present needs and interests of a group have a significant impact on collective memory. This is true of both literary and oral cultures. One might fairly expect it to be also true of scribal cultures.

Collective Memory Eight Decades after Halbwachs

It is over eight decades since Maurice Halbwachs first began writing about the concept of collective memory. In the interim, the idea of collective memory has been "tried for size" on a wide variety of disparate social and historical situations, and its characteristics and boundaries have become more clearly understood.

The case study of the collective memory of Abraham Lincoln examined earlier in this chapter has shown that, while the present does influence collective memory of past events and persons, there are limits to the changes that can be made to collective memory—limits imposed by the nature of the event or person. Similar comments could be made on the events at Masada. Some elements of the actual story may be ignored, but there are limits to what changes can take place to collective memory. Even so, these two case studies, along with the other evidence cited in this chapter, have shown two crucial elements in Halbwachs's theory of collective memory to be true. First, there is some experimental evidence that supports his contention that various groups share common memories and concerns. This is true particularly of events that took place during the late teens and early twenties of individuals in a particular group. Second, collective memories of past events and persons are shaped by present needs.[14]

Collective memory still remains a "slippery concept," but there is good reason for its widespread adoption. Memory is not entirely a private matter. It is frequently formed, rehearsed and thought about in social contexts—family, church, and nation. Something as private as autobiographical memory is expressed in terms of language: a social construct. Furthermore, there is a sense in which a group made up of individuals has a collective memory that might consist of shared experiences, knowledge of past events and people, common skills, attitudes, and beliefs. This collective memory is strongly shaped by the needs of the present. The collective memory of a group such as the earliest followers of Jesus can give it cohesion and identity.

---

14. "Facts are lost or retained in specific circumstances and in specific ways. They are lost whenever, in a new external context, old information is no longer meaningful; or, alternatively, because they do not fit into the new internal context designed to hold the information" (Fentress and Wickham 1992, 73). Cf. the words of James Wilkinson, "Beliefs are instruments of power or of self-preservation—that memory functions as a shield in the present rather than as a bond with the past" (Wilkinson 1996, 87). Other aspects of Halbwachs's arguments have been found to be less convincing. While memories are often social, one cannot say that memories are entirely social. True, they are mainly expressed in language, a socially generated convention of meaning attached to individual words ("In very fundamental ways, languages are collective memories" [Padden 1990, 190]). Yet some memories are generated and considered outside of social interaction. Memory is partly private and partly social. One cannot exclude one or the other of these elements as Halbwachs tried to do.

Part 2
Jesus Traditions as Memory

6
Collective Memory as an Explanation of Gospel Origins

Significant challenges must be faced when applying to the Jesus traditions what has been discovered in part 1 about the qualities of individual and collective memories. Granted, it has been established that eyewitness memories of significant events persist with remarkable accuracy, even over the time periods envisaged between the events of Jesus' ministry and the writing of the Gospels. Indeed, quite a lot has been discovered about what is likely to have shaped the formation of such recollections. It may even be granted that a number of eyewitnesses would still be alive at the time the Gospels were written (see appendix A). Such eyewitnesses would not only have been available for consultation by the Evangelists, but their presence would have served as an inhibition on any really wild flight of imagination as they told the story of Jesus. But several issues remain that need careful scrutiny. For example, how does one distinguish materials within the Gospels that are based on eyewitness memories from those that are derived from other sources? Indeed, how can one be sure that a description of a particular incident is based on something that actually happened during the ministry of Jesus, rather than an imaginative story that someone has made up about Jesus? What role might have been played by collective memories, and which groups were the source(s) of the collective memories that made their way into the Jesus traditions in the Synoptic Gospels? What of the impact of the frailties of human memory, frailties such as transience, suggestibility, and bias? These and other issues will be dealt with systematically in the chapters in part 2.

Collective Memory and Gospel Studies

There have been a number of significant studies of the Gospel traditions that invoke some aspect of memory, although twentieth-century works tended to employ considerations relating more to collective than to individual memory. While the qualities of the individual eyewitness memories that contributed to the collective memories of Jesus will be explored in the next chapter, it is appropriate to begin by reviewing the use that has been made of concepts analogous to collective memory in assessing the Jesus traditions.

While the explicit use of the terminology associated with collective memory is a relatively recent phenomenon in Gospel studies, concepts related to collective memory plays a crucial role the explanations of the origins of the Gospel traditions provided by Martin Dibelius, Rudolf Bultmann, Birger Gerhardsson, Rainer Riesner, Kenneth Bailey, and James D. G. Dunn. Of these writers, only Dunn explicitly references the work of Halbwachs, but all of them develop models that in some way draw upon the concept of the collective preservation of oral traditions.

For example, Dibelius and Bultmann suggest that new Jesus traditions were generated by the early groups of Jesus' followers as they encountered new circumstances with their associated challenges. Over time, a considerable body of tradition was built up in these groups, traditions that were drawn upon by the Evangelists as they composed their Gospels. Thus, for both Dibelius and Bultmann, the development and preservation of the traditions are collective processes, and although they did not use the terminology, their explanation of Gospel origins is centered on the concept of collective memory.

For their part, Gerhardsson, Riesner, and Bailey emphasize a more formal process for the transmission of the Jesus traditions than that envisaged by Dibelius and Bultmann, but again, this process takes place in groups and is monitored and preserved in group circumstances. The key groups envisaged by both Gerhardsson and Riesner are circles of disciples receiving formal instruction. The disciples around Jesus were taught by him to memorize his teachings. In their turn, the disciples taught their own followers to memorize the teachings that had been entrusted to them. The teachings of Jesus were thus preserved in the memories of groups, and it was formally transmitted and monitored for accuracy through group processes. The traditions not only made up the common memories of the group, but they provided guidance, coherence, and definition to that group. By any measure, these common traditions that are thus postulated form a collective memory of the disciples and their students.

Kenneth Bailey also invokes a formal process of passing of tradition, one based on first-hand observations that he made during his career as a missionary of the formation and preservation of collective memories in traditional village life in Egypt, Lebanon, and Palestine. At formal village meetings, different traditions and stories are shared by those individuals deemed by the group to remember them best. But the group monitors the accuracy of each recounting and vigorously corrects any deviation from the generally accepted memory. Thus the memories involved are the memories of the group. Dunn builds on this model, linking it to small groups of the early followers who would naturally swap their memories of the teachings of Jesus and stories about him at their informal and formal gatherings. In this manner, the Jesus traditions were persevered in the memories of group of his earliest followers.

Thus, while they do not use the terminology, many of the underlying concepts of collective memory form the basis of much of the argumentation of Dibelius, Bultmann, Gerhardsson, Riesner, and Bailey. This chapter will recount these various explanations of the origins and preservation of the Gospel traditions put forward by these writers and evaluate each one for its strengths and weaknesses, starting first with *formgeschichtliche* ("form-historical") explanations of Gospel origins.

Confabulation and *formgeschichtliche* Explanations of Gospel Origins

Both Rudolf Bultmann and Martin Dibelius propose that the origins of the traditions in the Synoptic Gospels are to be found in the early Christian community, not in the ministry and teachings of Jesus. Bultmann is particularly clear about this. He writes, "I do indeed think that we can now know almost nothing concerning the life and personality of Jesus, since the early Christian sources show no interest in either, are moreover fragmentary and often legendary; and other sources about Jesus do not exist" (Bultmann 1935, 8).[1] These words might be taken as a summing up

---

1. These particular words of Bultmann are widely quoted. In their original context, though, he is only denying the possibility of dealing with the personality of Jesus. In his article he goes on to state that rather than discussing Jesus' personality or pronouncing value judgments, he plans to discuss the teachings of Jesus. These are

of Bultmann's larger assessment of the historicity of the traditions in the Synoptic Gospels. Rather than going back to Jesus, Bultmann places the source of the Gospel traditions in the life of the Christian communities. They grow out of the church's *Sitz im Leben* ("life situation"). Each of the different genres of the tradition (i.e., the various "forms" of the tradition) grew out of a different situation faced by the local Christian communities.

Bultmann explains his methodology in the following terms: "the proper understanding of form-criticism rests upon the judgment that the literature in which the life of a given community, even the primitive Christian community, has taken shape, springs out of quite definite conditions and wants of life from which grows up a quite definite style and quite specific forms and categories. Thus every literary category has its 'life situation' (*Sitz im Leben*: Gunkel)" (Bultmann 1968, 4). For example, Bultmann suggests that controversy and scholastic dialogues found in the Synoptic Gospels are examples of typically rabbinic disputes and so must find their *Sitz im Leben* "in the discussions the [Palestinian] Church had with its opponents, and certainly within itself, on questions of law" (1968, 41).[2] Many of the "Synoptic sayings can be understood in relationship with Jewish 'Wisdom' and that we must therefore consider the possibility that they may in part derive therefrom." The parables may have "been taken from the Jewish tradition by the Church and put into Jesus' mouth," at least those that are not "*community formulations*." Some miracle stories and legendary motifs derive from the Palestinian church and some from the Hellenistic church (Bultmann 1968, 108, 203, 205, 240, 302–7, emphasis original).

Bultmann summarizes his analysis of the Synoptic Gospels by saying, "throughout the synoptics three strands must be distinguished: old tradition, ideas produced in and by the Church, and editorial work of the evangelists" (Bultmann 1952, 1:3). It is clear that for Bultmann little, if any, of the "old tradition" in the Synoptic Gospels can be attributed to Jesus. Rather, he considers most of the "old tradition" to derive from Judaism.

---

arrived at by noting the different layers of tradition that are evident in the Gospels, and relying on the earliest layer. He observes: "Naturally we have no absolute assurance that the exact words of this oldest layer were really spoken by Jesus" (Bultmann 1935:13). While his words are therefore quoted out of context, they do sum up his attitude towards what can be known of the historical Jesus revealed in this instance and in his other writings.

2. He also states, "We can firmly conclude that the formation of the material in the tradition took place in the *Palestinian Church*" (Bultmann 1968, 48).

The bulk of the materials in the Synoptic Gospels, he suggests, were "produced in and by the Church" (1952, 1:3). Thus for Bultmann, what is found in the Synoptic Gospels is a record of the life of the church, not the life of Jesus. He asserts that his analysis of the different forms found in the Synoptic traditions reveals this history. Thus it is very fitting that he describes his methodology as *Formgeschichte* ("form history").

It is sometimes easy to miss the larger picture as Bultmann proceeds methodically through the Synoptic materials, first analyzing each particular form, then asserting its likely origin. In this regard, Martin Dibelius gives greater assistance to his readers in enabling them to see the link between the life situation of the church and the development of traditions to meet the needs of that situation. His major work, *Die Formgeschichte des Evangeliums* [*The Form History of the Gospels*] was first published in 1919 and a much expanded second edition in 1933.[3] In it, Dibelius examines the forms found in the Gospel traditions and attempts to locate the *Sitz im Leben* that might lie behind the form.

For Dibelius, paradigms, tales, legends, and the sayings of Jesus all have a different *Sitz im Leben*. For example, paradigms such as the healing of the paralytic (Mark 2:1–12), the healing of the withered hand (3:1–6), and the tribute money (12:13–17) are well-suited for use in sermons. They are short stories that exist in isolation, have an external rounding-off, are brief and simple, have a definitely religious coloring to the narrative, and usually reach their point and conclude with a word of Jesus. On the other hand, tales such as the stories of the leper (Mark 1:40–45), the storm (4:35–41), and the walking on the sea (6:45–52) have their *Sitz im Leben* in the activities of storytellers and teachers. Although sometimes it is possible to see that a tale has developed from a paradigm, a tale is an individual story complete in itself and is told with the more secular motive of entertainment. Tales often include a miraculous act. Legends, such as the story of Jesus at twelve years of age (Luke 2:31–52), the calling of Nathanael (John 1:45–51), and the story about blind Bartimaeus (Mark 10:46–52), like other legends, are stories that give information about larger-than-life heroes. The passion story is unique among the Gospel traditions and grows out of very early preaching that always included the story of the crucifixion of Jesus. Finally, the sayings of Jesus had their own path of trans-

---

3. The English translation, *From Tradition to Gospel* (Dibelius 1971), is based on the 1933 edition, with some further changes made by Dibelius.

mission. "From a very early date, viz. already in the time of Paul, words of Jesus had been collected for hortatory purposes" (Dibelius 1971, 15, 243). Finally, Dibelius lists what he considers to be full-blown myths, such as the baptism of Jesus (Mark 1:9–11), the temptations (Matt 4:1–11), and the transfiguration (Mark 9:2–8).

Dibelius thinks the oldest traditions are those associated with preaching, which he defines very broadly. Preaching may refer to "preaching to non-Christians and also to a Christian congregation, as well as to the teaching of catechumens." Of all the forms, paradigms are closest to sermons and thus, in Dibelius's thinking, are the oldest forms of the tradition. Yet this is the tradition of the Greek-speaking pre-Pauline Hellenistic Christianity, not the Aramaic-speaking traditions associated with the early believers at Jerusalem. Dibelius returns several times to the question of historical authenticity of the Gospel traditions. Toward the end of the book he states, "the weightiest part of the tradition had been developed at a time while eyewitnesses still lived, and when the events were only about a generation old. It is not to be wondered that this part of the tradition remained relatively unaltered" (1971, 295). Yet in his analysis, Dibelius usually points out the problems of identifying reliable tradition. The traditions are not those of the Aramaic-speaking part of the church but have already been translated. Even paradigms show evidence of change and additions. As he says in chapter 2, "the materials which have been handed down to us in the Gospel lived in these decades an unliterary life or had indeed as yet no life at all" (1971, 9). Dibelius writes little about the process by which materials that had "as yet no life at all" eventually found their way into the Gospels, but what he says is consistent with the process of confabulation. The early Christians were interested in stories about Jesus and the early disciples, and storytellers and teachers provided what was missing. The early church faced difficult decisions about such things as to whether or not they should pay the temple tax, so traditions grew that answered these questions.

Though they did not use the term, collective memory lies at the heart of both Bultmann's and Dibelius's model of the development of the traditions that are found in the Synoptic Gospels. For them, the Gospel traditions are not just drawn from the collective memory of the early Christian communities; they are a product of that collective memory! The time period between Jesus and the writing of the Gospels had been so great that virtually nothing of the actual memory of Jesus remains. Those few vague authentic memories that survive are overwhelmed by the needs of the earliest Christians in their proclamation of the gospel. As a consequence, new stories and sayings to meet their urgent needs were developed. Thus for both Dibelius and Bultmann, the traditions found in the Gospels are not just those memories of Jesus that are preserved in collective memory. To a large extent, the traditions themselves are a product of the "collective mind," confabulations, if you will. But in the light of what else is known about collective memory, can such wholesale confabulation of collective memories be supported?

Confabulations in Collective Memories

A process not that dissimilar to that posited by Bultmann and Dibelius can be observed in the social interaction of some humans as they try to compensate for deficits in their memories. This is described as confabulation. The term can carry the implication of a deliberate lie, although in neuropsychology it is used in a neutral way to describe a symptom that accompanies many neuropsychological disorders and some psychiatric ones. In this type of confabulation, "there is no attempt to deceive and the patient is unaware of the falsehoods" (Moscovitch 1995, 226), yet, as may be observed in the case of patient HW (a sixty-one-year-old with severe brain injuries), it can be very evident to others around the patient that what is being said is unlikely to be true. The following is part of an interview with HW:

> Q: Can you tell me a little bit about yourself? How old are you?
> A: I'm 40, 42, pardon me, 62.
> Q: Are you married or single?
> A: Married.
> Q: How long have you been married?
> A: About 4 months.
> Q: What's your wife's name?
> A: Martha.
> Q: How many children do you have?
> A: Four. (He laughs.) Not bad for 4 months!
> Q: How old are your children?
> A: The eldest is 32, his name is Bob, and the youngest is 22, his name is Joe. [These answers are close to the actual age of the boys] (He laughs again.)
> Q: How did you get these children in 4 months?
> A: They're adopted.
> Q: Who adopted them?

A: Martha and I.
Q: Immediately after you got married you wanted to adopt these older children?
A: Before we were married we adopted one of them, two of them. The eldest girl Brenda and Bob, and Joe and Dina since we were married.
Q: Does it all sound a little strange to you, what you are saying?
A: (He laughs.) I think it is a little strange.
Q: Your record says that you've been married for over 30 years. Does that sound more reasonable to you?
A: No.
Q: Do you really believe that you have been married for 4 months?
A: Yes.
Q: You have been married for a long time to the same woman, for over 30 years. Do you find that strange?
A: Very strange. (Moscovitch 1995, 227–28)

That patient HW is confabulating is clear from the inconsistencies in his explanations. Confabulations in less brain-damaged patients need not be so evident but are no less unconsciously inconsistent with verifiable facts. One cannot but feel a certain sympathy with the situation of HW and others who need to confabulate because some of their memory systems are malfunctioning. Many crucial long-term memories are not available to such individuals, and in some cases the ability to monitor a memory for plausibility is greatly diminished. Confabulations are a way to make good deficits in memory. If something is missing, then a somewhat coherent response is produced to a current stimulus by putting together fragments of existing information. The end result, though, is a confabulation.

Innocent confabulation is not confined to those individuals who have significant memory impairment, as Jean E. Fox Tree and Mary Susan Weldon discovered in an experiment aimed at investigating what factors influenced the retelling of urban legends (Tree and Weldon 2007, 459–76). Of significance here, is that when asked to recall an urban legend they had encountered ten weeks before, "Only 3 of the 65 recalled stories contained no confabulated details. The average number of confabulated details was 3.88, SD 2.86, range 0–16" (2007, 469).[4] Nor should these results be surprising, given what has been discovered about the reconstructive nature of

---

4. Tree and Weldon manipulated the number of details provided to flesh out the story in the original stimulus but discovered that the number of confabulated details was unaffected by the number of genuine details initially provided.

human memory. When retelling a story, the basic gist of the story needs to be filled out with corroborating details. Confabulation is further evidence of the human capacity to form meaning.

By suggesting that the early church made good the deficits in its collective memory of Jesus by developing stories and sayings to fit their current needs, Dibelius and Bultmann posit that a mechanism exists in collective memories that is similar to that of confabulation in individuals. One might fairly ask whether such a mechanism is likely in collective memory. To be sure, details will vary with each retelling of an account. Furthermore, the needs of the present do impact collective memories (such was the conclusion reached in the previous chapter). But do the needs of the present actually give rise to the invention of completely new stories about the past, to "confabulations"?

That collective memories can be sometimes completely fabricated is demonstrable and is one of the ways in which Roy Baumeister and Stephen Hastings suggest that collective memories might be distorted (1997, 277–93). As a case in point, they cite the fact that George Washington did not, in fact, ask Betsy Ross to sew the first American flag. This story was invented in 1976 by some of Betsy Ross's descendants to create a tourist attraction in Philadelphia. Further examples can be found. Despite strong contemporary opinion (i.e., collective memory), the traditional Scottish kilt is not in fact traditional dress for the highland Scots, who, in reality, were more Irish than Scottish. Rather, it was a variation of belted plaid, which was originally the dress of the poor who could not afford the expense of trousers or breeches. The kilt was invented soon after 1726 by the Quaker Thomas Rawlinson for the workers at an iron-smelting furnace that he established at Glengary. Rawlinson hired a tailor "to abridge the dress [the belted plaid] and make it handy and convenient for his workmen." It was only after a period when traditional dress had been banned and forever abandoned by the poorer classes that the kilt became popular among the gentry. Associating a particular tartan with a tribe has no historical roots but probably is to be traced to the highland regimental uniforms and some rather creative work by the two brothers Allen that was taken up by the Highland Society of London (Trevor-Roper 1983, 22).[5]

---

5. A detailed account of the invention of the kilt and the traditions of the tartans can be found in Trevor-Roper 1983, 15–41. In my personal files, I have some of the research done on the history of the McIvers by my father, Robert Donald McIver, including a full description and sample of the McIver tartan. Until reading Trevor-

Yet, even though one can demonstrate that collective memory can be fabricated, Baumeister and Hastings conclude:

> Still, it seems that by and large outright fabrication of collective memory is rare. The implication may be that collective memories are to some extent constrained by the facts. Facts may be deleted, altered, shaded, reinterpreted, exaggerated, and placed in favourable contexts, but wholesale fabrication seems to lie beyond what most groups can accomplish. Presumably, a thorough historical search would eventually uncover an example or two of fabrication, but these would be extreme exceptions. Fabrication is thus not one of the standard techniques of altering collective memory for self-serving ends. (1997, 282)

Rather than outright fabrication, Baumeister and Hastings suggest that collective memory is changed to meet the demands of the present by a number of means. One can selectively omit aspects of earlier events and biography, as, for example, leaving out proslavery acts or opinions of favorite American historical figures. One can exaggerate or embellish, such as exaggerating the role of Britain and the United States in winning World War II, when in fact the Red Army bore the brunt of the war and all the best German divisions were fighting in Russia. One can connect one event to other events, such as linking the dropping of the atomic bombs on Japan to the attack on Pearl Harbor. One can blame the enemy, such as when Germany attacked Russia in World War II despite a nonaggression pact. One can blame circumstances, such as attributing the demise of the native Americans mainly to disease, while ignoring "deliberate policies of genocide, subjection, and extermination" (Baumeister and Hastings 1997, 290). One can provide a contextual frame by choosing which causal nexus to emphasize, such as the different causes attached to the American Civil War. In northern states the Civil War was said to be about slavery. In the southern states the war was said to be about living according to local values and cultures. Thus are collective memories transmuted to fit the needs of the present. Baumeister and Hastings, together with many historians, call this a process of "distortion." But, as with the frail-

---

Roper's article, I had had a sneaking pride in knowing that there was an authentic McIver tartan. Yet another illustration of the fact that more accurate historical knowledge does not guarantee increased happiness.

ties of individual human memory, this process can in fact have positive as well as negative impact. Such is the argument of Michael Kammen (1995, 329–45).

Kammen gives several case studies from American history. The Puritan fathers, for example, immigrated to America because it apparently was hopeless to stay in England to try to reform that morally corrupt society from within. Their purpose was to create a model theocratic community; at least, such was their self-rhetoric. One might expect that the success of Oliver Cromwell and the establishment of a Puritan-led nation would lead many of the American Puritans to wish to return to England to contribute to this new society, but now they saw their mission as the conversion of the heathen peoples in the new world. "[M]emories can readily, with scant embarrassment or challenge, be quietly repressed within a generation and replaced by alternative explanations" (Kammen 1995, 331). This change is not necessarily a cynical manipulation of a dominant social group. It is hardly reprehensible, although it might not be morally neutral. On the other hand, some changes to collective memory can be seen as having a positive impact. Andrew Jackson and Abraham Lincoln were presidents in a country that "had staked its own claim to independent nationhood upon Lockean principles of the right to revolution." They responded "by invoking a political fiction…: the notion of a 'Perpetual Union,'" a notion that required "an astonishing revision of historical reality" but one "that seems to have troubled no one in the North and perplexed few people even in the South" (Kammen 1995, 337). As for morality, Kammen concludes: "Call it casuistry or sophistry, but not cynicism or hypocrisy. Those who rationalized the Union believed every word that they said and wrote." He notes, "Frequently … the willful alteration of collective memory becomes a necessity for a viable, progressive society. How else can it coherently adapt to change, often desirable change, without being plagued by a sense of inconsistency or sham?" (Kammen 1995, 340).

While some changes in collective memory might be desirable, it is not infrequently the case that politicians and others attempt to distort collective memory for their own purposes. Modern Western civilization is characterized by its tolerance of a number of competing voices to counterbalance these attempts. Collective memories are often contested memories.

"The past, anthropologist Arjun Appadurai has suggested, is a 'scarce resource,' and conflict over its ownership is recurrent. … Contest, conflict, controversy—these are the hallmark of studies of collective memory"

(Schudson 1995, 361).⁶ Peter Burke considers that historians have an important role in the wider societal debate. He agrees that some changes in collective memory are beneficial. Amnesty after war or major changes in government can be seen as "the official erasure of memories of conflict in the interests of social cohesion." But any number of things, including writing and print, act to resist too great a manipulation of the collective memory. He says, "historians also have a role to play in this process of resistance. Herodotus thought of historians as the guardians of memory, the memory of glorious deeds. I prefer to see historians as the guardians of the skeletons in the cupboard of the social memory, the 'anomalies' … which reveal weaknesses in grand and not-so-grand theories" (Burke 1997, 57–59).

Thus far, then, collective memories appear to be largely free of actual confabulation (see Rodríguez 2010, 50–64), yet this positive evaluation of the essential authenticity of collective memories must be balanced against their known frailties. Not only does the present strongly shape the collective memory of the past, but some aspects of group behavior can entrench false perceptions of reality in the collective memory of some groups. Take, for example, the kind of phenomena on which Leon Festinger based his theory of cognitive dissonance. He suggests five conditions that need to be present for a group to entrench their false perception of reality: (1) a strongly held belief must have some relevance to action; (2) because of that belief, a person must have taken some important action difficult to undo; (3) the belief must be "sufficiently specific … so that events may unequivocally refute the belief"; (4) "such undeniably disconfirmatory evidence must occur and must be recognized by the individual holding the belief"; and (5) "The individual believer must have social support" (Festinger, Riecken, and Schachter 1956, 4).⁷ Festinger gives several historical examples that under such conditions a group can not only survive the disconfirmation of one of their core beliefs, but the confirmation itself may stimu-

---

6. Cf. the comment of John Bodnar: "The story of the Vietnam Veterans Memorial underscores a very fundamental point. The shaping of a past worthy of public commemoration in the present is contested and involves a struggle for supremacy between advocates of various political ideas and sentiments" (Bodnar 1992, 13).

7. See also Festinger's more theoretical and discursive *A Theory of Cognitive Dissonance* (Festinger 1957); and the review of subsequent research into the theology in Joel Cooper's *Cognitive Dissonance: Fifty Years of a Classic Theory* (Cooper 2007).

late the group into energetic proselytization.[8] He suggests that individuals in such groups experience significant cognitive dissonance between their beliefs and reality. This dissonance can be reduced by the social support of others who believe as they do. Thus recruitment of others into the group becomes a natural outgrowth of the impulse to reduce cognitive dissonance. In this way, false perceptions of reality can be entrenched in the collective memory of some groups.

Thus, it might be concluded that, while collective memories appear to be generally resistant to outright confabulation, they are susceptible to shaping by present circumstances, and there are some conditions in which false perceptions of reality become entrenched in collective memory. This being said, what should be concluded about the process of the formation of the Gospel traditions suggested by Dibelius and Bultmann? Several observations conspire to make unlikely their suggestion that the Gospel traditions derive from the early Christians' activities in proselytizing where new traditions were confabulated to meet new situations. While it is possible to document the occasional complete fabrication in collective memories, collective memories do not usually work in this manner. To be sure, aspects of a historical figure that do not fit current ideology and interests are ignored, and those that do fit are emphasized. But in collective memory, traditions about past events and figures generally correspond in important ways to what actually happened and the personality and achievements of individuals from the past. Such a wholesale invention of tradition as proposed by Dibelius and Bultmann appears inconsistent with what else is known about collective memory. In other words, despite some valuable contributions in their analysis of the forms of tradition found in the Gospel traditions, the model developed by Dibelius and Bultmann to account for the development of the Gospel traditions must be rejected.

---

8. Most of Festinger's examples relate to failed predictions of dates among religious groups. Anabaptists predicted that Jesus would return in 1533; in 1648, Sabbatai Zevi proclaimed himself to be the predicted Jewish Messiah who would issue in an era of redemption that did not arrive; William Miller predicted Jesus would return in 1843 (later changing the date to 1844). Each of these dates was disconfirmed, but after disconfirmation the movements gained in vigor. Sabbatai Zevi only proclaimed himself as Messiah outside of his own circle of disciples after 1648, and his movement became very influential in Smyrna. The Millerite movement was at its strongest after 1843 (Festinger, Riecken, and Schachter 1956, 7–23).

Jesus as Teacher, and the Disciples as Preservers of the Jesus Traditions

By emphasizing the teaching activities of Jesus and the role taken by the disciples in the transmission of his ideas, several scholars have built a collective memory model of the preservation of the Gospel traditions quite different from that of Dibelius and Bultmann. In this model, the circle of disciples and their immediate followers developed a carefully controlled collective memory of the teachings and activities of Jesus. Among those who develop such a position are Harald Riesenfeld, Birger Gerhardsson, Rainer Riesner, and Armin Baum.

Harald Riesenfeld's ideas are succinctly expressed in an address to the opening session of the Congress of the Four Gospels in 1957 and published in a small book entitled *The Gospel Tradition and Its Beginning: A Study in the Limits of "Formgeschichte"* (Riesenfeld 1957). In it he attacks the then-prevailing model of the transmission of the material given by scholars espousing the methodology of *Formgeschichte*. As has already been noted, for Dibelius and Bultmann the creative *Sitz im Leben* of the Gospel narratives about Jesus and the teaching attributed to him is to be found in teaching activities of the earliest Christians, in the catechal instruction they provided to new converts, and in the controversies that surrounded them. Informed by the post-Easter faith, these early Christians developed the teaching of Jesus into the form that is to be found in the Gospels, and many of the accounts of miracles and the like were free inventions of these early preachers to give account of who Jesus was. At least, such was the position of Dibelius and Bultmann. Riesenfeld attacks this viewpoint by saying:

> I cannot enter here into a detailed critique of these theories. The very existence of such an anonymous creative generation in primitive Christianity presupposes, in view of what we know from the New Testament about the apostles and the other members of the early Christian community, a truly miraculous and incredible factor in the history of the Gospel tradition. (Riesenfeld 1957, 9)

Indeed, as Riesenfeld goes on to point out, when one looks at the records of early Christian preaching that are available today (those recorded in Acts, for example), what is striking is that there is a complete lack of the kinds of materials found in the Gospels. "Mission preaching was not the

Sitz im Leben of the Gospel tradition" (1957, 13). Even in the preaching intended for the Christian communities themselves, which can be studied in Paul's letters and in such books as James, while there are allusions to the words of Jesus, explicit quotations of his words are lacking.

Instead of looking to preaching as the *Sitz im Leben*, Riesenfeld looks to another model drawn from the practices of Judaism, where preaching was likewise prominent. Within Judaism, "in New Testament times the specifically Jewish tradition, at any rate, was not possessed and shaped by an unlimited and undefined anonymous multitude" (1957, 18). Rather, "[t]he bearer of the tradition and the teacher (*rabbi*) watched over its memorizing by his approved pupils (*talmd*) and what was passed on in this way was, in the matter both of content and form, a fixed body of material" (1957, 18).

Riesenfeld then applies this model to Jesus and his disciples. Jesus, as rabbi, teaches his disciples, getting them to memorize his words. Thus the Christian tradition derives from Jesus himself. What the bearers of the tradition (his disciples and those whom they instructed) did was to preserve them faithfully. To consider that the early church created these traditions is to ignore the realities of the times in which they lived.

Birger Gerhardsson's well-known monograph, *Memory and Manuscript* (1998 [orig. 1961]), is more a prolegomenon to the question of the possibility of oral transmission of the traditions found in the Synoptic Gospels than its detailed exposition.[9] The book deals extensively with the first-century Jewish transmission of written and oral traditions and with setting up a model from the New Testament of how traditions were preserved in early Christianity, but it deals specifically with the Gospels only in a short chapter at the end. However, the whole work is of importance to the question of oral transmission of the Gospel material, and enough is said about the Gospels to get a good idea of his thinking about them.

Gerhardsson deals separately with the transmission of the written and the oral Torah within first-century Judaism. In discussing both he emphasizes the importance of the process of education and discusses it in detail (1998, 56–66, 113–70). Elementary education (*bet sefer*) started with the teaching of written Torah, and advanced education (*bet hammidrash*) consisted of study of both the written and the oral Torah. The *bet sefer* taught

---

9. In his last chapter, Gerhardsson says, "We ought now to proceed to the synoptic material, but this would require an independent monograph" (1998, 324).

the correct reading of the written text of the sacred writings that eventually made their way into the Hebrew Bible. As was the case with Hellenistic schools, memorization played a basic educational role in both the *bet sefer* and the *bet hammidrash* (1998, 62–65, 113–15). In the entire classical world, material was first committed to memory before any attempt was made to understand it. Thus even texts that had become garbled or whose meaning was lost could still be transmitted (1998, 126). Oral Torah was preserved only by memorization. Considerable effort was given to preserving the exact wording of the teacher, who assisted by abbreviating and condensing his thoughts and arranging mnemonic helps. Although the tradition frowns on the practice, at times written notes must have been made to assist in the process of memorization. The basic method of memorization and maintenance was that of repetition.

In part 2 of his book, Gerhardsson deals with the transmission of tradition in early Christianity. The early fathers of the postapostolic church are nearly unanimous in their reporting of the importance and reliability of tradition. Not only this, but they all attribute the writing of the Gospels to either apostles or close acquaintances of the apostles. The picture of the early church found in Luke is very interesting to Gerhardsson. As he reconstructs it, the twelve apostles, located at Jerusalem, formed a *collegium* (led by Peter) and were those entrusted with the preservation of tradition and the ordering of the new group of believers.[10] Their function is perhaps seen most clearly in the early Christian general session recorded in Acts 15. Paul, while not part of the original circle of the twelve, still claims that he is an eyewitness, and even though he claims independence from the twelve, he still submits his gospel to them to ensure its correctness.

Gerhardsson then builds on this information to form a picture of the formation of the Gospels. He insists that one must pay close attention to the milieu in which the early church worked. They were initially all Jews and were all products of its system of education to a greater or lesser extent. The way they would preserve tradition would be closely modeled upon their background. What was distinctive is that for them Jesus was *the* authority. They preserved his insights into Torah and his other teachings. At times mnemonic arrangements can be detected. The Jesus traditions

---

10. He develops these ideas particularly in Gerhardsson 1998, 214–45 (although the term *collegium* is used more frequently later in the book, e.g., see the summarizing statement on p. 329).

would have the character of oral Torah to the early believers. It would be carefully taught by teachers, using all the methodologies known to them (particularly memorization). As recently as 2005, Gerhardsson was still insisting:

> My thesis is still that the most important carriers of this text material were early, well-informed adherents of Jesus—in the beginning above all "the twelve"—and that these men "worked with the word of the Lord" according to a common Jewish model.... They handled and transmitted an oral tradition ... in principle memorized. (Gerhardsson 2005, 18)

Rainer Riesner is another who has placed great importance on Jesus' role as a teacher who set himself the goal of forming a collective memory of his important teachings within the circle of his disciples. His published PhD dissertation, *Jesus als Lehrer* (*Jesus as Teacher*),[11] is now in its fourth edition. Riesner provides an analysis of the term "teacher" as it was applied to Jesus. This term is not a christological title but something that describes important activities of Jesus. The practice of teaching in local synagogues is an important background to the ministry of Jesus and quite consistent with what is known of synagogue practice at the time. Teaching and preaching outdoors for crowds, though, is distinctive to Jesus. Jesus taught in a vivid style and arranged his teachings in memorable forms of poetry or parables. Like Gerhardsson, Riesner emphasizes that Jesus taught his disciples by asking them to memorize his teachings. As he says,

> Perhaps the least persuasive point in my reconstruction of the origins of Gospel tradition was for many colleagues the assumption that Jesus encouraged his disciples to learn by heart some of his carefully formulated teaching summaries. I still believe that in New Testament research there are more improbable hypotheses than this. That rote-learning formed an important factor in the Hellenistic schools on all levels was recently admitted by Klaus Berger. Learning by heart was an important part of all ancient education from the elementary to the academic niveau. (Riesner 1991, 203)

---

11. Rainer Riesner, *Jesus als Lehrer: Eine Untersuchung zum Ursprung der Evangelien-Überlieferung* (Riesner 1981). An English summary of many of Riesner's important ideas may be found in Riesner 1991, 185–210; 2008, 624–30; and German summary may be found in Riesner 2002.

Riesner places particular stress on the fact that, before Jesus sent out his disciples to go before him through the villages of Galilee (Matt 10:5–15; Mark 6:7–13; Luke 9:1–16), he would have ensured that they would have been able to repeat back to him essential parts of his teaching (Riesner 1984, 453–75, 500–501; 1991, 197–201; 2008, 627–28).[12] Thus, even before the Easter event, Riesner insists that the disciples would have mastered a considerable and well-defined body of Jesus' teaching. He even suggests the possibility that some of the teachings of Jesus may have been preserved in written form during his ministry by some of his sedentary followers.[13]

In his book *Der mündliche Faktor und seine Bedeutung für die synoptische Frage* (*The Orality Factor and Its Meaning for the Synoptic Question*), Armin Baum builds on the work of Riesner in several ways. For example, he points out that:

> The synoptic tradition as a whole contains about 30,000 words. The words of Jesus amount to about 15,000 words. In the ancient Jewish world it was not regarded as an extraordinary achievement to learn such a *large number of words* by heart. The rabbis knew not only their holy scriptures (containing about 300,000 words) by heart, but in addition substantial parts of oral torah. ... In this time period an average Jew would certainly have been able to commit all the synoptic words of Jesus to memory, or at least a considerable part of them. (Baum 2008a, 404)

Much of Baum's work relates to the features of Jesus' teachings that make it ideal for memorization, as well as analyzing various parts of the rabbinic traditions that report the same or very similar stories and legal determinations. Such comparison reveals that the phenomena observable in the parallels between the rabbinic traditions show many similarities to those found within the Synoptic Gospels (Baum 2008b, 1–23).

Reisenfeld, Gerhardsson, and Riesner provide an important reminder of the importance of the circle of disciples that Jesus gathered around himself. They highlight the possibility that it is not unlikely that Jesus deliberately fostered the formation of a controlled set of collective memories

---

12. In making this suggestion, Riesner is building on the work of Heinz Schürmann 1960, 361–69.

13. "In view of the widespread literacy in Jewish Palestine and the high-class background of some of Jesus' adherents it seems not too far fetched that, as has been suggested by some scholars, some of his teachings may have been written down even before Easter by such sedentary sympathizers" (Riesner 1991, 196).

within his disciples, and this is an insight that will be further explored in a later chapter. Kenneth Bailey and James Dunn, on the other hand, have pointed to other processes whereby the community of early Christians may have formed collective memories of Jesus and his teachings.

Kenneth Bailey's Description of Formal, Controlled Oral Traditions

Kenneth Bailey suggests that, just as archaeologists can understand some styles of ancient building techniques by studying existing traditional Arab villages near a site, so also those studying the Gospel traditions could benefit from examining how traditions are preserved in Middle Eastern cultures. From his forty-year experience observing Middle Eastern culture as a teacher of New Testament in Egypt, Lebanon, and Palestine, Bailey distinguishes three methods by which oral traditions are passed along (Bailey 1991, 34–54; 1995, 363–67). First is what Bailey describes as "informal uncontrolled oral tradition," such as the rumors and atrocity stories that came to the author in Beirut, Lebanon, between 1975 and 1984. In one such atrocity story, the three people killed by a random shell while waiting in line outside a bakery quickly became a story of three hundred massacred in cold blood. Bailey suggests that such informal and uncontrolled oral traditions correspond to the model proposed by Dibelius and Bultmann. On the other hand, there exists "formal controlled oral traditions." It is not uncommon to memorize the entire Qur'an, as did Taha Hussein of Eygpt as an eight-year-old boy, who was also required to learn a collection of one thousand couplets of Arabic verse, each of which defines some aspect of Arabic grammar. In a Syrian Orthodox seminary in Lebanon, young students learn to sing ancient hymns by the hour, all without books. But for Bailey, neither of these types of transmission corresponds well with what we can observe in the Gospels. There is too much similarity between the parallel Gospel accounts for informal uncontrolled oral transmission and too much variation for formal controlled oral transmission.

Bailey recounts in detail a third way in which oral traditions are transmitted: "informal controlled oral tradition," which is found in a gathering called a *hafalat samar*. In the time described by Bailey, and before the widespread introduction of television, in the average simple village, extended families and at times the whole village would often gather in the evening and spend their time listening to stories and the recitation of poetry. There is no set teacher, thus the tradition is informal, but important traditions are generally recited by the older men, the more gifted men, and the socially prominent men. Women and young people can have their own *hafalat samar*, at which occasions other speakers would recite. There are a number of different types of material recited: short proverbs, story riddles, poetry, parables and stories, and accounts of important figures in the history of the village or community, particularly its founder. The various types of material are afforded different amounts of flexibility. Poetry and proverbs are recited with no flexibility—if the reciter makes a mistake, he or she is corrected by a chorus of voices. Parables and recollections of important historical events or people allow for some flexibility. Bailey describes this process as continuity and flexibility, *not* continuity and change, as the essential components of the story must remain, or again, the community corrects the reciter. On the other hand, there is total flexibility in the telling of casual news of the day, jokes, atrocity stories, and the like.

Bailey gives examples of how effective this form of oral tradition can be for preserving large amounts of material for long periods of time. The large amount of material that can be preserved might be illustrated by a collection of some six thousand Palestinian Arab proverbs, of which over four thousand had been collected orally and had been in current usage. Long periods of time can be detected in some of the stories. Stories are rarely told accompanied by formal dates, but their age might be indicated by a comment that a particular story comes from the time "back when we spoke Coptic" (i.e., before the fifteenth century), or by the remark that another story comes from "back when 'Antinus was founded" (second century), or yet another story comes from the days of Turkish rule. Very old stories indeed, but all told in the present tense.

Bailey notes that the types of materials found in the Gospels—aphorisms, parables, stories of the founder—are exactly the type of materials transmitted by the informal but controlled oral tradition of the *hafalat samar*. The community exercised control over the accuracy of the tradition recited in the *hafalat samar*, ensuring some materials were preserved verbatim and others with some flexibility. It is this same flexibility, while preserving the essence of the meaning, that is observed in the Gospel parallels. Bailey further suggests that at least until the disruption of the 66–70 war, the Christian communities would have considered the oral tradition to be intact and would have felt no need to actually write them down. He concludes that, while other processes, such as the pedagogy of the rabbinic schools, might contribute some materials to the Gospel traditions, the concept of informal but controlled tradition may well "provide a methodological framework within which to perceive and interpret the bulk of the material before us" (Bailey 1991, 41).[14] Bailey's report has strongly influenced how James D. G. Dunn reconstructs the transmission of the traditions concerning Jesus, to whom we now turn.

Collective Memory in James D. G. Dunn's *Jesus Remembered*

In a series of publications spanning over twenty-five years, James D. G. Dunn has emphasized the importance of the fact that the traditions about Jesus were kept in oral form for a long time before they were written in the Gospels (e.g., Dunn 1987; 2000, 287–326; 2003a, 139–75; 2003b, 173–254; 2005, 35–56; 2007, 179–94). For Dunn, there are several inputs into the oral traditions found in early Christianity. Important roles were played by the apostles, particularly Peter (2003a, 151–53). Nor should one overlook the significance of teachers as "the congregation's repository of oral tradition" (Dunn 2003b, 176; see also 180–81). Yet one cannot help but gain the impression that Dunn places more emphasis on the role of the Christian communities in the preservation of traditions than the role of apostles or teacher.[15] Dunn observes that Jesus made a great impression on all those he met. While at first these impressions would be memories of individuals, "tradition-forming is a *communal* process" (2003b, 240). As Dunn says, "I simply do not believe that Peter, Mary of Magdala and the like stored up many memories of Jesus' mission, which were only jerked into remembrance by 'oral history' inquiries of a Luke or a Matthew. They had already fed these memories into the living tradition of the churches, as major contributory elements in the forming and shaping that tradition" (2004, 483–84). Dunn is thankful to Bailey for providing the "possibility

---

14. Diana Allan reports that while she had expected to find oral performance in community gatherings among Palestinian refugees in Lebanon, such did not take place in modern Lebanon. "Few families or village networks have the space or resources to maintain daiwans (traditional meeting places, normally limited to men) or *Qu'at* (village halls) anymore" (Allan 2005, 51), and the younger generation gains their understanding of current events from television (2005, 47–56).

15. An observation also made by Samuel Byrskog (2004, 467–68). In his reply to Byrskog, Dunn first cites "the importance of the case made by Maurice Halbwachs and others on the creative character of 'social memory.'" He then states that he does emphasize the role of teachers, apostolic custodians, and church-founding apostles, "but on the other hand, it is not really possible to speak of *tradition* except as community tradition" (Dunn 2004, 481–82).

... of envisaging a realistic *Sitz im Leben* for the performance of the earliest tradition" (Dunn 2004, 479; see also 2003b, 205–9).

Dunn gives several examples from the parallels between the Gospels to illustrate that, even though he still thinks that Q and Mark were used as literary sources for Matthew and Luke (Dunn 2003b, 143–61),[16] oral traditions contributed significantly more to the writing of the Gospels than is usually thought. Take the Lord's Prayer, for example. A literary dependence provides a poor explanation of the variations that can be observed in the parallels between Matt 6:7–15 and Luke 11:1–4. "What failure in historical imagination is it that could even suggest to us that Matthew, say, only knew the Lord's prayer because he read it in Q?" (Dunn 2003a, 166). "Almost certainly, the early Christian disciples … *knew it because they prayed it*, possibly on a daily basis" (2003b, 227). Indeed, as one looks at the parallels between Matt 8:23–27, Mark 4:35–41, and Luke 8:22–25 (the stilling of the storm); Matt 17:14–18, Mark 9:14–27, and Luke 9:37–43 (the healing of the possessed boy); Matt 18:1–5, Mark 9:33–37, and Luke 9:46–48 (the dispute about greatness); and the other examples that Dunn provides in parallel columns in which the common words and phrases are underlined, one can see the principle of "variation within the same" (2003b, 212) that is so characteristic of oral traditions.[17]

Dunn suggests that several significant corollaries flow out of noting the important contribution of oral traditions into the Gospels. First, oral performance is not like reading a text. Second, it is essentially communal in character, and the community in which it is found acts to keep the traditions stable, even though, third, there are one or more within a particular community that might be recognized as responsible for remembering and performing particular traditions. Fourth, the oral origins of the traditions subvert the search for the "original version," so characteristic of much research on the Synoptic Gospels, and fifth, oral traditions are character-

---

16. Note also the list of parallels given in Dunn 2003b, 144 n. 15, which he says "can hardly be explained by other than literary dependence."

17. In Dunn 2003b, 224–38, the parallel passages are cited in English (cf. Dunn 2005, 103–20; 2003a, 158–70, which give many of the same examples, but this time giving the parallels in Greek). In *Oral Tradition and Literary Dependency* (Mournet 2005, 174–90), the published version of his PhD dissertation, Dunn's student Terence C. Mournet discovers redundancy, flexibility, and stability to be the characteristics of oral tradition.

ized by "a combination of *fixity* and *flexibility*, of *stability* and *diversity*" (Dunn 2003a, 150–56).[18]

Oral tradition's characteristic stability yet diversity means, Dunn insists, that one should not look specifically at the details of the Gospel tradition but at the broad picture, at themes that are widespread. He borrows Keck's terminology and suggests that he wishes to look for the "characteristic Jesus," not the "dissimilar Jesus." His criterion is that "any feature which is *characteristic of Jesus within the Jesus tradition and relatively distinctive of the Jesus tradition* is most likely to go back to Jesus, that is, to reflect the original impact made by Jesus' teaching and actions on several at least of his first disciples" (Dunn 2003b, 333). Yet, Dunn insists, this is not Jesus himself that we are listening to in the Gospels, but "Jesus remembered" (Dunn 2003b, 327–36). Bengt Holmberg has challenged Dunn on this point. Holmberg insists that "we have not completed our work as historians working on Jesus unless we push forward from the statement that a certain motif … appears frequently in the Jesus tradition because that was how Jesus was *remembered* to have spoken, to a judgment about whether he actually spoke like that or not" (Holmberg 2004, 450). Dunn, however, does not retreat from his position, even though he admits that this means that "our discerning of this Jesus will always be at least a little out of focus" (Dunn 2004, 475).

Even though the terminology is rarely used, the writings of Dunn form an excellent, well-considered example of the use of collective memory to explain Gospel origins.[19] In his model, Jesus' impact on his first followers and others who interacted with him very quickly formed the basis of community traditions even before the events of the crucifixion. These tradi-

---

18. See also Dunn's emphasis that the Gospel traditions are "not layers, but performances," in Dunn 2000, 322–23; 2003b, 248–49.

19. Dunn does explicitly recognize the importance of Halbwachs's conceptions of collective memory (Dunn 2004, 481–82). He also defines Christian tradition in a way that is quite close to the concept of the collective memory of the early Christian communities. For example, in a footnote to the comment on p. 173 of Dunn 2003b, he says: "Few, if any doubt that behind the written sources there was earlier tradition." He defines tradition in the following manner: "At one end of its spectrum of usage 'tradition' has to be distinguished from individual memory, though it could be described as corporate memory giving identity to the group which thus remembers. At the other end it has to be distinguished from formal rules and written law, though its being written down need not change its character, initially at any rate." Dunn also uses the terminology "shared memory" (2003b, 241).

tions were preserved in community meetings not unlike the *hafalat samar* as described by Bailey. These communities preserved the traditions in oral form. In other words, they preserved them in a form in which stability met flexibility, in a form of variations within the same. For Dunn, this is the bedrock on which the Gospel traditions are founded.

Conclusions

Though a "slippery phenomenon" (Kansteiner 2002, 180), collective memory has proved to be a very useful tool for evaluating several significant contributions to the debate as to how the memories of Jesus were preserved (in the case of Bailey and Dunn) or lost (in the case of Bultmann and Dibelius). It has been discovered that, while the processes of confabulation in the collective memory of early Christianity that were proposed by Bultmann and Dibelius are a possible explanation of the origins of the Gospel traditions, it is a highly unlikely one. The collective memories found in early Christian communities may well have been shaped by the interests and needs that were present during the formation, preservation, and eventual writing down of those traditions. But like such shaping in almost all collective memories, some essential characteristics of the original would have been preserved. Collective memories are suited to present circumstances precisely because there was something in the original that was apposite. Thus a knowledge of the characteristics of collective memory enabled the decisive rejection of the reconstruction put forward by Bultmann and Dibelius.

The models proposed by Riesenfeld, Gerhardsson, and Riesner also receive correction from both the insights from collective memory and what has been discovered in earlier chapters about the transience of memory. Gerhardsson, in particular, proposes a rather mechanical process of memorization that appears to understand the disciples transmitting the teachings of Jesus with near-verbatim recall, something that can be shown to be quite possible where a written text is available but highly unlikely in the absence of such a text. Ian Hunter has pointed out that "the human accomplishment of lengthy verbatim recall arises as an adaptation to written text and does not arise in cultural settings where text is unknown" (Hunter 1985, 207). One cannot assume that memorization in the type of oral context in which Jesus and his disciples operated was done at the level of verbatim recall (see also ch. 9). Furthermore, the insights provided from a consideration of the workings of collective memory reveal that greater attention needs to be given to the adaptations that collective memory makes to the present context in which a group preserves oral materials than is acknowledged by Gerhardsson.

The model for the preservation of the Jesus traditions proposed by Dunn is much more consistent with what might be expected of collective memories. There can be hardly any dispute that these traditions were kept for a long period in oral form as Dunn assumes. It is also self-evident that in a society without television, radio, and even good means of night-time illumination, opportunities for telling stories in communal gatherings in the evening would have existed in any community group. Furthermore, among the followers of Jesus, it can almost be guaranteed that these community gatherings would have repeated stories about Jesus and sayings attributed to him. The nature of collective memory means that the traditions preserved in such groups would need to correspond in some significant manner to Jesus himself and what he said and did. This much, then, can be accepted with a relative degree of confidence. On the other hand, while Dunn acknowledges the importance of Jesus deliberately forming in his inner circle of disciples a specific set of memories of his key teachings, their role seems to be somewhat undervalued by Dunn.

What is needed is a fresh look at the Jesus traditions in the Synoptic Gospels, one that has been informed by what has been discovered in earlier chapters about the qualities of individual eyewitness memories, as well as what is known of the characteristics of collective memories. What is sought is a model that gives adequate attention to the dynamic nature of human memory but also gives adequate attention to the significant influence of eyewitnesses and trained tradents such as the disciples and other early teachers within Christianity. The development of such a model will be attempted in subsequent chapters, beginning with a consideration of how the qualities of human memories would have shaped the individual eyewitness memories that made their way into the collective memories of the earliest followers of Jesus.

7
Eyewitness Memory and the Gospel Traditions

Characteristics of Written Texts Derived from Eyewitness Traditions

Later in this chapter it will be argued that the Jesus traditions moved from eyewitness memories into the collective memories of groups of early followers of Jesus and from thence into the written text of the Gospels. An important consideration, therefore, is whether it is possible to identify elements of eyewitness accounts in the written texts of the Gospels. In other words, what form might traditions and written texts be expected to take if they are derived from eyewitness memories? Here is where the experimental evidence presented in part 1 bears fruit.

A range of different types of memory appeared in the experiments reported in chapters 2 and 3. They include short-term memory for nonsense syllables, episodic memory, visual memory, long-term memory of a second language, flashbulb memories and other personal event memories, memories of linked lists, memories of historical events, and the like. With the exception of the memory of nonsense syllables, the material in the Gospels potentially includes eyewitness memories of each of these types. Nevertheless, it is the characteristics of human autobiographical memory (i.e., episodic memory) that are most likely to be helpful in reconstructing the characteristics of materials that come from eyewitness recollection, particularly the subset of episodic memories that are personal event memories.

The experiment into his own autobiographical memory conducted by Willem A. Wagenaar reported in chapter 2 provides several important clues as to what might characterize eyewitness memories. Wagenaar's experiment tracked his own success in reconstructing past episodes in the four categories *who, what, where,* and *when*. He reports that he was most successful in recalling *what*, was more vague with regard to *where*, and least successful in recalling *when*. One would therefore expect that eyewitness memories would be rich in descriptions of what happened but lack much in the way of reliable temporal references. Indeed, both of the case studies cited in chapter 1 showed that this was in fact true of eyewitness testimony. Witnesses gave estimates of one crucial time interval in the foiled gun-shop robbery in Burnaby, Vancouver, that ranged from 5 seconds to 2 minutes, and John Dean's testimony contained many "time-slice" errors. Ample evidence suggests that eyewitness memory is much less reliable with respect to time than in describing what happens. Other characteristics of eyewitness testimony grow out of the discussions of chapter 3, where it was discovered that the subset of autobiographical memories that can be categorized as personal event memories have distinctive characteristics. They are intense memories of a very short period, full of sensory information, and often including irrelevant details. They are often without further narrative context. In fact, these are characteristics that they share with most types of human autobiographic memory: episodic memory is granular in the sense that it consists of memories of specific moments and incidents, often with uncertain anchoring to a specific point in time and space.

As eyewitness memories are embodied in traditions and texts, they retain the characteristics just described. Thus, the following criteria might be used to identify written material that is potentially based on some form of eyewitness recollection:

1. It consists of narratives of events, places, and people.

2. These narratives are particularly vague with respect to time and often with respect to place.

3. The narratives usually lack further narrative context.

4. The narratives usually describe events that took place over a short time period.

5. The narratives can be full of sensory information and often contain irrelevant details.

Naturally, not all texts that have these traits are necessarily derived from eyewitness accounts. On the other hand, texts that are based on eyewitness accounts will almost always show this particular set of attributes. Thus the qualities advanced above might be described as necessary but not sufficient criteria. Their absence will strongly count against the presence of eyewitness sources. Their presence may suggest the possibility of eyewitness sources, and thus identifying their presence is the first step in identifying the possibility that eyewitness traditions were incorporated into the documents. Subsequent arguments will need to be considered before the possibility of eyewitness sources in a written text becomes a probability.

The Pericope Form and Eyewitness Traditions in the Gospels

Significantly, it is precisely the kinds of phenomena typical of eyewitness memory that characterize many of the traditions found within the Synoptic Gospels. The traditions are granular, in that outside of the passion narrative they consist largely of a series of pericopes. Each pericope describing an event in the life of Jesus is usually very brief, often contains short dialogues or sensory imagery, and appears with little regard to context.

The account in Luke 6:1-5 of the incident in the grainfield provides a brief example of such a pericope. This incident is introduced with a generic reference to time, "And it came to pass one Sabbath" (Ἐγένετο δὲ ἐν σαββάτῳ), not untypical of the way many incidents are introduced in the Gospel accounts (see the use of "and it came to pass," Καὶ ἐγένετο, in Luke 7:11; 8:1; 9:18, etc. and ἐγένετο δέ in Luke 2:1; 11:14, etc.).[1] If the location in time is vague, so also is the location in space: Jesus and his disciples were crossing an otherwise unidentified grainfield. The rest of the description, though, is very vivid. The actions of the disciples are described (they plucked ears of grain, rubbed them between their hands, and ate the kernels), and, unusually, so is their motivation (they were hungry). This is followed by an extended dialogue between Jesus and the Pharisees, purportedly quoted verbatim. The next incident described in Luke 6:6-11 also relates to a Sabbath controversy, this time about whether it is lawful to heal on the Sabbath. But again, while the incident is vividly described, it is introduced with only a vague reference to time and place: "It came to pass on a different Sabbath he went into the synagogue in order to teach" (6:6).

The Sabbath controversies in Luke 6:1-11 might serve as exemplars of many like accounts of Jesus' deeds and words. They are fragmentary

---

1. Matt 12:1 introduces the incident with the phrase, "At that time" (Ἐν ἐκείνῳ τῷ καιρῷ), linking the two Sabbath controversies in Matt 12:1-14 with Jesus' statement about rest in Matt 11:25-30 (McIver 1995, 231-43, esp. 234-35 and the literature cited there).

and are introduced without much context and only a vague reference to time. On the other hand, they contain vivid details, including some of the actions of the participants and what they said. Their form is consistent with what might be found in eyewitnesses' personal event memories. In other words, the Sabbath controversy stories have the characteristics that might be expected if they were recalled from the memory of an eyewitness to the events.

If human memory is vague with regard to a temporal framework, so also are most of the incidents recorded in the Synoptic Gospels. Time references are usually vague. Accounts are linked together with such phrases as "that same day" (Matt 13:1; 22:23; Luke 24:13), "the next day" (Mark 11:12; Luke 9:37), "after six days" (Matt 17:1 // Mark 9:2). Less definite time references are frequently found, such as "at that time" (Matt 11:25; 12:1; 14:1; 18:1; Luke 1:39; 10:21; 13:31; 14:17), "in those days" (Matt 3:1; Luke 2:1; 6:12), and "then" (Matt 3:13; 4:1; 9:37; 11:20). But while there is a general connectedness between the events, outside of the passion narrative one is never presented with a coherent narrative of Jesus' doings linked by a reliable time-line, only discrete events in his life and ministry. In other words, as might be expected of accounts based on human memory, the Gospels are granular, made up of loosely linked but vivid incidents. These are the very characteristics that might be expected of eyewitness accounts. But does their presence in the Gospel traditions establish that the traditions are either eyewitness memories or built on eyewitness memories? Not everyone thinks so. For example, at the beginning of a three-part series of articles on "Eye-Witness Testimony and the Gospel Tradition," D. E. Nineham outlines the qualities of the Synoptic traditions that led him to share the widespread opinion that actual eyewitnesses had little to do with the traditions that were incorporated into the Synoptic Gospels. He says:

> The formal, stereotyped, character of the separate sections, suggestive of long community use, the absence of particular, individual details such as would be irrelevant to community edification, the conventional character of the connecting summaries, all these point to a development which was controlled by the impersonal needs and forces of the community and not immediately by the personal recollections and interests of the individual eye-witness.[2]

---

2. Nineham 1958, 13. Parts 2 and 3 of his article are found in Nineham 1958, 243–52, and 1960, 253–64.

Later he argues, "all, or practically all, the material in Mark seems to be in the *pericope* form and so presumably has passed through the formalizing process of community tradition, just like the similar material in Matthew, Luke and Q." For Nineham, the pericope form is an indication of lack of eyewitness input.[3]

Nineham has taken the very features that point to the possibility that eyewitness sources may lie behind the pericope form and argues from it that the form is most appropriate to community use and for remembering in an oral context. Clearly Nineham is mistaken in using the traits of pericopes to argue that they could not derive from eyewitness accounts. But on the other hand, it is true that, in their present form in the Gospels, most pericopes are very concisely expressed, thus easily remembered. Most of them are also directly suited to the needs of the communities of faith. These characteristics are what one might expect of material that has been previously incorporated into community traditions. Yet at the same time, the same pericopes appear to have characteristics typical of human episodic memory. What should be made of this dual aspect of the pericope form? Perhaps a general consideration of the conditions under which the Gospel traditions would have been preserved may assist in providing a preliminary answer to this question.

From Eyewitness Memory to Written Gospels

The number of eyewitnesses present at a particular incident in Jesus' ministry would have fluctuated, and the number of separate incidents observed by any one individual would vary considerably. For example, the inner circle of disciples would have witnessed much more of his life than those who only lived at Jerusalem and followed Jesus to the site of crucifixion. Even so, it is not unlikely that in excess of sixty thousand individuals were able to witness one or other significant moment in the life of Jesus

---

3. It is difficult to know, however, what would constitute adequate evidence of eyewitness input for Nineham. Presumably, if the absence of "particular and individual details" is an indication of lack of eyewitness input, their presence may be taken as such evidence. However, when he discusses the "vivid circumstantial details in St. Mark's narrative," instead of discovering these to be the "particular and individual details" of eyewitness reports, they become instead an indication of "signs of the comparative lateness of the materials in which they occur ... attempts to lend greater verisimilitude to the very bare narrative of the traditional *pericope*" (1958, 20, 22).

(see appendix A). Jesus' sayings and doings would be a constant topic of interested conversation among a considerable subset of all those who were eyewitnesses. In particular, it is nearly impossible to deny that significant collective memories of Jesus and his doings would grow among those who considered themselves to be his followers.

When individual eyewitness accounts were incorporated into the collective memories of the groups of early followers of Jesus is unknown and probably unknowable. One would expect that the process would have been well underway even during his lifetime and would have received significant acceleration in the immediate post-Easter period. During that time, stories about Jesus and the events of the crucifixion and resurrection appearances would have been discussed obsessively among his followers as they each tried to make sense of what had recently transpired. Nor should this kind of process be thought of as being confined to Jerusalem. Christianity had several centers from the earliest time period. For example, it is hard to ignore the possibility that there were several significant groups of early followers of Jesus in Galilee. Another group of early followers of Jesus appear to have been based at Syrian Antioch, a strong center of missionary outreach from very early times (e.g., Acts 13:1-3; Gal 2:11-12), and other groups formed as Christianity quickly spread to other major urban centers. The strong social cohesion known to exist in first-century Mediterranean groups, and visible in the book of Acts, undoubtedly led to a strong collective memory of the teachings and deeds of the one central to the existence of the groups: Jesus. That eyewitness accounts both contributed to this process and ensured that the traditions did not stray too far from the reality of the memories of Jesus can be taken for granted. So, it is hard to gainsay the observation that there was considerable eyewitness input in the early formation of traditions about Jesus. Indeed, it is possible to name some of those who are likely to have contributed to the tradition.

As Samuel Byrskog has suggested, it is true that not every eyewitness who saw or heard Jesus would have contributed to the formation of the early Christian's collective memories about Jesus and the subsequent outgrowth of the traditions that were used in the Synoptic Gospels.[4] Nor would every follower of Jesus be a contributor. On the other hand, it is

---

4. Byrskog 2002, 65-94, has a very helpful discussion of who exactly might have been the principal eyewitness contributors to the traditions of Jesus and his teachings.

hard to deny some significant role to those whom Jesus himself had especially chosen and trained to be eyewitnesses and teachers: the eleven surviving disciples of Jesus.[5] They had accompanied Jesus for a significant time during his public ministry, and while not present at the crucifixion, they were there for all the other significant events reported in the Gospels. This is particularly true of Peter, who had prominence both among the disciples during the ministry of Jesus and in the early church. Nor should one neglect the role of the women who were associated with Jesus in his public ministry (Luke 8:1–3; Matt 27:55), who are mentioned specifically as eyewitnesses of the crucifixion (Mark 15:40–41; Luke 23:55), and who primarily were the first bearers of the news and witnesses of the resurrected Jesus (Luke 24:1–11; Matt 28:1–10). Nor are these women anonymous: Mary Magdelene, Mary the mother of James the younger and of Joses, and Salome are among those named (Mark 15:40). These women, therefore, were the eyewitnesses from whose reports the important narratives of the crucifixion and resurrection were built.

Eyewitnesses, then, must have been significant contributors to the communal memories of Jesus in the early post-Easter period, but what of the time when the Gospels were written down? What is the likelihood of eyewitness input at the latter time period? Evidence presented in appendix A shows that, even though life expectancy was much shorter in the ancient world than it is in the Western world today, there would still have been some surviving eyewitnesses at the time the Synoptic Gospels were likely to have been written, although not a great number. Furthermore, if, as appears likely, some or all of the Gospels originated outside of Jerusalem or Galilee, then to be consulted, eyewitnesses would need to have traveled at some time to the centers in which the Gospel originated. Opportunities for travel were available in the Roman Empire, but travel was usually difficult, dangerous, and expensive, so a high proportion of the local

---

5. Byrskog, 2002, 70, downplays the possible contribution made by the eleven disciples. He says, "Just as the old form-critics have been criticized for assuming that the transmission of the Jesus tradition was merely a collective enterprise integrated within the various activities of the entire communities of believers, so one may also question the possibility of a collective oral history within the group of disciples. The disciples never formed such a coherent group of persons, even less were they trained in the techniques of memory and transmission." Given the role the eleven surviving disciples played as teachers and leaders in the early Christian communities, and the group dynamics of the small band of followers, Byrskog's assessment appears unlikely.

populations were static. Furthermore, as Nineham points out, many of those visible moving among the Gentile churches in the Pauline letters and Acts—Paul, Barnabus, Timothy, Titus, Tychicus, Priscilla, Aquila, and Apollos—were not eyewitnesses, Peter being the notable exception. Not only this, but the actual memories of the eyewitnesses would themselves have been shaped by constant repetition (their own and others) of the stories about Jesus. Thus it is likely that eyewitnesses contributed less to the final formation of the Gospels than they had to the formation of the earliest collective memories of the post-Easter believers. Yet their contribution is unlikely to have been zero, or they would not have received the prominence they were given in Luke 1:2. True, Luke mentions that he has drawn material from oral traditions derived from the "ministers of the word." Further, from the acknowledgement of "many who have undertaken to compile a narrative" (1:1), it also appears likely that Luke had some written documents available to him. Even so, he still insists that eyewitnesses contributed significantly to his account.

A process such has been described above would account for the dual characteristics of the pericope forms found in the Synoptic Gospels. That much of the material originated in eyewitness memory accounts for the characteristics of eyewitness memories that may be found in the Gospel pericopes, characteristics such as the fact that what is related in the Synoptic traditions consist of details of incidents without much in the way of information as regards to time or place. That the pericopes that make up the Synoptic Gospels appear to have been shaped in ways suitable for remembering and to have been selected so as to meet the needs of the community out of which the Gospel account grew grows out of the reality that these memories survived in the collective memories of the groups of early followers of Jesus for a considerable length of time before they were drawn upon by the Evangelists as they fashioned their Gospels.

But it should be remembered that, while observing these characteristics in the Synoptic Gospels establishes the possibility that they are based originally on eyewitness accounts, the potential impact of the frailties of human memory have yet to be considered, particularly the frailty of suggestibility. This will be a matter taken up in the next chapter. Sufficient for the argument at this point is to establish that what is observable in the Synoptic Gospels is consistent with what would be expected of material that derives from eyewitness accounts.

The Apophthegmata (or Chreiai) as a Case Study of Potential Eyewitness Material

The Synoptic Gospels include several different types of materials about Jesus or attributed to him. They include aphorisms, parables, short stories about Jesus attached to sayings (the apophthegmata), miracle stories, the passion narrative, and so forth. A case will be made in chapter 9 that the aphorisms and parables attributed to Jesus are most likely to be traced to a stream of tradition that began with Jesus teaching his disciples and was transmitted via means of teaching. But because they are stories *about* Jesus, it is most likely that the apophthegmata, miracle stories, and passion narrative stem from the memory of those around Jesus, rather than from his teaching ministry and the stream of tradition that flowed from it. Of significance here is that the apophthegmata are natural candidates for the types of materials that are likely to have developed in the collective memory of the earliest followers of Jesus. This point is argued by Michael Winger in the following terms:

> If we encountered Jesus, what would we remember? It would be natural to remember some things he said, but it would be extraordinary to remember nothing else. Which would be more striking to a witness, the words by which Jesus rebuked a rich man, or the rich man's shrinking back in confusion? A well-balanced phrase or the event in which the phrase was situated? These questions do not have categorical answers, but one reason to suspect that events were more prominent than sayings for the original witnesses is that it is very difficult to remember exactly what someone has said. … The first memories of Jesus were probably not transcripts of his sayings. We can assume that these memories included some of his words, but not words only. Where he spoke, how, to whom, the impact of his words, especially on the witnesses themselves—all of this had to be remembered. This forms the starting point for tradition, and if Jesus' deeds include more than speeches, as all our sources testify, deeds and words must have been remembered together. (Winger 2000, 683, 685)

Because of their frequency of occurrence in the Gospels and the fact that they also fit a genre known elsewhere in the ancient world, apophthegmata have the potential to form a useful set of case studies against which to gauge the qualities of the Gospel traditions that could be traced back to eyewitness memories.

The apophthegm is a form found outside of the Gospels. The term chreia (χρεία) or apophthegm (ἀπόφθεγμα) was used by Greek authors of the Roman period to describe a brief anecdote from famous personages and thinkers that usually climaxed in a memorable utterance. A first-century handbook of prose composition and rhetoric attributed to Aelius Theon defines a chreia in the following manner: "A chreia (*khreia*) is a brief saying or action making a point, attributed to some specified person or something corresponding to a person, and maxim (*gnômê*) and reminiscence (*apomnêmoneuma*) are connected to it. Every brief maxim attributed to a person creates a chreia" (the *Exercises* of Aelius Theon).[6] The following chreia concerning Aristotle may serve as an example. "Being once reproached for giving alms to a bad man, he rejoined, 'It was the man and not his character that I pitied'" (Tannehill 1984, 1792–1829). In this example, the introductory narrative is brief indeed, but enough is said to provide a meaningful context for the saying from Aristotle. Aelius Theon suggests that there are three general categories of the chreia: some are verbal, some describe an action, and others are mixed. He provides several examples of each kind. He illustrates a verbal chreia with the following anecdote: "Diogenes the philosopher, when asked by someone how to become famous, replied that it was by thinking least about fame." Verbal chreias are further subdivided. For example, one based on an enthymeme (a statement for which one premise is omitted) is illustrated by the following interchange: "When his acquaintance Apolodorus said to him, 'The Athenians have unjustly condemned you to death,' Socrates broke into a laugh and said, 'were you wanting them to do so justly?'" Aelius Theon explains the missing premise from the second chreia as "It is better to be condemned unjustly than justly" (Kennedy 2003, 16, 18).

The term apophthegm is not used by Aelius Theon, but it is used to describe such things as collections of the aphorisms and anecdotes of the more prominent fourth-century Egyptian hermits and monks called the *Apophthegmata patrum*. These stories with attached sayings vary in length.

---

6. From the translations of Aelius Theon's *Exercises* found in Kennedy 2003, 15. See the full discussion of chreia by Aelius Theon in Kennedy 2003, 23, that by Aphthonius the Sophist in Kennedy 2003, 97–99, and Nicolaus the Sophist in Kennedy 2003, 139–42. A Greek version with facing English translation of Aelius Theon's, Aphthonius's, and Nicolaus's comments on chreia may be found in Hock and O'Neil 1986, 82–107, 224–29, 252–65.

Some are quite short, as, for example, the following story about Abba John the Dwarf (a fourth/fifth-century Eygptian ascetic monk): "One of the Fathers asked Abba John the Dwarf, 'What is a monk?' He said, 'He is toil. The monk toils at all he does. That is what a monk is'" (Ward 1975, 93). Many others, though, are between fifty and one hundred words in length, and some of the longer can extend over two pages when printed. One or two such apophthegmata cannot represent so diverse a collection of stories, but the following two stories about Poemen (the Shepherd; ca. fourth or fifth century[7]) capture some of the combination of story and dialogue that is found in many of them:

> One day the priests of the district came to the monasteries where Abba Poemen was. Abba Anoub came and said to him, "Let us invite the priests in today." But he stood for a long time without giving him any reply, and, quite offended, Abba Anoub went away. Those who were sitting beside Poemen said to him, "Abba, why didn't you answer him?" Abba Poemen said to them, "It is not my business, for I am dead and a dead man does not speak." ...
>
> Abba Joseph asked Abba Poemen, "How should one fast?" Abba Poemen said to him, "For my part, I think it better than one should eat every day, but only a little, so as not to be satisfied." Abba Joseph said to him, "When you were younger, did you not fast two days at a time, abba?" The old man said: "Yes, even for three days and four and the whole week. The Fathers tried all this out as they were able and they found in preferable to eat every day, but just a small amount. They have left us this royal way, which is light." (Ward 1975, 164, 171)[8]

Many of the shorter apophthegmata in the *Apophthegmata patrum* could equally well be classified as chreiai by the definitions of Theon; thus, if they are not exactly synonymous, the terms *apophthegm* and *chreia* have a considerable overlap in meaning. That the term *apophthegm* is used to describe stories attached to sayings that are both longer and shorter in

---

7. Poemen was a name adopted by several monks, and it is hard to know exactly who among them is the object of the stories found in the *Apophthegmata patrum* (Ward 1975, 16).

8. Reading several pages from almost anywhere in this collection gives a good idea of what is encompassed by the term *apophthegm*. See also Budge 1934, which is arranged thematically, rather than by the monk from whom the sayings derived, which is the organizational principle found in the text translated by Ward 1975.

length may mean that it is the most suitable term to describe many of the stories with their attached sayings of Jesus that are found within the Synoptic Gospels, which themselves vary considerably in length. Thus, while it is tempting to use the term *chreiai* of these types of pericopes, the rest of this discussion will use the term *apophthegmata*.[9]

The Synoptic traditions contain a considerable number of apophthegmata (or chreiai[10]) that climax in a saying of Jesus, some very short and some more elaborate. They include correction stories (e.g., Matt 18:1-4, 21-22), commendation stories (e.g., Mark 3:31-35; 14:3-9), quest stories (e.g., Luke 19:1-10), objection stories (e.g., Mark 2:15-17, 23-28), and inquiry stories (e.g., Mark 7:17-23; 10:10-12; Luke 17:5-6).[11]

The examples of the inquiry story in [Matt 22:15-22 //] Mark 12:13-17 // Luke 20:20-26 (represented in tables 7.1 and 7.2) and the correction story in Matt 8:18-22 // Luke 9:57-62 (tables 7.3 and 7.4) might serve to illustrate several of the characteristics of the genre as it is found in the Gospel traditions.[12] Versions of these stories are found in more than one

---

9. The term *apophthegm* is familiar in Gospel studies in that it was the term used by Rudolf Bultmann in his classification of the teachings of Jesus found in *The History of the Synoptic Tradition* (Bultmann 1968, 27-69).

10. Papius states that the Gospel of Mark derives from Peter's interpreter, Mark. He then goes on to say that "Peter ... used to give his teachings in the form of *chreiai*, but had no intention of providing an ordered arrangement of the *logia* of the Lord." Richard Bauckham, following Nineham, argues convincingly that as used by Papius χρεῖαι should be understood in the technical sense it is used by the rhetoraticians (Bauckham 2006, 203, 214-17). If so—and Bauckham's case is convincing—then the classification of many of the Gospel traditions about Jesus as chreiai is very ancient. Incidentally, the plural of χρεία is, naturally, χρεῖαι. While one might expect an anglicized plural *chreiai* (as indeed is found in Hock and O'Neil 1986, 95), translations such as that by Kennedy (e.g., 2003, 17) use the plural form "chreias." Sometimes the anglicized plural of *apophthegm* is *apophthegms* (e.g., Bultmann 1968, 27-69). In this chapter, though, the plural *apophthegmata* will be used, as it has the virtue of more closely resembling the Greek plural (ἀποφθέγματα).

11. The classification is that of Tannehill 1984, 1792-1829. Rudolf Bultmann classifies apophthegms under the headings "Controversy Dialogues, Scholastic Dialogues, and Biographical Apophthegms" (1968, 39-61).

12. There is little unanimity in the secondary literature as to which descriptive label best describes a particular Gospel apophthegm. For example, the "inquiry story" of Matt 22:15-22 // Mark 12:13-17 // Luke 20:20-26 is classified as an inquiry story apophthegm by Tannehill, a controversy dialogue apophthegm by Bultmann, and a paradigm by Dibelius (Tannehill 1984, 1820; Bultmann 1968, 48; Dibelius 1971, 43). The short sayings in Matt 8:18-22 // Luke 9:57-62 are classified as correction story

Gospel, and if the Gospels were completely independent of each other, then one could take each of the Gospel versions as separate instances of the same underlying collective memory of the incident in the ministry of Jesus. But this is not the case. While the controversy about which Gospel was written first and how the others relate to it continues after more than a century of vigorous debate, all participants in the debate—including those that argue for a strong oral component in the process—are in agreement that there is some close relationship between the three Synoptic Gospels. In a way, this makes any differences that emerge in the comparison of two or more versions of an apophthegm the more remarkable. Even though there is a close connection between the Gospels, the apophthegms are recorded in the Gospels in a way that closely preserves the sayings of Jesus, while at the same time allowing flexibility in the language to describe the incident. These characteristics are visible in the following tables.

In tables 7.1 through 7.4, two versions of the apopthegmata are placed side by side. This is the only possible option for Matt 8:18–22 // Luke 9:57–62, as Mark does not record this incident. On the other hand, the story recounted in Mark 12:13–17 // Luke 20:20–26 is also found at Matt 22:15–22. For simplicity of comparison, only two versions are shown at one time, and because the other combinations (Matt 22:15–22 // Luke 20:20; and Matt 22:15–22 // Mark 12:13–17) do not provide much further data, for conciseness they are not reported here. So that the common elements between the parallels are easily observed, the words that are in exactly the same grammatical form are underlined. Where two or more words are found in verbatim sequence, they are underlined with a continuous line. The Greek text is the Gramcord version of the 4th edition United Bible Societies text, and the English text is that of the Revised Standard Version. Here, then, is the comparison between Mark 12:13–17 and Luke 20:20–26, which illustrates two versions of an inquiry story apophthegm:

---

apophthegms by Tannehill and biographic apophthegms by Bultmann (Tannehill 1984, 1798–99; Bultmann 1968, 56). Dibelius gives far fewer examples in his category "paradigms," which corresponds most closely to what is described here as apophthegms. He does consider the parallel as a New Testament example of a chreia, as he discusses Greek analogies (Dibelius 1971, 161).

Table 7.1. A Greek-Text Example of an Inquiry Story Apophthegm
(Mark 12:13–17 // Luke 20:20–26)

Mark 12:13–17	Luke 20:20–26
13 Καὶ <u>ἀποστέλλουσιν</u> πρὸς αὐτόν τινας τῶν Φαρισαίων καὶ τῶν Ἡρῳδιανῶν <u>ἵνα</u> <u>αὐτὸν</u> ἀγρεύσωσιν <u>λόγῳ</u>. 14 καὶ ἐλθόντες <u>λέγουσιν</u> <u>αὐτῷ· διδάσκαλε, οἴδαμεν ὅτι</u> ἀληθὴς εἶ καὶ οὐ μέλει σοι περὶ οὐδενός· οὐ γὰρ βλέπεις εἰς <u>πρόσωπον</u> ἀνθρώπων, <u>ἀλλ' ἐπ' ἀληθείας τὴν ὁδὸν τοῦ θεοῦ διδάσκεις· ἔξεστιν δοῦναι</u> κῆνσον <u>Καίσαρι ἢ οὔ</u> δῶμεν ἢ μὴ δῶμεν 15 ὁ δὲ εἰδὼς <u>αὐτῶν</u> τὴν ὑπόκρισιν <u>εἶπεν</u> <u>αὐτοῖς·</u> τί με πειράζετε φέρετέ <u>μοι</u> <u>δηνάριον</u> ἵνα ἴδω. 16 οἱ δὲ ἤνεγκαν. καὶ λέγει αὐτοῖς· <u>τίνος</u> ἡ <u>εἰκὼν</u> αὕτη <u>καὶ</u> ἡ <u>ἐπιγραφή</u> οἱ δὲ <u>εἶπαν</u> αὐτῷ· <u>Καίσαρος.</u> 17 ὁ δὲ Ἰησοῦς <u>εἶπεν</u> <u>αὐτοῖς·</u> <u>τὰ Καίσαρος ἀπόδοτε Καίσαρι καὶ τὰ τοῦ θεοῦ τῷ θεῷ.</u> καὶ ἐξεθαύμαζον ἐπ' αὐτῷ.	20 Καὶ παρατηρήσαντες <u>ἀπέστειλαν</u> ἐγκαθέτους ὑποκρινομένους ἑαυτοὺς δικαίους εἶναι, <u>ἵνα</u> ἐπιλάβωνται <u>αὐτοῦ</u> <u>λόγου,</u> ὥστε παραδοῦναι αὐτὸν τῇ ἀρχῇ καὶ τῇ ἐξουσίᾳ τοῦ ἡγεμόνος. 21 καὶ ἐπηρώτησαν <u>αὐτὸν</u> <u>λέγοντες·</u> <u>διδάσκαλε, οἴδαμεν ὅτι</u> ὀρθῶς λέγεις καὶ διδάσκεις καὶ οὐ λαμβάνεις <u>πρόσωπον,</u> <u>ἀλλ' ἐπ' ἀληθείας τὴν ὁδὸν τοῦ θεοῦ διδάσκεις·</u> 22 ἔξεστιν ἡμᾶς <u>Καίσαρι</u> φόρον <u>δοῦναι ἢ οὒ</u> 23 κατανοήσας δὲ <u>αὐτῶν</u> τὴν πανουργίαν <u>εἶπεν</u> πρὸς <u>αὐτούς·</u> 24 δείξατέ <u>μοι δηνάριον· τίνος</u> ἔχει <u>εἰκόνα καὶ ἐπιγραφήν</u> οἱ δὲ <u>εἶπαν· Καίσαρος.</u> 25 ὁ δὲ <u>εἶπεν</u> πρὸς <u>αὐτούς·</u> τοίνυν <u>ἀπόδοτε τὰ Καίσαρος Καίσαρι καὶ τὰ τοῦ θεοῦ τῷ θεῷ.</u> 26 καὶ οὐκ ἴσχυσαν ἐπιλαβέσθαι αὐτοῦ ῥήματος ἐναντίον τοῦ λαοῦ καὶ θαυμάσαντες ἐπὶ τῇ ἀποκρίσει αὐτοῦ ἐσίγησαν.

Table 7.2. An English-Text Example of an Inquiry Story Apophthegm
(Mark 12:13–17 // Luke 20:20–26)

Mark 12:13–17	Luke 20:20–26
13 And they <u>sent</u> to him some of the Pharisees and some of the Herodians, to entrap him in his talk. 14 And <u>they came and said to him, "Teacher, we know that you</u> are true, and care for no man; for you do not regard the position of men, <u>but truly teach the way of God. Is it lawful</u> to pay taxes <u>to Caesar, or not?</u> 15 Should we pay them, or should we not?" <u>But</u> knowing their hypocrisy, <u>he said to them,</u> "Why put me to the test? Bring me <u>a coin,</u> and let me look at it."	20 So they watched him, and <u>sent</u> spies, who pretended to be sincere, that they might take hold of what he said, so as to deliver him up to the authority and jurisdiction of the governor. 21 <u>They</u> asked <u>him, "Teacher, we know that you</u> speak and teach rightly, and show no partiality, <u>but truly teach the way of God. 22 Is it lawful</u> for us to give tribute <u>to Caesar, or not?"</u> 23 <u>But he</u> perceived their craftiness, and <u>said to them,</u>

16 And they brought one. And he said to them, "<u>Whose likeness and inscription</u> is this?" <u>They said</u> to him, "<u>Caesar's.</u>" 17 Jesus <u>said to them,</u> "<u>Render to Caesar the things that are Caesar's, and to God the things that are God's.</u>" <u>And they were</u> amazed at him.	24 "Show me <u>a coin. Whose likeness and inscription</u> has it?" <u>They said,</u> "<u>Caesar's.</u>" 25 He <u>said to them,</u> "Then <u>render to Caesar the things that are Caesar's, and to God the things that are God's.</u>" 26 <u>And they were</u> not able in the presence of the people to catch him by what he said; but marveling at his answer they were silent.

That there is a close connection between both versions of this story is evident from the comparisons shown in tables 7.1 and 7.2. At the level of gist, the two versions are almost identical. Furthermore, they share much common vocabulary and expression. Even so, considered from the perspective of exact details and verbatim parallels, there are a number of interesting differences between the two versions. Both Mark and Luke report that the question put to Jesus was at the behest of the chief priests and scribes (the antecedent of "they" in Mark 12:13 and Luke 20:20; cf. Mark 11:27 and Luke 20:19), but "they" are reported to have sent "some of the Pharisees and some of the Herodians" (Mark 12:13) or "spies" (Luke 20:20). Matthew 22:15 reports that it was the Pharisees who sent some of their disciples with the Herodians to put the question to Jesus. Other details in the surrounding story also show small differences. On the other hand, the parts of the parallel involving dialogue have a much closer relationship to each other than the rest of the accounts. This is particularly true of the climactic saying of Jesus, "Render to Caesar the things that are Caesar's, and to God the things that are God's." Aside from the position of the word ἀπόδοτε, this saying is reported verbatim in the two accounts. In sum, the narrative elements of the two versions of this apophthegm have a gist relationship, while the sayings of Jesus, particularly the climactic one, have a near verbatim relationship between the two Gospels. It is not unlikely that these were the qualities of the apophthegm as it circulated in collective memory prior it is being recorded in the Gospels. After all, if the story element of an apophthegm was reproduced with a gist relationship between two closely related texts, one would hardly expect any closer relationship to exist in various versions of the apophthegm circulating in collective memory prior to their being written down. In particular, one would not expect that the story element of the apophthegm would have circulated in collective memory verbatim. This may not have been true of the saying, "Render to Caesar the things that are Caesar's but to God the things that are God's." This short saying is in the form of an aphorism with a strong element of parallelism. Both of these qualities lend themselves to verbatim reproduction. Thus, while it is difficult to say so with any certainty, it is not unlikely that the sayings element of this particular apophthegm circulated in collective memory with near verbatim accuracy.

The apophthegm represented in Matt 8:18–22 and Luke 9:57–62 contains one of the longest verbatim parallels between the Gospel accounts, and shares more common vocabulary than is typical in parallels between the Synoptic Gospels.[13] Even so, one can see that it is the words of the dialogue that are best preserved. Thus, the characteristics observed in the apophthegm observed in Mark 12:13–17 // Luke 20:20–26 are also visible in Matt 8:18–22 // Luke 9:57–62:

---

13. The Greek text of the first of the correction stories in the parallel between Matt 8:18–22 and Luke 9:57–62 has twenty-four words in common verbatim sequence. This is one of the twenty parallels between the Synoptic Gospels that have the longest verbatim sequences. The table found in McIver and Carroll 2002, 681, reveals that the longest common verbatim sequence between Gospel accounts is thirty-one words found in Matt 10:16–25 // Mark 13:3–13. After this there are parallels that have twenty-nine, twenty-eight, twenty-eight, twenty-six, and twenty-six words in verbatim sequence and four parallels that have twenty-four words in verbatim sequence. These are unusual parallels between the Synoptics for the number of words that they share in verbatim sequence, as the median number of words in verbatim sequence of all the pair-wise parallels between the Synoptic Gospels is seven words. Perhaps it is of significance that almost all of the examples of apophthegms cited in the text have an above-average number of words in verbatim sequence and percentage of common vocabulary in their parallels between the Gospels. In the Greek text Mark 12:13–17 and Luke 20:20–26 (found in table 7.1), the longest common verbatim sequence is nine words, while 47 percent of the vocabulary of the Markan version is shared with the Lukan version (48 percent of Luke). This inquiry story is found in the triple tradition (Matt 22:15–22 // Mark 12:13–17 // Luke 20:20–26), so there are two further sets of statistics to report for the longest common verbatim sequence (twelve in the case of Matt 22:15–22 // Mark 12:13–17, nine in the case of Matt 22:15–22 // Luke 20:20–26), and for the percentages of common vocabulary (58 percent and 66 percent respectively, in the case of Matt 22:15–22 // Mark 12:13–17, and 33 percent and 38 percent respectively in the case of Matt 22:15–22 // Luke 20:20–26). The statistics for these parallels, then, are mostly in the upper quartile of all parallels between the Synoptic Gospels—the relevant statistics of the upper quartile are ten words in verbatim sequence and 53 percent common vocabulary.

Table 7.3. A Greek-Text Example of a Correction Story Apophthegm
(Matt 8:18–22 // Luke 9:57–62)

Matt 8:18–22	Luke 9:57–62
18 Ἰδὼν δὲ ὁ Ἰησοῦς ὄχλον περὶ αὐτὸν ἐκέλευσεν ἀπελθεῖν εἰς τὸ πέραν. 19 καὶ προσελθὼν εἷς γραμματεὺς εἶπεν αὐτῷ· Διδάσκαλε, ἀκολουθήσω σοι ὅπου ἐὰν ἀπέρχῃ. 20 καὶ λέγει αὐτῷ ὁ Ἰησοῦς· Αἱ ἀλώπεκες φωλεοὺς ἔχουσιν καὶ τὰ πετεινὰ τοῦ οὐρανοῦ κατασκηνώσεις, ὁ δὲ υἱὸς τοῦ ἀνθρώπου οὐκ ἔχει ποῦ τὴν κεφαλὴν κλίνῃ. 21 ἕτερος δὲ τῶν μαθητῶν (αὐτοῦ) εἶπεν αὐτῷ· Κύριε, ἐπίτρεψόν μοι πρῶτον ἀπελθεῖν καὶ θάψαι τὸν πατέρα μου. 22 ὁ δὲ Ἰησοῦς λέγει αὐτῷ· Ἀκολούθει μοι καὶ ἄφες τοὺς νεκροὺς θάψαι τοὺς ἑαυτῶν νεκρούς.	57 Καὶ πορευομένων αὐτῶν ἐν τῇ ὁδῷ εἶπέν τις πρὸς αὐτόν· ἀκολουθήσω σοι ὅπου ἐὰν ἀπέρχῃ. 58 καὶ εἶπεν αὐτῷ ὁ Ἰησοῦς· Αἱ ἀλώπεκες φωλεοὺς ἔχουσιν καὶ τὰ πετεινὰ τοῦ οὐρανοῦ κατασκηνώσεις, ὁ δὲ υἱὸς τοῦ ἀνθρώπου οὐκ ἔχει ποῦ τὴν κεφαλὴν κλίνῃ. 59 Εἶπεν δὲ πρὸς ἕτερον· Ἀκολούθει μοι. ὁ δὲ εἶπεν· (Κύριε,) ἐπίτρεψόν μοι ἀπελθόντι πρῶτον θάψαι τὸν πατέρα μου. 60 εἶπεν δὲ αὐτῷ· Ἄφες τοὺς νεκροὺς θάψαι τοὺς ἑαυτῶν νεκρούς, σὺ δὲ ἀπελθὼν διάγγελλε τὴν βασιλείαν τοῦ θεοῦ. 61 Εἶπεν δὲ καὶ ἕτερος· Ἀκολουθήσω σοι, κύριε· πρῶτον δὲ ἐπίτρεψόν μοι ἀποτάξασθαι τοῖς εἰς τὸν οἶκόν μου. 62 εἶπεν δὲ (πρός αὐτόν) ὁ Ἰησοῦς· Οὐδεὶς ἐπιβαλὼν τὴν χεῖρα ἐπ' ἄροτρον καὶ βλέπων εἰς τὰ ὀπίσω εὔθετός ἐστιν τῇ βασιλείᾳ τοῦ θεοῦ.

Table 7.4. An English-Text Example of a Correction Story Apophthegm
(Matt 8:18–22 // Luke 9:57–62)

Matt 8:18–22	Luke 9:57–62
18 Now when Jesus saw great crowds around him, he gave orders to go over to the other side 19 And a scribe came up and said to him, "Teacher, I will follow you wherever you go." 20 And Jesus said to him, "Foxes have holes, and birds of the air have nests; but the Son of man has nowhere to lay his head." 21 Another of the disciples said to him, "Lord, let me first go and bury my father."	57 As they were going along the road, a man said to him, "I will follow you wherever you go." 58 And Jesus said to him, "Foxes have holes, and birds of the air have nests; but the Son of man has nowhere to lay his head." 59 To another he said, "Follow me." But he said, "Lord, let me first go and bury my father." 60 But he said to him, "Leave the dead to bury their own dead; but as for you, go and proclaim the kingdom of God."

22 <u>But</u> Jesus <u>said to him</u>, "Follow me, and <u>leave the dead to bury their own dead.</u>"	61 Another said, "I will follow you, Lord; but let me first say farewell to those at my home." 62 Jesus said to him, "No one who puts his hand to the plow and looks back is fit for the kingdom of God."

As may be observed in tables 7.3 and 7.4, most of the parallels between Matt 8:18–22 and Luke 9:57–60 consist of dialogue, and this dialogue is preserved with near verbatim accuracy. But despite the close connection that exists between the two Gospels, the actual frame for the dialogue provided in the two accounts varies considerably. Matthew reports, "Now when Jesus saw great crowds around him, he gave orders to go over to the other side," while Luke provides the following general setting: "As they were going along the road, a man said to him." The Lukan version gives one further correction story not found elsewhere (Luke 9:61–62).

Other apophthegmata also find varied expression in the Gospel parallels. Sometimes these changes give a different impression of the meaning of the crucial saying. For example, one might consider Matt 9:14–17 // Mark 2:18–22 // Luke 5:33–39 and the saying of Jesus that grew out of the question asking him why the disciples of John the Baptists fasted but his disciples did not. In all three accounts, Jesus answers the question with two illustrations, the first explaining that the weddings guests do not fast while the bridegroom is with them, the second speaking about not patching old garments with new cloth or placing new wine in old wineskins. In Matthew and Mark, the comment on the cloth reads, "No one sews a piece of unshrunk cloth on an old cloak; otherwise, the patch pulls away from it, the new from the old, and a worse tear is made" (Mark 2:21, NRSV; cf. Matt 9:16). But in Luke 5:36 this saying is expressed in the following manner: "No one tears a piece from a new garment and sews it on an old garment; otherwise the new will be torn, and the piece from the new will not match the old." Clearly, this is a version of the saying found in Mark and Matthew. But it is expressed in such different terms as to change the actual image conveyed, if not the underlying meaning. Furthermore, sometimes the actual meaning can change between versions of the same saying. In the apophthegm in Mark 9:38–41, Jesus is reported to say, "Who is not against us is for us," while in the parallel version in Luke 9:49–50 Jesus is reported saying, "whoever is not against you is for you." While these two sayings are not entirely contradictory, there is a substantial difference between them.

Thus the parallels observable in tables 7.1 through 7.4 represent the Gospel apophthegmata in general. While there is considerable variation in the wording of the narrative section of the apophthegmata where two or more versions exist, the gist of such narrative parallels is usually preserved well, although sometimes the same saying can be framed by a different introduction. On the other hand, the short sayings of Jesus attached to apophthegmata are among those that show the longest sequences of verbatim parallels of all of the Gospel materials.

The concise nature of the apophthegm as well as the close linkage between a story and a saying of Jesus make it an ideal unit to retain in memory and consequently give a greater expectation that apophthegms in the Jesus traditions would have been remembered reliably. Indeed, they are the kind of stories that circulate widely in an oral culture. Furthermore, they are ideal for incorporating into the post-Easter oral traditions about Jesus and his teaching. But showing that they are consistent with what might be expected to be preserved in the collective memory of the early followers of Jesus does not, in itself, prove that they report actual memories of real events that took place in Jesus ministry. One has to consider the possibility that the frailties of human memory observed in chapters 2–4 may have shaped them in such a way as to produce an unreliable account of what happened. The possibility still exists that some of the incidents recorded in the apophthegmata are the products of the imagination of early Christians and do not, in fact, go back to Jesus at all. These are issues that will be taken up in the next chapter.

8
MEMORY FRAILTIES AND THE GOSPEL TRADITIONS

The qualities of human memory shape how eyewitnesses remember events. Consequently, texts that derive content from eyewitness memories are likely to mirror the characteristics of the original eyewitness memory. The previous chapter has put forward evidence that many of the traditions found within the Synoptic Gospels do exhibit some of the characteristics one might expect of texts that derive from human memories and that the apophthegms in particular are the kind of materials that one would expect to have been derived from eyewitness memories. This chapter considers the impact that the known frailties of human memory might have had on any eyewitness memories incorporated into the Gospel accounts, particularly the frailties of transience, suggestibility, and bias. It also considers the question as to whether the stories recorded in the Gospels may have had their source in the imagination of the early church rather than in the ministry of Jesus.

TRANSIENCE AND THE GOSPEL TRADITIONS

Human memory is largely transient. In other words, most of what is experienced is rather rapidly forgotten. This would have been true also for the eyewitnesses of the various events in Jesus' earthly ministry. The question might fairly be asked: What impact might the transience of human memory have had on the contribution of individual eyewitness testimony to the formation of the Gospel traditions? Indeed, could any authentic eyewitness memory survive the long period envisaged between the events described in the Gospel traditions and their writing down in the Gospels?

Most of the experiments reported in the chapters 1–3 throw light on this question, at least from the perspective of the memories of individuals. In chapter 2, for example, it was noted that individual eyewitness memories of episodes from their past—their episodic memory—follow the characteristic Ebbinghausian forgetting curve for the first three to six years. In other words, there is a rapid loss of some memory of events, but this rate of loss slows over time. Furthermore, there is experimental evidence that suggests up to 50 percent of distinctive episodes may be remembered five years later, something also true for eyewitnesses' memories of events significant enough to form personal event memories. On the other hand, it appears highly likely that specific eyewitness memories surviving the first three to five years become stable from that time forward for the next twenty-plus years, after which time they slowly decline. Thus, as far as the frailty of transience is concerned, the critical period in the memories of the individual eyewitness of Jesus is not the thirty to sixty years that elapsed before the writing of the Gospels. The critical period is, in fact, the first three to six years after the death and resurrection of Jesus. This is the time during which the memory frailty of transience would have had its greatest impact and when crucial details may have been forgotten.

These observations have direct applicability to the episodic memories of the eyewitnesses of Jesus' earthly ministry. Considered as individuals, then, this means that individual eyewitnesses of Jesus would have quickly forgotten much of what they observed. Yet after a short time, the rate of forgetting would slow, so that what had been retained after the initial period of rapid loss would only slowly be forgotten thereafter. Furthermore, it is inconceivable that stories about Jesus were not discussed regularly by his early followers, and thus individual eyewitnesses would receive reinforcement of their memories of a particular incident in the life of Jesus. Out of this process would also emerge a relatively coherent collective memory of the event in the groups of early followers of Jesus.

Thus it is likely that recollections of up to 50 percent of the events of Jesus life that were witnessed by those still alive when the Gospels were written could have survived in the memory of those eyewitnesses over the thirty to sixty years that had intervened since the crucifixion-resurrection. Whatever else is made of this datum, it is clear that the events reported in the Gospels form but a fraction of the total number of memories of his doings that would have survived in the memories of eyewitnesses (see John 21:25).

Personal Event Memories, the Gospel Traditions, and Transience

But what of the extensive research into flashbulb and other personal event memories reported in chapter 3 and also shown to exhibit the frailty of transience? Can one find evidence of flashbulb and other personal events in the Synoptic Gospels? A case could, and will, be made that traces of personal event memories can be detected in the Gospels, but it is hard to identify any event that would fit the category of flashbulb memory, at least according to the strict definition of Brown and Kulik. After all, the crucial characteristic of flashbulb memories are that they are memories of *reports* of events of great personal significance, not a direct memory of the events themselves, while the Gospel materials are written about the events themselves, not a report of the event. Thus they represent the viewpoint of one present and observing the event—an eyewitness.[1] On the

---

1. A case could conceivably be made that Acts 12:12–17 does report somebody's flashbulb memory of an event. Five of the six "abstract canonical categories" (see chapter 3 for further details) are present in Acts 12:12–17. The "ongoing event" was the prayer of the many believers who had gathered at the house of Mary the mother of John (the "place"), and the "informant" was none other than Peter himself. The "affect in others" was that they first responded by suggesting to the maid Rhoda, who brought them the news, that she was out of her mind. When they finally met Peter, they were amazed; the "aftermath" was Peter's escape and the execution of the sixteen hapless guards; while the "idiosyncratic information" is that when the servant girl Rhoda went to the gate and discovered Peter, instead of opening the gate, she left him there and ran to tell the others. Yet even this account does not quite match the strict definition of flashbulb memories put forward by Brown and Kulik, which restricted flashbulb memories to memories of events where the individuals were not eyewitnesses The account appears to be based on the memories of one of those gathered in the prayer room. Peter's experience in prison could have come either from Peter's memories or from memories of what he said at the meeting. However, as the account in Acts ceases at the moment Peter leaves the house of Mary the mother of John, it is more likely that the present account comes from one of those actually at the prayer meeting. Furthermore, this individual does not appear to be the narrator. After all, the one item missing of the six "canonical abstract categories" is the "personal affect" of the event. So a better case could be made that Acts 12:12–17 may have been based on the memories of an eyewitness than on somebody's flashbulb memory of hearing of the event. It therefore does not strictly qualify as a flashbulb memory. Moreover, the version in Acts is not actually narrated by the possessor of the eyewitness memory. Thus, given that the best possibility has turned out not to be a flashbulb memory, it could be argued that

other hand, a number of Gospel accounts could fit the category of personal event memory.

David Pillemer argues that memories of personal trauma, flashbulb memories, memories of critical incidents, and moments of insight are but varieties of a class of memories he describes as personal event memories (Pillemer 1998, 30–49).[2] As has already been noted, Pillemer develops the following criteria by which they may be recognized. An event is a personal event memory if it: (1) is the memory of a specific event, (2) contains a detailed account of the personal circumstances, (3) is accompanied by sensory images and emotional content, (4) recounts action that is of short duration, and (5) is represented as truthful (Pillemer 1998, 50–51).

Embedded in Pillemer's conception of personal event memories are categories that naturally fit many of the pericopes found in the Synoptic Gospels. For example, there are a number of accounts that might fit Pillemer's category of "memory directive." It could be argued that the calling of Peter, Andrew, James, and John as found in Matt 4:18–22 // Mark 1:14–20 is based on somebody's "memory directive." After all, it has most of the expected characteristics of one. It was a specific event; it contains a detailed account of the rememberer's own personal circumstances (Peter and Andrew were casting their nets by hand; James and John were in their father's boats preparing their nets); the words of Jesus were of momentous and life-changing import for the participants and are quoted ("Follow me, and I will make you fishers of men"); and the immediate consequences are expressed (Andrew and John left their father and the boats).

Such things as the life-changing challenge of Jesus to Matthew to leave his tax table (Matt 9:9), the memorable teachings of Jesus, and the various healing miracles all fit the general categories developed by Pillemer. But what can be said about their reliability? One might argue that what has been discovered to be true of one type of personal event memory—flashbulb memories—is highly likely to be true of other types of personal event memories. After all, the distinctive features of flashbulb memories—their short time frame, their vivid details, and their emotional content—are true of all the various kinds of memories considered by Pillemer to be examples of personal event memories. Thus, one might conclude that the measures

---

there are no flashbulb memories at all in the New Testament, at least according to the strict definition originally put forward by Brown and Kulik

2. One might compare the grouping of eyewitness memory, flashbulb memories, and memory for traumatic events by Schooler and Eich 2000, 379–92.

of reliability found for flashbulb memories, and reported in chapter 3, could fairly be expected to be true of other personal event memories. It was discovered that such memories can persist for a long time—over fifty years in one experiment—and that they can contain vivid details not available to those who have not experienced the event. This was true also of the studies into eyewitness memory reported in chapter 1. While not 100 percent accurate, they usually correctly report the gist of the event witnessed and even at the level of details have a very high percentage of accurate recall (up to 80 percent when measured by very stringent criteria).

It might be concluded, then, that much of the episodic memories of the eyewitnesses of Jesus would have been of such a nature as to form personal event memories. What has been discovered about personal event memories allows at least three more observations about the contribution that the memories of eyewitnesses may have made to the formation of the Gospel traditions. First, while their memories are often likely to be accurate in the details recounted, they would have been most reliable at the level of gist. Second, eyewitness memories tend to be concentrated around moments of time. Personal event memories are characterized by the recollection of emotional reactions and vivid details concentrated in a very short period of time. Eyewitness memory, then, is granular. It remembers short moments in great detail. What connects these moments often has to be reconstructed by the individual eyewitness from clues found in the details recollected. Of significance is the observation that was made in the previous chapter that the various pericopes that make up the Synoptic Gospels exhibit a similar granularity. Third, in some regards, personal event memories can be misleading. While they are long-lived, their very vividness leads the one who possesses such a memory to overestimate their reliability. They were revealed in chapter 3 to be no more nor less reliable than memories of more mundane events. They are equally subject to transience, especially over the long period. On the other hand, studies on personal event memories do show that humans can accurately remember some details over periods as long as fifty or more years. This lends more credibility to the observation made already: those eyewitness memories of Jesus' ministry that survived intact for the first five or so years would likely have lasted over the lifetime of that eyewitness.

Fourth, while it has been noted that a number of the pericopes in the Gospels could have derived from the personal event memories of eyewitnesses, because they are narrated in the third person, such pericopes are not presently formulated as direct eyewitness reports. So, while eyewitnesses may well have contributed to the process of the formulation of the tradition, the present form of the tradition shows that it has been somewhat shaped. Thus, while eyewitnesses may prove to be an important part of the picture of how the Gospel traditions were formed, their contribution is likely to be greatest at the time the traditions were initially formed.

Source Documents and the Frailty of Transience

Before leaving matters relating to the transience of memory, it is perhaps appropriate to consider the possibility that the Evangelists drew upon earlier written records as they composed their Gospels. Perhaps the existence of earlier written records might remove the need to consider the transience of the memories of the eyewitnesses to Jesus' earthly ministry.

There is a well-known and widely utilized principle in historiography: more attention should be given to written and other sources that are dated closer to the event they describe than should be given to later sources.[3] As a consequence, the status of the Gospel of Mark changed remarkably once it was widely thought that Mark was the first Gospel to be written and was used as one of the documentary sources for Matthew and Luke.[4] It is probably fair to say that this principle lies behind the impulse that has generated the considerable volume of research and publication that are devoted to Q. In the opinion of many, Q is a very early document and can therefore reveal Christianity's nature at a very early date.[5]

---

3. The comment of Markus Bockmuehl is apposite: "For good reasons, students of history are trained to privilege primary sources dating from the period under investigation. Nevertheless we will do well to ponder for a moment what a poor track record the authors of such contemporary sources have as guides to the history of their own times" (2007, 345).

4. E.g., "St Mark's Gospel suffered relative neglect for centuries. ... But the discovery of Mark's priority transformed the situation. Since the end of last century its importance as the earliest gospel and the primary source of information about the ministry of Jesus ... has been widely acknowledged" (Cranfield 1959, 10).

5. Burton L. Mack, for example, says, "With Q in view the entire landscape of early Christian history and literature has to be revised," and concludes that "[t]he remarkable thing about the people of Q is that they were not Christians. They did not think of Jesus as a messiah or the Christ. They did not take his teachings as an indictment of Judaism. They did not regard his death as a divine, tragic, or saving event" (Mack 1993, 7, 4). With some others working on Q, Mack finds that Q itself reveals a development in the thought of the early followers of Jesus. The earliest traditions, Q^1,

MEMORY FRAILTIES AND THE GOSPEL TRADITIONS   149

Perhaps, then, priority of interest should be given to distinguishing as carefully as possible the written documents that appear to lie behind some of the parallels between the Gospels.[6] Such might appear to be the case, until one considers what has been noted about human memory in chapters 2–4. Memory is characterized by a rapid loss that starts immediately after an experience. As a result, humans forget most things that occur, a characteristic that frustrates nearly everyone from time to time but one that allows attention to be given to events of greater significance. Generally speaking, recent events are more significant than distant events, so it is a positive quality of memory that they are remembered more clearly. Some distant events, though, are of very great significance, and personal event memories are but one form of the long-term memories that form a person's self-identity and provide expertise and wisdom to handle contemporary problems. Even these long-term memories tend to fade over time, but a significant finding of chapter 2 is that long-term memories become stable after about three to five years.

Thus, the important question becomes: How early are the documents from which the Evangelists copied? Might they, in fact, come from a period earlier than three years after the events they describe and the giving of the sayings they include? Perhaps they might even be earlier, from the time of the ministry of Jesus. At least, such is the suggestion put forward by Alan Millard. He says,

> Jesus' followers and audiences included people of various occupations who would use writing, tax collectors … centurions … unnamed court-

---

consists largely of wisdom sayings and reveals a group of wandering Cynic look-alikes. Q^2 adds prophetic idiom to the wisdom sayings of Q^1 and contains a strong emphasis on final judgment. This reconstruction depends entirely on whether or not Q can be reconstructed with any confidence—an exercise fraught with methodological difficulties—and, further, on the very dubious and indemonstrable assumption that wisdom preceded the apocalyptic worldview in early Christianity. See also Crossan 1998, 239–25 and *passim*, as an example of another writer who relies heavily on Q (along with the Gospel of Thomas and some other noncanonical sources that he argues contain traditions earlier than those found in the Synoptic Gospels) to reconstruct early Christian history.

6. See McIver and Carroll 2002, 667–87; 2004, 1251–69, where it is argued that, while oral processes were perhaps more important in the formation of the Synoptic Gospels than is generally thought, there are some parallels that show clear evidence of processes of copying from previous documents.

iers and officials ... scribes.... To imagine any of these people going out with papyrus roll, pen and ink to take down the words of a travelling preacher would be absurd. To imagine some of them opening notebooks they carried for their day-to-day business, perhaps hung at the belt, and jotting down a few of the striking sayings they had heard, or writing a summary of what they had experienced while it was fresh in the memory is quite feasible. ... This is not to say the Evangelists began to compose the Gospels in Jesus' lifetime, but that some, possibly much, of their source material was preserved in writing from that period, especially accounts of the distinctive teachings and actions of Jesus. (Millard 2000, 223–24; see also 185–229, esp. 223–29)[7]

Millard builds his case on three things: (1) some of Jesus' followers used writing in their day-to-day employment, (2) nothing would be more natural than that such folk would take notes as they listened to Jesus, and they would feel the urge to quickly turn these notes into written records, and (3) a number of such records would have found their way to the places in which the Evangelists were living as they composed their Gospels.

The first point, that there were some among the followers of Jesus who wrote as part of their livelihood, is probably correct. For example, Matthew the tax collector (Matt 9:9; 10:3), was one of the inner circle of disciples. He would have used writing each day while working in that role. Nor should one restrict the ability to write to Matthew alone. Jesus and his disciples moved in a scribal society, and there would be those around him that would have used writing often. Despite this, the rest of Millard's suggestions are frankly implausible.[8] Even those who used writing as part of their regular employment in the first century did so on very specific occasions. Few contemporary written records survive from first-century Palestine, although many more have survived from Egypt. Surviving written records include census returns, tax records, contracts of sale and rent of land, marriage contracts, school exercises, and copies of works of lit-

---

7. See the arguments advanced to support the suggestion that one or more of the disciples of Jesus would have taken written notes in Eddy and Boyd 2007, 249–52.

8. Cf. the words of Jens Schröter: "Zunächst sollte nicht bestritten werden, daβ es eine Phase der mündlichen Tradierung der Jesusüberlieferung gegeben hat. Daβ der Beginn des Traditionsprozesses in schriftlichen Werken zu suchen sei, ist dagegen schon historische unwahrscheinlich und widerspricht zudem dem Charakter der Evangelien, die sich kaum anders denn als an die Jesusverkündigung gebundene Werke adäquat verstehen lassen" (1997, 57).

erature. Notable also are the very rare examples of religious literature that was found at Qumran near the Dead Sea and Nag Hammadi in Egypt. Not even among the writings derived from schools does one find the kinds of lecture notes envisaged by Millard (see, e.g., Cribiore 1996). With the possible exception of wax tablets, writing in the first centuries of the Common Era was slow and cumbersome. Outside of actual exercises in writing, teaching took place in a largely oral context. It is different today. All but a few modern students take advantage of inexpensive high-technology pens, abundant and cheap paper, and the surface provided to support writing in a lecture hall, where they take written notes of lectures as a later aide-memoir. Nor is it infrequent that someone listening to a modern sermon will also take notes. But such note taking is highly unlikely among the type of people pictured as listening to Jesus. Nor would large numbers of them retreat to their homes at night to write diaries and sort out their jottings to create coherent accounts of what they had just heard that day. Archaeology is revealing a great deal about the Galilee of the time of Jesus, even the small villages in which he moved. The vast majority of houses were just not equipped for writing and storage of written materials. Such things can be found in major centers such as Sepphoris and Tiberias— places remarkably absent from the list of locations in which Jesus is found in the Gospels. It must be emphasized that, while Jesus lived in Roman Palestine, a scribal society, he moved in circles where almost all everyday interactions took place in an oral context. Consequently, that written records of Jesus' teachings and doings were composed during the time of his ministry appears highly unlikely. Even had they existed, Millard still needs to account for their transit from Galilee to the locations in which the Evangelists were composing their Gospels.

Nor does it appear likely that any potential written sources that may have been drawn upon by the Evangelists Matthew and Luke would have been composed within three years of the crucifixion and resurrection. The urgency of the expectation of the soon return of Jesus would hardly create an environment where it was felt necessary to invest the time and labor necessary to produce and then copy written records.[9] Furthermore,

---

9. After rehearsing such texts as 1 Thess 4:17; 1 Cor 7:29–31; Phil 4:5; and Rom 13:11–12, Werner Georg Kümmel concludes, "but in view of all these texts, there can be no doubt that Paul is basically moulded in his thinking by the expectation of the imminent consummation of salvation" (Kümmel 1973, 144). Cf. the words of James D. G. Dunn, "In fact, there is a striking consistency in imminence of expectations

the first Christian writings to have survived come from the period when Christianity had begun to spread throughout the urban centers surrounding the Mediterranean Sea.

Two main considerations lead to the conclusion that only little, if any, benefit can be expected from pursuing an investigation of the documents used as written sources by one or more of the Synoptic Evangelists. First, it is impossible to delimitate accurately the extent and content of such documents.[10] Second, it is highly unlikely that they derive from the first three to five years after the events they describe and the sayings of Jesus they record. From the perspective of what is known about human memory, while earlier documents may reveal much about the community in which they arose, unless they were written within the first three to five years of the event, preferably within a few weeks or months, it is unlikely that they are historically more accurate than any other document written within the lifetime of the original eyewitnesses. Thus it must be concluded that it is

---

throughout the undisputed letters of Paul. Paul's sense of 'eager expectation' (*apekdechomai*) of the final denouement is as fresh in the later letters as in the early" (Dunn 1998, 311). Dunn also observes, "Given the new theological departure which it constituted, it is somewhat surprising that the coming (*parousia*) of Christ is a topic which has commanded relatively little attention among NT scholars in the past few decades" (Dunn 1998, 296).

10. I think little confidence can be given to the task of defining accurately the compass of Q. One can be confident of some of the parallels it is likely to include (such as Matt 3:1–12 // Luke 3:1–20; Matt 7:7–12 // Luke 11:9–13; Matt 8:5–13 // Luke 7:1–10; Matt 8:18–24 // Luke 9:57–62; Matt 11:1–19 // Luke 7:18–35; Matt 11:25–30 // Luke 10:21–24; Matt 12:38–42 // Luke 11:29–32; Matt 24:45–51 // Luke 12:41–48), but a considerable number of the parallels considered as potentially included in Q exhibit a very loose, gist relationship and may equally come from oral sources unrelated to Q. Yet even this is a more positive estimate of the usefulness of the Q hypothesis than is expressed by many working in Gospels studies who have challenged whether or not Q exists. These challenges not only come from the many scholars espousing the Griesbach hypothesis; it has even come from those who adopt a documentary explanation and Markan priority. For example, Mark Goodacre argues that Mark was written first and known to the other two Gospel writers and that Luke used Matthew, which for Goodacre means that the Q hypothesis is not necessary (Goodacre 2001, 2002). As might be surmised from McIver and Carroll 2002, 667–87; 2004, 1251–69, I am of the opinion some document, somewhat like Q, exists but remain very agnostic as to whether or not it is possible to determine its extent. In any event, Q is a very precarious foundation indeed on which to build a reconstruction of Christianity, especially one as radical as proposed by Burton Mack and others.

not possible to minimize the impact of the frailty of memory transience by relying on source documents that may lie behind the surviving Gospels.

Suggestibility and the Gospel Traditions

Several possible ways to induce false memories were described in chapter 4, including the use of memorized lists (the Deese, Roediger, and McDermott False Memory Procedure [DRM]), imagination of bizarre events, doctored photos, plausible (but false) childhood events, leading questions, and social contagion. The ease with which false memories are induced might lead to a general suspicion of the accuracy of any eyewitness reports, including those of the eyewitnesses of Jesus' earthly ministry. This, in fact, is the conclusion reached by Judith C. S. Redman, who points out that "inaccuracies can, and almost inevitably will, arise in eyewitness testimony before it *becomes* valuable community tradition that is seen to be in need of preservation." Her view of the impact that such eyewitness inaccuracies would have had on the Gospel traditions may be summed up by her comments in the following sentence: "it seems likely that the answer to the question How much can we reliably know about the Jesus of history from the Gospels in the light of Bauckham's work [on Eyewitnesses]? Is *still* 'not much'" (Redman 2010, 192–93).[11] In saying this, Redman has highlighted the challenge to the potential accuracy of the Gospel traditions posed by the fallibilities of human memory. But does what has been discovered about the ease with which false memories may be induced in experiments actually support Redman's conclusions?

While the DRM false memory procedure might be interesting in its own right, and while the ability to induce false memories by social contagion is fascinating, it might fairly be asked: What do these and the other experimental procedures described in chapter 4 have to do with this study of the nature of the Gospel traditions? After all, doctoring photos to induce false memories of a childhood balloon ride, for example, seems to be far removed from the types of processes out of which the Synoptic Gospels emerged. This question will be addressed in due course, but first there is an equally important question that must be addressed: What have doctored photos, misleading questions, and memorizing lists of words and all the

---

11. Cf. the words of April D. DeConick: "To trust the eyewitnesses because testimony asks to be trusted in nonsense. Whatever memories are preserved in the gospels, they are reconstructed and highly interpreted memories" (DeConick 2008, 179).

other diverse ways that have been shown to generate false memories have in common? The answer is that they all are able to induce false memories because they share the same characteristic of plausibility.

It is clear that there are a range of procedures that consistently induce memory errors. It is noteworthy, though, that these "errors" are induced because they are a natural fit to the stimulus. For example, it is true that the word "sleep" did not occur in the lists of words used in the DRM false memory procedure, but it was recalled because of its strong association with the words "bed, pillows, rest, sheets, snore, drowsy," and so on, the words actually on one of the lists. It must be emphasized that reproducing such a list from memory does not illicit random words such as "fireman" or "Neptune." In other words, while including the word "sleep" might strictly be called an error, it is not a gross error. It is a memory error that is closely related to what was originally learned.[12]

The same can be said of the false memories elicited by leading questions. That participants in the experiment described in chapter 4 "remembered" seeing video of the El Al plane hitting an apartment building in Amsterdam is demonstrably false. No such video exists. However, they *had* actually repeatedly seen video reconstructions and video of the apartment buildings. Their false memories are consistent with their prior real experiences. Likewise, the experiments that elicited social contagion of memory work because the suggested objects could plausibly belong to the set of objects shown on the original slide. While these experiments *do* elicit false memories, they *do not* show that memory is entirely erratic. Consistency appears to underlie the induced false memories. Of course, one could wish that no false memories could be induced at all, especially memories that grow out of events that are imagined rather than experienced. But some comfort may be derived from the observation that there does appear to be a certain limit on what might be incorporated as a false memory.

The relevance of these observations to the dependability of the Gospel traditions is evident. If the traditions are to be considered reliable, it is only so because the memories on which they are built are reliable. But

---

12. Matthew B. Reysen reports that in his experiments, "the likelihood that participants will incorporate misleading information into their own memory reports is dependent on the plausibility of the misleading information.... the transfer of incorrect information from confederates to participants is largely confined to instances in which the confederate's misinformation was plausible" (2007, 64).

can memories be considered to be reliable if it can be shown that it is possible to induce false memories that are indistinguishable from true memories by those who possess them? Thus it is important to have a good knowledge of the kind of errors that can be incorporated into eyewitness memories. While eyewitness testimony has been shown to have a first-order faithfulness to events that happened, there is already one conclusion from the research adduced in chapter 4 that must be squarely faced: to the extent that they are built on eyewitness memories, the Gospel accounts are highly likely to contain some errors at the level of detail. Furthermore, some errors can be demonstrated.

Take, for example, the accounts of the healing of the Gadarene/Gerasene demoniac(s) recounted in Matt 8:28–34 // Mark 5:1–20 // Luke 8:26–39, which must contain at least one and probably more errors of detail. Did this incident take place in the country of the Gadarenes (Matt 8:28) or the Gerasenes (Mark 5:1 // Luke 8:26)? Were there two demoniacs (Matt 8:28) or only one (Mark 5:2 // Luke 8:27)? While it is possible to suggest that Gadarenes and Gerasenes might be two different names for the same group of people, there is no credible way to explain why Matthew's account describes two demoniacs, while those in Mark and Luke describe only one demoniac. There was either exactly one or exactly two demoniacs, and at least one of these accounts contains an error of detail. Nor are the differences in the details observable in this parallel an isolated example of variability between parallel accounts in the Synoptic Gospels. In fact, variability of language and detail is characteristic of the parallel accounts, [13] and some of this variability almost certainly contains errors of detail. For example, variations in name and number such as those just noted may be observed elsewhere. Was the transfiguration six days after the promise of Jesus that "some standing here will not taste death until they see that the kingdom of God has come with power" (Mark 9:1–2; cf. Matt 16:28–17:1), or was it eight days later (Luke 9:28)? Was it Thaddeus (Matt 10:3; Mark 3:18) or Judas the son of James (Luke 6:15; cf. Acts 1:13) who was a disciple of Jesus? Did Jesus approach a tax collector called Matthew and invite him to become a disciple (Matt 9:9), or was he called Levi (Mark 2:14; Luke 5:27)? Who were in the line of male ancestors of

---

13. Alan Dundes argues that the variations in number, name, and sequence found in the Bible are evidence that it grew out of oral processes (which he labels "folklore"). Of interest here is the number of such variations that he notes in the Gospel accounts (see Dundes 1999, 21, 25–30, 33–37, 49–51, 57–63, 81–86, 103–11).

Jesus? Was it the line of kings that included David, Solomon, Rehoboam, Abijah, Asa, Jehoshaphat, Joram, Uzziah, Jotham, Ahaz, Hezekiah, Manasseh, Amos, Josiah, and so on (Matt 1:6–11), or did the line extend from David through the commoners Nathan, Mattatha, Menna, Melea, Eliakim, Jonam, Joseph, Judah, Simeon, Levi, Matthat, Jorim, Eliezer, and so on (Luke 3:29–30)? Did Jesus give his teaching of the beatitudes on a mountain (εἰς τὸ ὄρος, Matt 5:1) or on a level place (ἐπὶ τόπου πεδινοῦ, Luke 6:17). Did the beatitudes consist of a list of nine "happinesses" (μακάριοι, Matt 5:3–11) or four "happinesses" and four "woes" (μακάριοι ... οὐαί, Luke 6:20–26)? While some of these variations may have perfectly natural explanations (e.g., Thaddeus and Judas might be two names given to one individual, as might Matthew and Levi), it is almost certain that some of these details are incorrect (there was either one or two demoniacs; it was either six or eight days later, etc.).

What should be made of these variations in detail and likely errors of fact? Here is where the research cited earlier in chapter 4 is of great significance. Errors of memory are induced because they are plausibly consistent with what else is known. Thus, with regard to the errors of detail that are almost certainly to be found within the Gospel accounts, the important thing that should be noted is that these "errors" could be present only because they are plausible in the light of what else was known about Jesus and his doings. In other words, they are not inconsistent with the larger picture of Jesus. The kinds of variations that can be noted in the various parallel accounts are variations in detail and fall short of substantial change. As emerged in chapter 1, they are precisely the type of variations that one might expect of various eyewitness reports of the same event. Thus, while exact certitude about every detail of the Gospel narratives is just not possible, the larger picture that emerges is likely to be true. Only those details that were plausible in the light of what else was known about Jesus would have been incorporated. It might be wished that it were possible to state that there were no errors in these details in the Gospel accounts, but human memories do not work that way. But given the types of false memories that can be induced in humans, at least what is recorded in the Gospels is highly likely to be *consistent* with what actually happened.

Suggestibility and the Possibility of Nonauthentic Jesus Tradition

The previous chapter has examined two indications that many of the Gospel traditions may have been based on eyewitness memories. The pericope form is typical of the kinds of materials based on the memory of events, and the apophthegmata are not only of a form amenable to preservation in memory, but they are plausibly the exact type of matter that one would expect to develop in the collective memory of Jesus' early followers. But neither of these observations was used as a basis for claiming that this material must therefore be based on authentic memories of Jesus. It is not unknown for legendary stories to develop around figures of the past, and perhaps the very suggestibility of human memory may be the mechanism for the development and acceptance of some of these stories. Such has frequently been argued in the academic study of the Gospels.

The experimental and other evidence reported in previous chapters gives some pointers as to the likelihood that much extraneous material might be incorporated into the collective memories of Jesus and his deeds. Evidence was provided that, indeed, sometimes completely fabricated materials are incorporated into collective memory. But it was also observed that such instances are quite rare. Collective memories are much more likely to be shaped by the needs of the present and by adaptation of actual memories of the events described rather than outright invented. Just as with the contradictory details discussed in the previous section, if there was nonauthentic Jesus tradition circulating in the collective memory of his early followers, then it must have had considerable congruence with what he actually did and said. Just as individual details are selected for their consistency with actual memories of what took place, so also stories in collective memory accumulate because they correspond in a significant way to what is remembered of the actual person and events. This, naturally, does not preclude that one or other incident reported in the Gospels did not happen in the life of Jesus, but it makes much less likely than has sometimes been considered.[14] The process of wholesale fabrication of the Jesus traditions envisaged by Dibelius and Bultmann is highly unlikely.

---

14. Ulrich Luz also considers it highly unlikely that the Evangelists themselves would have created new traditions: "As I see it, the number of instances in Matt. 1–26 of Matthew inventing stories with no reference to tradition are relatively few" (2005, 57–58). See also Rodríguez 2010, 50–64.

Bias and the Gospel Traditions

Thus far this chapter has dealt with the memory frailties of transience and suggestibility. The third type of memory frailty considered in chapters 2–4 is that of bias.[15] Several factors might be considered to have the potential to introduce bias into the Gospel traditions, but few are as potent as the potential of theological and community interests. It might fairly be asked whether or not there is evidence in the Gospel accounts of theological interest and whether evidence can be adduced that these interests are likely to have introduced bias.

One of the characteristics of collective memory discovered in chapter 5 is that only those memories relevant to the present circumstances of individuals are retained as live memories, and this is especially true in the absence of written records. Thus, collective memory has a dynamic relationship to the past determined by the needs of the present. With the traditions about Jesus, this process would naturally be tempered by the high regard in which Jesus was held and the process of deliberate transmission of his teachings undertaken by the apostles and other teachers visible within the Christian communities. Furthermore, some of the events described in the Gospels are sufficiently memorable that one could imagine that they would be preserved out of their uniqueness and interest. Even so, the memories about Jesus that would have the greatest likelihood of being retained in the traditions that made up of the collective memory of early Christians would be those of greatest relevance and interest to early Christian communities. Moreover, as the various Evangelists were composing their Gospels, they would perforce select from the range of traditions available to them those they considered most relevant. Their own interests would be an important factor in determining what they considered to be most relevant. These interests would intersect in significant ways the interests of their surrounding community, which in their turn would suggest to the Evangelists which of the traditions might be of greatest relevance to their potential readers. As a result, each Evangelist has his own distinctive understanding of Jesus and his mission.

Such factors would be influential in determining which materials were selected for inclusion in the various Gospels. Take, for example, the Gospel of Matthew. It is rather unlikely that Matthew was ignorant

---

15. See chapter 4 particularly.

of the parables of the Good Samaritan and the Prodigal Son, but these are parables that only Luke considered important enough to include in his Gospel (Luke 10:30-37; 15:11-32). On the other hand, only Matthew considered it important to include a number of sayings that relate to the community of believers. These include sayings relating to community discipline (Matt 18:10, 14-20, 28-31), true and false prophets (7:15, 21-23; 10:41; 24:10-12, 14), Christian scribes (13:51-52), the mixed nature of the community (13:24-30, 36-43, 47-50; 25:1-13), and the leadership role of Peter (14:28-31; 16:17-19; 17:24-27). Other sayings unique to Matthew touch on Jews and Gentiles and their relationship to the saved community. These include sayings that initially limit the missionary activity of the disciples to the Jews only but that later expand to include all Gentiles (Matt 10:5b-6, 23; 15:23-24; 24:14; 28:16-20), a number of sayings relating to controversies between Jesus and the (scribes and) Pharisees (5:20; 15:12-13; 16:12; 23:1-3, 5, 8-10, 15, 16-22, 27-28, 32-33), and the recounting of several incidents that would have special relevance to Jews (5:33-37; 6:1-4, 16-18; 9:27-31; 17:24-27; 19:28b; 21:14-17, 43). A third group relates to the law (Matt 5:17, 19-20, 21-24, 27-28; 7:21-23; 12:5-7, 11; 15:12-13, 41; 21:28-32) and associated matters, such as righteousness (3:14-15; 5:10, 20; 10:41), forgiveness (6:15; 18:21-22, 23-35), prayer (6:5-8, 10b; 18:19-20),[16] and practical injunctions (5:4-5, 7-10, 14, 16, 21-24, 27-28, 33-37, 41; 6:1-4, 16-18). A fourth group concerns the end of the age. They speak either of the closeness or the delay of the second coming (Matt 10:23; 16:3; 25:1-13) or about judgment (12:36-37; 16:27; 18:23-35; 19:28b; 24:10-12, 14; 25:31-46). Furthermore, there is a considerable interest in the kingdom of heaven (Matt 13:24-30, 36-52; 16:19; 17:24-27; 18:3-4, 23-35; 19:12, 28b; 20:1-16; 21:14-17, 43; 25:1-13). That the texts unique to Matthew show such well-developed themes makes it almost certain that there was a deliberate process of choice involved in their inclusion.[17] The basic insight of *redactionsgeschichtlich* approaches to the Gospels—that the Evangelists were not mere collectors of tradition but theologians in their own right—appears to be borne out by the evidence of the Gospel of Matthew. Similar cases have been made for Mark and Luke.

---

16. Note that Luke also seems to have a particular interest in prayer. The three parables in Luke 11:5-13; 18:1-8, 9-14 all relate to prayer and are unique to Luke.

17. This observation provides the starting point from which it is possible to delineate some of the features of the community within which Matthew was written. See McIver 1989, 4-75; 1997b; 1999.

The Evangelists, then, were selective of the traditions available to them. Their choice of material appears to be influenced by a combination of the needs of their community as they perceive them, their own particular interests, and their theological perspectives. But does this mean that the traditions they selected are unreliable or less reliable than if they were not motivated by the needs of their community or their theology? An answer to this question lies in what has already been observed: while unhistorical information can make its way into collective memories, such occurrences are very rare indeed. Collective memories might be shaped by the needs of the present, but they are rarely invented from scratch. There almost always is something in the original historical person or event that corresponds in some significant way to the current collective memory of that person or event (Schwartz 2000, 293–312; 2008, 219–68). The same is highly likely to be true of the sayings and deeds of Jesus. While the needs of the community and the theological interests of the Evangelists would be used in the selection and presenting of the traditions, the product of such selection and shaping probably corresponds very significantly to what Jesus actually said and did. One should not minimize the fact that such a process undoubtedly gives an incomplete picture of the totality of the sayings and doings of Jesus, but what is recorded is highly likely to be trustworthy.

Conclusions

The memory frailties of transience, suggestibility, and hindsight bias investigated in earlier chapters were discovered to have more impact on the details of memories rather than on the general gist of what is remembered. The two case studies of eyewitness memories cited in chapter 1 illustrate how these general observations about individual memory are reflected in the actual testimony offered by eyewitnesses. Their memories were discovered to be substantially correct—the eyewitnesses to the shooting in Burnaby remembered up to 80 percent of details accurately, for example. While this is not 100 percent accuracy, and it can prove very difficult to determine which parts of eyewitness testimony belong to the 80 percent that is accurate as opposed to the 20 percent that is not, it does mean that eyewitness testimony can be considered to have general reliability. It is particularly good at the level of gist rather than detail. Thus eyewitness memory may be considered to be accurate more often than not. By preserving the gist of events, human memory demonstrates a "first-order" faithfulness to the past. If this is true of eyewitness testimony in general, it is therefore true of the contributions that the individual eyewitnesses would have made to the formation of the traditions found in the Synoptic Gospels. Their memories would have been accurate more often than not. They would be most reliable in reporting the gist of the event and what happened and least reliable about matters relating to time. Their contribution would have had a "first-order" faithfulness to the events in Jesus' life that they had witnessed.

This chapter—and the one preceding it—have dealt with the potential impact that the strengths and frailties that the memories of individual eyewitnesses may have had on the Jesus traditions and how these individual memories have been formed into the collective memories of groups of the earliest followers of Jesus. The next chapter adds another element to the model being developed—that of the teaching activities of Jesus and his disciples.

9
Collective Memory, Jesus as Teacher, and the Jesus Traditions

Several elements of the model being developed to account for the formation of the Jesus traditions found within the Gospels have already emerged from chapters 7 and 8. The model is built on the observation that eyewitness accounts of Jesus' doings would have been shared among groups of his earliest followers, thereby forming the basis for a strong collective memory of Jesus. Yet, of necessity, many important elements of the process suggested for the formation of collective memories about Jesus have been left vague. The formation of collective memory can be an ill-defined amorphous process, and any model built on an ill-defined process must likewise remain somewhat ill-defined.

Such would remain the case except for an important stream of evidence that will be considered in this chapter: that Jesus was a teacher who gathered around him a group of disciples. This further information will allow considerable clarification of the process by which many of the collective memories of Jesus' teaching were formed. After all, the more formal instruction given by Jesus to his disciples, as well as their firsthand experience of his day-to-day ministry, would have formed within the group of disciples a large, well-defined group of common remembered experiences. The information about the teachings of Jesus and his doings would then have been distributed by the inner group of disciples to other groups of earliest followers of Jesus by several processes, including a process of formal instruction. Such memories from the inner group of disciples formed a relatively well-defined collective memory shared among themselves, a collective memory about which much can be said with relative confidence.

Jesus as a Teacher

By any measure, the teaching activities of Jesus are a prominent theme of the Gospels. As Stephen D. Jones so cogently points out,

> The church today, so diverse in all of its expressions, likely converges around the theological confession of Jesus as Lord and Savior. ... Yet there are only three occurrences of the title Savior, referring to Jesus, in the four Gospels (Luke 1:69, 2:11; John 4:42). Yet they speak frequently of Jesus as Lord and rabbi. Jesus is addressed as Lord no fewer than 83 times, and as rabbi or teacher 56 times. (The next most frequently used title for Jesus is the enigmatic Son of man, found no fewer than 37 times.) (Jones 1997, 1)

The pattern of word usage found in the New Testament confirms Jones's assertion regarding the prominence given to Jesus' teaching activities in the Gospels and also reveals that the title "teacher" is attributed to him with great frequency. A Gramcord search reveals that the verb διδάσκω ("to teach") occurs fifty-five times in the New Testament, and all but nine are direct references to Jesus' teaching activities. In addition, there are forty-eight occurrences of the title διδάσκαλος ("teacher"), all but five of which are references to Jesus. The phrase ἐπί [or ἐν] τῇ διδαχῇ αὐτοῦ ("at [in] his teaching") also occurs seven times with reference to Jesus' teaching. This might be compared with the fact that out of 138 uses of the word in the New Testament, Jesus is identified as προφήτης ("prophet") eight times[1] in the Synoptic Gospels and five times in John. Furthermore, the verb θεραπεύω ("to heal") occurs forty-two times, thirty-five of which refer to the healing activities of Jesus; further, while the verb κηρύσσω ("to preach") occurs sixty times, it is only used nine times in reference to the preaching activities of Jesus. Thus, while Jesus is reported to have engaged in a number of activities, including healing and preaching, it is his teaching activities that are given most prominence in the Gospels. But what was Jesus actually doing that was perceived by his contemporaries as teaching?

Sufficient evidence survives about teaching methodologies from the ancient world to enable relatively secure conclusions to be drawn concerning the methodology Jesus used in his teaching activities. Confidence in this matter is possible because both the content and pedagogical method

---

1. Or twelve times, if one also counts Matt 13:57; 16:14; and Mark 6:4; 6:15.

showed remarkable uniformity over the entire period of the Roman Empire.² As it developed among the Greeks and later flourished amongst the Romans, "Basic education relies heavily on memory and recitation, limits attendance to those who can pay, offers strictly restricted instruction in writing, and defines grammar in terms of the sounds of the spoken language" (Lentz 1989, 56). Yet it should be emphasized that this focus on memory did not necessarily imply verbatim memorization. "Ancient theory and practice focus on the memory of things or arguments associated with *topoi*, not on the verbatim memory that we often associate with the term. ... memory does not necessarily require the verbatim recitation that modern preconceptions demand" (Lentz 1989, 92).³ A teaching process that revolved around memorization, then, was the fundamental pedagogy used to educate the elite in the ancient Roman world. Further, while memory lay at the root of the pedagogies used, verbatim memorization was not the goal of ancient education; rather, its goal was mastery of content. Memory was merely the means by which the content was retained, which was probably a practical result of the scarcity of written materials. Books were relatively rare, and one could not always rely on them being available for perusal.⁴

---

2. "[A]t any time from the early third century BCE until the end of the Roman empire, you could be fairly sure of finding a teacher, or more than one, in most towns and many villages.... what they taught, at any given level, recurs again and again in the surviving evidence in remarkably similar forms across vast geographical distances, a wide social spectrum and a timespan of nearly a thousand years" (Morgan 1998, 3; see also Atherton 1998, 217).

3. An exception to this general trend against verbatim memorization is the case of the rhapsodes. In the sixth and fifth centuries, these popular reciters of poetry "were to some extent composers as well as reciters," but after about 450 B.C.E., the rhapsodes became "mere" reciters. Their repertoire included the works of Homer, recited verbatim and with some style. They flourished in Greek culture well into the period of the Roman Empire. So Lentz 1989, 35–45, esp. 42; the cited words are found on 37, in a block quotation in which Lentz cites Frederick Beck, *Album of Greek Education* (Sydney: Cheiron, 1975).

4. Even for those who could read and write, what Mary Carruthers says of medieval times is even more apposite for the classical period: "Memory played a crucial role in pre-modern Western civilization, for in a world of few books, and those mostly in communal libraries, one's education had to be remembered, for one could never depend on having continuing access to specific material" (Carruthers 1990, 8).

Education in Palestine had its own distinct character, but such sources that survive[5] indicate that memorization played a crucial role there also. The basic methodology is illustrated by the following anecdote:

> R. Akiba stated: Whence is it deduced that a man must go on teaching his pupil until he has mastered the subject? From Scripture where it says, *And teach thou it to the children of Israel*. And whence is it deduced that it must be taught until the students are well versed in it? From Scripture where it says, *Put it in their mouths*. ...R. Pereda had a pupil whom he taught his lesson four hundred times before the latter could master it. On a certain day having been requested to attend to a religious matter he taught him as usual but the pupil could not master the subject. "What", the Master asked, "is the matter today?"—"From the moment", the other replied, "the Master was told that there was a religious matter to attend to I could not concentrate my thoughts, for at every moment I imagined, Now the Master will get up or now the Master will get up". "Give me your attention", the Master said, "and I will teach you again", and so he taught him another four hundred times. ... R. Hisda stated: The Torah can only be acquired with [the aid of] mnemonic signs, for it is said, *Put it in their mouths*; read not "*put it*" but "its mnemonic sign".[6]

---

5. While primary sources relating to education from times contemporary and earlier than the New Testament exist for many countries, this is not true of Palestine, where the only really useful sources are the rabbinic writings, which were not placed in written form until centuries after the time of the New Testament writings. Birger Gerhardsson argues for the basic conservatism of educational practice in the ancient world: "Education in antiquity was really not characterized by rapid changes. Least of all in such an utterly conservative milieu as that of Rabbinic Judaism.... nothing radically new was introduced by R. Aqiba; he must basically have adopted the traditional teaching method, and only developed and improved it" (1998, 77; see also the similar comments on 59, 113). While not everybody agrees with Gerhardsson in this matter, the extraordinary consistency of content and method in Greco-Roman education over many centuries and countries might be cited as evidence that educational practices in the ancient world were indeed very slow to change. In any event, if one is to speak of educational practices in Palestine, one is forced to deal primarily with the rabbinic data, as no other comparable source of information exists from the time of Jesus.

6. The translation is that of Israel W. Slotki, in *The Babylonian Talmud: Seder Mo'ed 'Erubin* (Epstein 1959, 382–83). The word play "put it" versus "its mnemonic sign" depends on the similarity in sound between שימה and סימנה. It might be wished that an account of teaching methods that was contemporary with Jesus and the disciples could be cited, but, unfortunately, the only clear information is to be found in later rabbinic sources. Given that the practice of memorization was found throughout

R. Pereda's pupil took an unusually large number of repetitions before he was able to repeat back to his teacher what he had "learned" (i.e., remembered, or memorized), but the anecdote illustrates the basic methodology adopted by all the rabbis. The teacher repeated something until the pupil could repeat it back to the teacher's satisfaction. In an oral context, this need not necessarily imply that the pupil repeated the materials verbatim, only that the basic ideas were preserved.

On the other hand, some kinds of materials lend themselves to more accurate and even verbatim memorization. Experiments have shown that structure and rhythm in the original tend to be reflected in what is memorized, hence orally transmitted poetry and songs have much higher verbatim agreement with an original than prose narrative (Rubin 1995, 65–121). Of particular importance for the Gospel materials is the observation that aphorisms are usually remembered with near verbatim accuracy or not at all (McIver and Carroll 2002, 667–87; 2004, 1251–69). Verbal materials can be remembered either verbatim or in gist—both forms of memory appear to be formed at the same time (Brainerd and Reyna 2004, 396–439; Brainerd 2005, 219–38; Reyna 2005, 241–56). Verbatim memory is much more short-lived than gist memory (Sachs 1974, 1967). Thus, the majority of long-term verbal memory is gist memory. Verbatim memory must be intentionally formed and then frequently rehearsed until it is settled into long-term memory. Consequently, while aphorisms are remembered with near verbatim accuracy, they need constant rehearsal before they are encoded and maintained in long-term memory. Thus materials such as the aphorisms found within the Gospels presuppose some process of frequent repetition and rehearsal such as might have taken place within the interaction between Christian teachers and their students and the exchange of memories about Jesus that must have taken place within the small circles of early followers of Jesus.

Putting these various elements together enables the following to be stated with some certainty. When Jesus is described in the Gospels as teaching his disciples, he was clearly engaged in activity that was recognized by his contemporaries as analogous to what other teachers found in the ancient world were doing. While pedagogical methods varied somewhat between various teachers and environments, common to all was the

---

the Roman world, though, it appears highly likely that rabbis contemporary to Jesus also taught their pupils by means of repetition.

effort expended by the teacher to enable his pupils to *remember* the principal components of his teaching. Jesus' disciples would have heard him speak often and thus would form clear memories of the principal topics on which he spoke. But in addition to this general instruction, it is highly probable that, like other Palestinian teachers, Jesus would have set up semiformal occasions where he asked his disciples to repeat back to him what he wished them to learn.

Collective Memories of Jesus' Teachings and the Jesus Traditions

Jesus is frequently portrayed as teaching in the Gospel accounts. While he taught the crowds as well as preached to them (e.g., Mark 4:2; 10:1; Luke 5:3; cf. Mark 1:38), the inner circle of the twelve disciples who accompanied Jesus throughout most of his ministry (see Acts 1:21-22) appears to have received special instruction (e.g., Matt 5:1; 13:10-23, 36). As a consequence of the time spent with Jesus and the special instruction they received, the twelve disciples would have developed a large pool of common memories. Their memories would have encompassed not only the events of Jesus ministry but also the materials deliberately imparted to them by Jesus by means of his specific instruction. It would be appropriate, then, to describe these common memories as the collective memory of Jesus possessed by the group of disciples. The component of their collective memories relating to Jesus' teachings was no doubt consolidated toward the end of Jesus' ministry before the disciples were sent out ahead of Jesus to prepare the villages to receive him (Matt 10:5-15; Mark 6:7-13; Luke 9:1-6). For this missionary activity in the pre-Easter period, the disciples would have needed to gather for themselves a body of Jesus' teaching adequate to support their own activities, and no doubt Jesus himself would have taken an interest in ensuring that they were adequately prepared for their task (Schürmann 1960, 361-69; Riesner 1984, 453-75, 500-501; 1991, 197-201; 2002, 26; 2008, 627-28). Both Mark and Luke describe the subsequent activity of the disciples as "preaching" (Mark 6:12; Luke 9:6); thus they may not have taken the role of teacher upon themselves at this time. Yet it is hard to imagine that in their preaching the disciples would not draw on the teachings of Jesus and, in so doing, consolidate their memories of his teachings. Thus, even before Easter, the disciples would have well-established memories of a significant body of Jesus' teaching, a collective memory deliberately fostered by Jesus through his teaching.

The crisis brought about by the crucifixion, resurrection, and ascension of Jesus would not destroy these memories, although it may have changed how the disciples themselves interpreted the teachings (e.g., Mark 9:9–10, 31–32; Luke 9:44–45; 18:31–34; cf. John 12:16; 13:7).

After Pentecost, the disciples are pictured doing what would naturally be expected of disciples when their master has departed: they become teachers in their own right (e.g., Acts 2:42; 4:2). Nor were the disciples the only teachers active among the early followers of Jesus. Indeed, there are a number of places in the New Testament that make reference to the activities of early Christian teachers (e.g., Acts 28:31; Rom 12:7; 1 Cor 14:6; 1 Tim 5:17). There are only hints of what content might have been included in the instruction given by these early Christian teachers, but one would expect that the disciples, at least, would have included significant parts of the teachings that they had received from Jesus in their own instruction to others. More important, by any analogy known from the ancient world, these teachers in early Christianity would have taught by repeating their instruction to their students until the students were able to repeat them back to the teacher's satisfaction that they had mastered the content.

Thus, one can perceive several streams by which tradition may have found its way into the Synoptic Gospels: a tradition handed down by teachers would have existed alongside the collective memory of the various groups of followers of Jesus identified in the previous chapters, and at later periods some written documents may have been available for consultation (e.g., Luke 1:1; McIver and Carroll 2002, 2004). It is likely that teachers played a significant part in gathering the various traditions about Jesus. Most important, we can see a line of tradition handed down from Jesus to his disciples, who in their turn instructed others. A case can thereby be made that such teachers constitute a clear line of transmission for the teachings of Jesus that extends from the time of Jesus to the time of the writing of the Synoptic Gospels. How many individuals make up this chain of tradents is ill-determined, although if one accepts the traditional ascriptions of authorship of the various Gospels and what is said of them by such writers as Papias and Irenaeus,[7] the chain of tradents is very short. Jesus to Matthew in the case of the first Gospel, and Jesus to Peter to Mark in the case of the second Gospel.

---

7. The comments on the authorship of the Gospels by Papias may be found in Eusebius, *Hist. eccl.* 3.39, that of Irenaeus in *Haer.* 3.1.1.

This model places the teachings of Jesus in fallible human memory. Werner Kelber highlights one of the ironies of the appearance of memory in considerations of the characteristics of the traditions about the teachings of Jesus:

> Gerhardsson envisioned a mechanical commitment of materials to memory and a passive transmission by way of continual repetition. Changes that did occur in the processing of traditional items remained confined to interpretive adaptations. On the whole, the work of memory as key arbiter of tradition was, therefore, characterized by fixity, stability and continuity, and the primary purpose of transmission was the deliberate act of communicating the legacy of Jesus for its own sake. No allowance is made, on this model, for memory's active participation in the operations of tradition. It is worth observing that the first and virtually only time memory is introduced as a key concept in the modern study of Christian origins, it is presented as cold memory, highlighting its retentive functions and reducing it to strictly preservative, reproductive purposes. As conceived by Gerhardsson, memory is the grand stabilizing agent in early Christian culture. (Kelber 2005, 232)

Kelber's implied criticism of Gerhardsson's model is quite consistent with research on memory presented earlier in this book. Memory is *not* characterized by fixity and stability. Quite the contrary. Memory does indeed have an "active participation in the operations of tradition," and this brings in its wake concomitant changes. As has been demonstrated in chapters 3 and 4 above, while memory is generally robust, specific memories are reconstructed from various subsystems in the human brain, and this reconstruction is capable of the creation of false memories, is subject to hindsight bias, and is highly selective in the preservation of only those things most relevant to the rememberer's current circumstances. Yet even conceding the possible presence of hindsight, bias, and selectivity, it should be noted that the two types of materials most characteristic of Jesus' teachings in the Synoptic Gospels—parables and aphoristic-like sayings—show great resistance to change in an oral environment.

Gospel Traditions of Jesus' Teaching: Parables

The parables form a significant component of the teachings of Jesus reported in the Synoptic Gospels. As with the apophthegmata considered in chapter 7, the fact that the three Synoptic Gospels bear some close relationship with each other adds extra significance to the variations found within the different versions of the parables recorded in the three Gospels. These differences underline Kelber's observation that memory is not characterized by fixity and stability. With some exceptions, most versions of the parables bear a gist relationship with the versions found in the other Gospels, not a verbatim relationship.

The amount of change that can be observed between the versions of the parables found in the different Gospels varies considerably. At one end of the spectrum is the parable of the Faithful or the Unfaithful Servant in Matt 24:45–51 // Luke 12:41–48, which shares so many common long verbatim sequences that I have argued elsewhere that this parallel is overwhelmingly likely to have been the result of a process of copying (McIver and Carroll 2002, 2004). The parable of the Fig Tree, found in the all three Synoptic Gospels (Matt 24:32–35 // Mark 13:28–31 // Luke 21:29–32) also shares long verbatim sequences and a very high percentage of common vocabulary. At the other end of the spectrum would be the parable of the Marriage Feast in Matt 22:1–14, which corresponds to some extent to the parable of the Great Banquet in Luke 14:15–24. But in this later case, there are sufficient differences between the two accounts to make it difficult to consider them versions of the same parable, despite the common theme of a rejected invitation (Matthew has a king, a marriage, cities destroyed by troops, and a man without a wedding garment; Luke has a man—presumably a commoner—who gave a banquet, and when rejected by his first guests extended his invitation to the poor, maimed, blind, and lame). Between these two extremes lie all three of the remaining parables that are found in all of the three Synoptic Gospels: the parable of the Sower (Matt 13:1–9 // Mark 4:1–9 // Luke 8:4–8), the parable of the Mustard Seed (Matt 13:21–32 // Mark 4:30–32 // Luke 13:18–19), and the parable of the Vineyard and the Tenants (Matt 21:33–46 // Mark 12:1–12 // Luke 20:9–19).[8] The parable of the Sower may stand as representative of the three parables,

---

8. One could make a case that the saying about new cloth and new wine in Matt 9:16–17 // Mark 2:21–22 // Luke 5:36–39 could be classified as a parable (it is described as a παραβολήν in Luke 5:36), in which case it would also be a parable of the triple tradition. In this book, though, it has been treated as an aphoristic-like saying. After all, the Hebrew מָשָׁל (mashal), which has been suggested as the best background for the New Testament usage of παραβολή, has a wide semantic domain in the Hebrew Bible that includes proverbs, by-words, prophetic figurative discourses, similitudes, and parables.

and the two versions of the parable of the Sower found in Mark 4:1–9 and Luke 8:4–8 may stand as representative of the three possible pairs in which they may be compared (i.e., of Matt 13:1–9 // Mark 4:1–9; and Matt 13:1–9 // Luke 8:4–8). As in tables 7.1–7.4 in chapter 7, so here, in order that the common elements between the parallels are easily observed, the words that are in exactly the same grammatical form are underlined. Where two or more words are found in verbatim sequence, they are underlined with a continuous line. The Greek text is the Gramcord version of the 4th edition United Bible Societies text, and the English text is that of the Revised Standard Version. Here, then, is the comparison of Mark 4:1–9 and Luke 8:4–8, which illustrates the gist relationship between two versions of the parable of the Sower that are found in Mark and Luke.

Table 9.1. The Parable of the Sower in Matthew and Mark (Greek)

Mark 4:1–9	Luke 8:4–8
1 Καὶ πάλιν ἤρξατο διδάσκειν παρὰ τὴν θάλασσαν· καὶ συνάγεται πρὸς αὐτὸν ὄχλος πλεῖστος, ὥστε αὐτὸν εἰς πλοῖον ἐμβάντα καθῆσθαι ἐν τῇ θαλάσσῃ, καὶ πᾶς ὁ ὄχλος πρὸς τὴν θάλασσαν ἐπὶ τῆς γῆς ἦσαν. 2 καὶ ἐδίδασκεν αὐτοὺς ἐν παραβολαῖς πολλά καὶ ἔλεγεν αὐτοῖς ἐν τῇ διδαχῇ αὐτοῦ· 3 Ἀκούετε. ἰδοὺ ἐξῆλθεν ὁ σπείρων σπεῖραι. 4 καὶ ἐγένετο ἐν τῷ σπείρειν ὃ μὲν ἔπεσεν παρὰ τὴν ὁδόν, καὶ ἦλθεν τὰ πετεινὰ καὶ κατέφαγεν αὐτό. 5 καὶ ἄλλο ἔπεσεν ἐπὶ τὸ πετρῶδες ὅπου οὐκ εἶχεν γῆν πολλήν, καὶ εὐθὺς ἐξανέτειλεν διὰ τὸ μὴ ἔχειν βάθος γῆς· 6 καὶ ὅτε ἀνέτειλεν ὁ ἥλιος ἐκαυματίσθη καὶ διὰ τὸ μὴ ἔχειν ῥίζαν ἐξηράνθη. 7 καὶ ἄλλο ἔπεσεν εἰς τὰς ἀκάνθας, καὶ ἀνέβησαν αἱ ἄκανθαι καὶ συνέπνιξαν αὐτό, καὶ καρπὸν οὐκ ἔδωκεν. 8 καὶ ἄλλα ἔπεσεν εἰς τὴν γῆν τὴν καλήν καὶ ἐδίδου καρπὸν ἀναβαίνοντα καὶ αὐξανόμενα καὶ ἔφερεν ἓν τριάκοντα καὶ ἓν ἑξήκοντα καὶ ἓν ἑκατόν. 9 καὶ ἔλεγεν· ὃς ἔχει ὦτα ἀκούειν ἀκουέτω.	4 Συνιόντος δὲ ὄχλου πολλοῦ καὶ τῶν κατὰ πόλιν ἐπιπορευομένων πρός αὐτὸν εἶπεν διὰ παραβολῆς· 5 ἐξῆλθεν ὁ σπείρων τοῦ σπεῖραι τὸν σπόρον αὐτοῦ. καὶ ἐν τῷ σπείρειν αὐτὸν ὃ μὲν ἔπεσεν παρὰ τὴν ὁδόν καὶ κατεπατήθη, καὶ τὰ πετεινὰ τοῦ οὐρανοῦ κατέφαγεν αὐτό. 6 καὶ ἕτερον κατέπεσεν ἐπὶ τὴν πέτραν, καὶ φυὲν ἐξηράνθη διὰ τὸ μὴ ἔχειν ἰκμάδα. 7 καὶ ἕτερον ἔπεσεν ἐν μέσῳ τῶν ἀκανθῶν, καὶ συμφυεῖσαι αἱ ἄκανθαι ἀπέπνιξαν αὐτό. 8 καὶ ἕτερον ἔπεσεν εἰς τὴν γῆν τὴν ἀγαθήν καὶ φυὲν ἐποίησεν καρπὸν ἑκατονταπλασίονα. ταῦτα λέγων ἐφώνει· ὁ ἔχων ὦτα ἀκούειν ἀκουέτω.

Table 9.2. The Parable of the Sower in Matthew and Mark (English)

Mark 4:1–9	Luke 8:4–8
1 Again he began to teach beside the sea. And a very large <u>crowd</u> gathered about him, so that he got into a boat and sat in it on the sea; and the whole crowd was beside the sea on the land. 2 And <u>he</u> taught them many things in <u>parable</u>s, and in his teaching he said to them: 3 "Listen! <u>A sower went out to sow</u>. 4 <u>And as he sowed, some seed fell along the path, and the birds</u> came and <u>devoured it</u>. 5 Other seed <u>fell on rocky</u> ground, where it had not much soil, and immediately <u>it</u> sprang <u>up</u>, since it had no depth of soil; 6 and when the sun rose it was scorched, and since <u>it had no</u> root <u>it withered away</u>. 7 Other seed <u>fell among thorns and the thorns grew</u> up <u>and choked it</u>, and it yielded no grain. 8 And other seeds <u>fell into good soil</u> and brought forth grain, growing up and increasing and <u>yielding</u> thirtyfold and sixtyfold and <u>a hundredfold</u>." 9 And <u>he said, "He who has ears to hear, let him hear."</u>	4 And when a great <u>crowd</u> came together and people from town after town came to him, <u>he</u> said in a <u>parable</u>: 5 "<u>A sower went out to sow</u> his seed; <u>and as he sowed, some fell along the path</u>, and was trodden under foot, <u>and the birds</u> of the air <u>devoured it</u>. 6 And some <u>fell on</u> the <u>rock</u>; and as it grew <u>up</u>, <u>it withered away</u>, because it had <u>no</u> moisture. 7 And some <u>fell among thorns; and the thorns grew</u> with it <u>and choked it</u>. 8 And some <u>fell into good soil</u> and gr<u>ew</u>, and <u>yielded a hundredfold</u>." As <u>he</u> said this, he called out, "<u>He who has ears to hear, let him hear.</u>"

It is noteworthy, given the close connections that exist between the three Synoptic Gospels, that the Evangelists appear to have concerned themselves only with a gist representation of the parable, not a verbatim representation. This observation is backed up by the following statistics. The longest common verbatim sequence in the Greek is six words, while the two versions share 30 percent (Mark) and 50 percent (Luke) common vocabulary. However, all of the details in each of the versions are presented in the same order. This is true of all the pair-wise comparisons that can be made between the three versions of the parable of the Sower (Matt 13:1–9 // Mark 4:1–9; Matt 13:1–9 // Luke 8:4–8; Mark 4:1–9 // Luke 8:4–8). They are all gist parallels. Despite the fact that Matt 13:1–9 shares ninety-six words in common with Mark 4:1–9, which as percentages are 73 percent

(Matt) and 64 percent (Mark), the longest common verbatim sequence is eight words.[9] Between Matt 13:1–9 and Luke 8:4–8 are forty-five words in common, which as percentages are 34 percent (Matt) and 50 percent (Luke), and the longest common verbatim sequence is five words.

But while the various versions of the parable of the Sower are found in gist parallels, they all follow exactly the same sequence in the details used. What is true of the parable of the Sower is true also of the discussion of the purpose of parables in Matt 13:10–17 // Mark 4:10–12 // Luke 8:9–10, the explanation of the parable of the Sower in Matt 13:18–23 // Mark 4:13–20 // Luke 8:11–15, the parable of the Mustard Seed in Matt 13:21–32 // Mark 4:30–32 // Luke 13:18–19, and the parable of the Vineyard and the Tenants in Matt 21:33–46 // Mark 12:1–12 // Luke 20:9–19. They are all gist parallels with relatively high common vocabularies, but their common verbatim sequences are very short and are generally restricted to common phrases. Yet the sequencing of details is exactly the same in all of the accounts.

What implications does this phenomenon have for the stability of parables? In the period of oral tradition, the very form of a parable means that it must be transmitted relatively coherently. Like a modern joke, a parable uses a short story to lead up to a punch-line. The story needs to be told coherently enough that the punch-line remains intelligible. The parables are expressed with great economy: they involve two, or at most three, characters, are told from a single perspective, and omit any participant, description of feelings and motives, character attributes, and events and actions that are not absolutely essential to the action (Bultmann 1968:188–190; see also Blomberg 1990, 1991). These qualities of a parable give them great stability in an oral environment. Indeed, Joachim Jeremias goes so far as to say, "The conclusion is inevitable that we are dealing with particularly trustworthy tradition. We stand right before Jesus when reading his parables" (1972, 12).[10]

---

9. The differences between the accounts are somewhat obscured in English translation, which has thirteen words in common verbatim sequence, at least in the RSV, which increases to forty-one words with one change, if one allows the change from the singular "seed" to the plural "seeds" and all subsequent changes from "it" to "they" as one change.

10. Ruben Zimmermann underlines the fact that parables are a form ideal for memorization and says, "Betrachten wir die Parabeln als Gedächtnisgattungen, können Vergangenheitsbezug und Gegenwartswirkung gleichermaßen zur Geltung

On the other hand, parables have not necessarily been immune from the frailties of human memory in their transmission. Take, for example, the parable of the Talents (Matt 25:14–30) or Minas (RSV "Pounds"; Luke 19:11–27). The basic storyline in the two parables is quite similar. An important personage goes away and entrusts his wealth to a number of servants. On his return, three of his servants provide different reports of their stewardship. One has made five further talents/ten minas, another two further talents/five minas, but the last servant hid the money. His master asked why he had not at least put the money with the money-changers. The money was taken from the last servant and given to the most successful servant, because "to everyone who has, more will be given, but from him who has not, even what he has will be taken away." Given these similarities, it is hard not to see Matt 25:14–30 and Luke 19:11–27 as two different versions of the same parable. If that is the case, though, then there are substantial differences in the two versions. For example, the monetary unit in Matthew, the talent, was worth more than fifteen years' wages for an average laborer, while a mina (RSV "pound"), while still a substantial amount, was equivalent to only three months of a laborer's wages. Matthew only mentions three servants; Luke has ten. In Mathew's account, one servant gets five talents, another two talents, and the final servant one talent. In Luke each of the ten servants receives one mina. The master in the version in Matthew is described as "a man," although given the amount of money he entrusts to his servants, he would be a wealthy man. In Luke, though, the master is a nobleman who goes to a far country to receive a kingdom, which he received despite the protests of the inhabitants of that country. When he returns, he orders those who opposed him slaughtered in his presence. These changes give the two versions of the parables quite a different flavor, although it must be admitted that the essential meaning of the parable is the same in both versions.

That when the Evangelists recorded the parables they were content with a gist representation makes it highly likely that such was the case while the parables were being taught by Jesus to the disciples and, in their turn, by the disciples to those who were interested. Yet by their very form, the central core of the parables (their gist) would be transmitted reliably and would be available to the Evangelists as they composed their Gospels.

---

kommen. Die Parabeln bewahren die Erinnerung an Jesus und seine Lebenswelten" (2008, 119).

The way in which aphorisms are transmitted in an oral context shows some interesting differences to that of parables.

Gospel Traditions of Jesus' Teaching: Aphorisms

A significant amount of the teachings of Jesus found in the Synoptic Gospels are found in an aphoristic-like form.[11] According to Rainer Riesner, of the 247 independent units that make up the sayings of Jesus in the Synoptics, 42 percent are one verse long; a further 23 percent are two verses long; only 12 percent are longer than four verses (1988, 392–93; cf. Gerhardsson 1986, 37). Many of the short sayings are formed as aphorisms: short, pithy sayings, with simple internal structure, and expressed using a remarkable amount of vivid imagery and rich in figures of speech. Aphorisms tend to be remembered primarily in verbatim memory (McIver and Carroll 2002, 2004). Such verbatim memories are very short-lived and will not be encoded into long-term memory without constant repetition (Sachs 1974, 1967)—the kind of repetition that has been previously shown to be a likely pedagogical method adopted by both Jesus and his disciples in their teaching activities. Once in long-term memory, aphorisms would usually be remembered accurately or—and this is the important point—*not at all*. This quality of human memory, together with their conciseness and rich imagery, make the aphorisms attributed to Jesus highly likely to be accurately transmitted once they are part of the tradition.[12] An examination

---

11. The description "aphoristic-like" is used deliberately here, although elsewhere in the book such sayings will usually be referred to as aphorisms. In his book *In Fragments: The Aphorisms of Jesus*, John Dominic Crossan provides an excellent introduction to the difficulties of classification of what he called the "prose miniature." The adage, aphorism, apothegm, epigram, fragment, *gnome*, proverb, maxim, and saying are all very similar. Perhaps an aphorism can be distinguished from a proverb in that a proverb tends to convey more collective wisdom, while an aphorism conveys more personal insight. An aphorism also often conveys paradox. But in the end, Crossan gathers most of the short saying of Jesus under the rubric of "aphorism" (1983, 3–36). In this manner, *aphorism* becomes a helpful term to describe a short saying rich in imagery and insight, and it will be so used in this book.

12. Alan Dundes highlights the remarkable persistence of recognizable forms of the proverb, "Do not be too sweet lest you be swallowed; do not be too bitter lest you be spat out." This proverb is first known from a fifth-century B.C.E. papyrus found in Elephantine in Upper Egypt. Recognizable forms of it have been found in an Arab manuscript from 1127 C.E., and it has been reported in Serbia in 1885, in India in

of the aphorisms attributed to Jesus in the Synoptic Gospels tends to support this assertion. In contrast to the parable parallels, which usually show a gist relationship, there is frequently a verbatim relationships between versions of the aphorisms found in two or more of the Gospels, as for example, the sayings found in the parallels between Matt 7:7–11 and Luke 11:9–13. This parallel, shown in tables 9.3 and 9.4, is coded according to the conventions already set out.

Table 9.3. A Greek-Text Example of the Stability of Aphorisms in the Synoptic Gospels (Matt 7:7–11 // Luke 11:9–13)

Matt 7:7–11	Luke 11:9–13
7 <u>Αἰτεῖτε καὶ δοθήσεται ὑμῖν, ζητεῖτε καὶ εὑρήσετε, κρούετε καὶ ἀνοιγήσεται ὑμῖν·</u> 8 <u>πᾶς γὰρ ὁ αἰτῶν λαμβάνει καὶ ὁ ζητῶν εὑρίσκει καὶ τῷ κρούοντι ἀνοιγήσεται.</u> 9 ἢ τίς ἐστιν <u>ἐξ ὑμῶν</u> ἄνθρωπος, ὃν <u>αἰτήσει ὁ υἱός</u> αὐτοῦ ἄρτον, μὴ λίθον <u>ἐπιδώσει αὐτῷ·</u> 10 <u>ἢ καὶ ἰχθὺν αἰτήσει,</u> μὴ <u>ὄφιν ἐπιδώσει αὐτῷ·</u> 11 <u>εἰ οὖν ὑμεῖς πονηροὶ</u> ὄντες <u>οἴδατε δόματα ἀγαθὰ διδόναι τοῖς τέκνοις ὑμῶν, πόσῳ μᾶλλον ὁ πατὴρ ὑμῶν ὁ ἐν τοῖς οὐρανοῖς δώσει</u> ἀγαθά <u>τοῖς αἰτοῦσιν αὐτόν.</u>	9 Κἀγὼ ὑμῖν λέγω, <u>αἰτεῖτε καὶ δοθήσεται ὑμῖν, ζητεῖτε καὶ εὑρήσετε, κρούετε καὶ ἀνοιγήσεται ὑμῖν·</u> 10 <u>πᾶς γὰρ ὁ αἰτῶν λαμβάνει καὶ ὁ ζητῶν εὑρίσκει καὶ τῷ κρούοντι ἀνοιγ(ής)εται.</u> 11 <u>τίνα</u> δὲ <u>ἐξ ὑμῶν</u> τὸν πατέρα <u>αἰτήσει ὁ υἱὸς ἰχθύν,</u> καὶ ἀντὶ ἰχθύος <u>ὄφιν αὐτῷ ἐπιδώσει</u> 12 <u>ἢ καὶ αἰτήσει</u> ᾠόν, <u>ἐπιδώσει αὐτῷ</u> σκορπίον 13 <u>εἰ οὖν ὑμεῖς πονηροὶ</u> ὑπάρχοντες <u>οἴδατε δόματα ἀγαθά διδόναι τοῖς τέκνοις ὑμῶν, πόσῳ μᾶλλον ὁ πατὴρ</u> (ὁ) <u>ἐξ οὐρανοῦ δώσει</u> πνεῦμα ἅγιον <u>τοῖς αἰτοῦσιν αὐτόν.</u>

Table 9.4. An English-Text Example of the Stability of Aphorisms in the Synoptic Gospels (Matt 7:7–11 // Luke 11:9–13)

Matt 7:7–11	Luke 11:9–13
7 <u>Ask, and it will be given you; seek, and you will find; knock, and it will be opened to you.</u> 8 For every one who asks receives, and he who seeks finds, and to him who knocks it will be opened.	9 And I tell you, <u>Ask, and it will be given you; seek, and you will find; knock, and it will be opened to you.</u> 10 For every one who asks receives, and he who seeks finds, and to him who knocks it will be opened.

1920, and in Kurdistan in 1937. As there is near zero probability that these various versions are dependent on each other, Dundes cites this as evidence for the remarkable preservation of a proverb in oral tradition for over a millennium and says that "[t]his is by no means an atypical example of the remarkable tenacity of tradition. Orally transmitted folklore such as proverbs and legends can survive relatively intact for centuries with no help from written sources" (Dundes 1999, 9–10).

9 Or <u>what</u> man of <u>you, if his son</u> asks him for bread, <u>will give him</u> a stone? 10 <u>Or if he</u> <u>asks for a fish, will give</u> <u>him a serpent</u>? 11 <u>If you then, who</u> <u>are evil, know how to give good gifts</u> <u>to your children, how much more</u> <u>will</u> your <u>Father</u> who is in <u>heaven give</u> good things <u>to those who ask him</u>!

11 <u>What</u> father among <u>you, if his son</u> <u>asks for a fish, will</u> instead of a fish give him <u>a serpent</u>; 12 <u>or if he asks</u> for an egg, <u>will give him</u> a scorpion? 13 <u>If</u> <u>you then, who are evil, know how to</u> <u>give good gifts to your children, how</u> <u>much more will</u> the <u>heavenly Father</u> <u>give</u> the Holy Spirit <u>to those who ask</u> <u>him</u>!

Further parallel sayings that show verbatim correspondence include the saying about serving two masters in Matt 6:24 // Luke 16:13; the saying about the greatness of the harvest found in Matt 9:37–38 // Luke 10:2; and the sayings about taking up a cross to follow Jesus found in Matt 16:24–28 // Mark 8:34–9:1. On the other hand, other aphorisms within the Gospel parallels have a mixture of verbatim and gist relationships, such as the set of aphorisms in Matt 5:13–16; 6:22–23 and Luke 11:33–36; 14:34–35, compared in tables 9.5 and 9.6.

Table 9.5. Greek-Text Examples of the Stability of Aphorisms in the Synoptic Gospels (Matt 5:13–16; 6:22–23 and Luke 11:33–36; 14:34–35)

Matt 5:13–16; 6:22–23

5:13 ὑμεῖς ἐστε <u>τὸ ἅλας</u> τῆς γῆς· <u>ἐὰν δὲ</u> <u>τὸ ἅλας μωρανθῇ, ἐν τίνι</u> ἁλισθήσεται εἰς οὐδὲν ἰσχύει ἔτι εἰ μὴ <u>βληθὲν ἔξω</u> καταπατεῖσθαι ὑπὸ τῶν ἀνθρώπων. 14 ὑμεῖς ἐστε τὸ φῶς τοῦ κόσμου. οὐ δύναται πόλις κρυβῆναι ἐπάνω ὄρους κειμένη· 15 οὐδὲ καίουσιν λύχνον καὶ τιθέασιν αὐτὸν ὑπὸ τὸν μόδιον ἀλλ' ἐπὶ τὴν λυχνίαν, καὶ λάμπει πᾶσιν τοῖς ἐν τῇ οἰκίᾳ. 16 οὕτως λαμψάτω τὸ φῶς ὑμῶν ἔμπροσθεν τῶν ἀνθρώπων, ὅπως ἴδωσιν ὑμῶν τὰ καλὰ ἔργα καὶ δοξάσωσιν τὸν πατέρα ὑμῶν τὸν ἐν τοῖς οὐρανοῖς…

Luke 11:33–36; 14:34–35

14:34 Καλὸν οὖν <u>τὸ ἅλας</u>· <u>ἐὰν δὲ</u> καὶ <u>τὸ</u> <u>ἅλας μωρανθῇ, ἐν τίνι</u> ἀρτυθήσεται 35 οὔτε εἰς γῆν οὔτε εἰς κοπρίαν εὔθετόν ἐστιν, <u>ἔξω βάλλουσιν</u> αὐτό. ὁ ἔχων ὦτα ἀκούειν ἀκουέτω.

11:33 Οὐδεὶς λύχνον ἅψας εἰς κρύπτην τίθησιν (οὐδὲ ὑπὸ τὸν μόδιον) ἀλλ' ἐπὶ τὴν λυχνίαν, ἵνα οἱ εἰσπορευόμενοι τὸ φῶς βλέπωσιν. 34 <u>ὁ λύχνος τοῦ</u> <u>σώματός ἐστιν ὁ ὀφθαλμός</u> σου. ὅταν <u>ὁ ὀφθαλμός σου ἁπλοῦς ᾖ, καὶ ὅλον</u> <u>τὸ σῶμά σου φωτεινόν ἐστιν· ἐπὰν δὲ</u> <u>πονηρὸς ᾖ, καὶ τὸ σῶμά σου σκοτεινόν</u>.

6:22 ʹΟ λύχνος τοῦ σώματός ἐστιν ὁ ὀφθαλμός. ἐὰν οὖν ᾖ ὁ ὀφθαλμός σου ἁπλοῦς, <u>ὅλον τὸ σῶμά σου φωτεινὸν ἔσται</u>· 23 ἐὰν δὲ ὁ ὀφθαλμός σου πονηρὸς ᾖ, ὅλον <u>τὸ σῶμά σου σκοτεινὸν</u> ἔσται. εἰ <u>οὖν τὸ φῶς τὸ ἐν σοὶ σκότος ἐστίν</u>, τὸ σκότος πόσον.

35 σκόπει <u>οὖν μὴ τὸ φῶς τὸ ἐν σοὶ σκότος ἐστίν</u>. 36 εἰ οὖν τὸ σῶμά σου ὅλον φωτεινόν, μὴ ἔχον μέρος τι σκοτεινόν, ἔσται φωτεινὸν ὅλον ὡς ὅταν ὁ λύχνος τῇ ἀστραπῇ φωτίζῃ σε.

Table 9.6. English-Text Examples of the Stability of Aphorisms in the Synoptic Gospels (Matt 5:13–16; 6:22–23 and Luke 11:33–36; 14:34–35)

Matt 5:13–16; 6:22–23	Luke 11:33–36; 14:34–35
5:13 You are the <u>salt</u> of the earth; <u>but if salt has lost its taste, how shall its saltness be restored? It is</u> no longer good for anything except to be <u>thrown</u> out and trodden under foot by <u>men</u>. 14 You are the light of the world. A city set on a hill cannot be hid. 15 Nor do men <u>light</u> <u>a lamp</u> and <u>put</u> <u>it</u> <u>under a bushel, but on a stand</u>, and it gives <u>light</u> to all in the house. 16 Let your light so shine before men, that they may see your good works and give glory to your Father who is in heaven. ... 6:22 The <u>eye is the lamp of</u> the <u>body</u>. So, if <u>your eye is sound, your whole body</u> will be <u>full of light; 23 but</u> if your eye is <u>not sound, your whole body</u> will be <u>full of darkness</u>. If then the light in you is darkness, how great is the darkness!	14:34 <u>Salt</u> is good; <u>but if salt has lost its taste, how shall its saltness be restored? 35 It is</u> fit neither for the land nor for the dunghill; <u>men throw</u> it away. He who has ears to hear, let him hear. ... 11:33 No one after <u>lighting</u> <u>a lamp</u> <u>put</u>s <u>it</u> in a cellar or <u>under a bushel, but on a stand</u>, that those who enter may see the <u>light</u>. 34 Your <u>eye is the lamp of</u> your <u>body</u>; when <u>your eye is sound, your whole body</u> is <u>full of light</u>; but when it is <u>not sound, your body</u> is <u>full of darkness</u>. 35 Therefore be careful lest the light in you be darkness. 36 If then your whole body is full of light, having no part dark, it will be wholly bright, as when a lamp with its rays gives you light.

These aphorisms are linked together differently in Matthew and Luke and are expressed in somewhat different words. Either what began as a verbatim memory has now become a well-remembered gist memory, or over time different lines of tradition have remembered these aphorisms slightly differently. But the essential meaning of the aphorisms is the same in both versions, and even some of the parallelism is preserved in both.

Yet even with aphorisms, sometimes the wording varies in a way that makes accommodation to the new circumstances in which the saying is heard. For example, in Matt 5:25 Jesus urges his followers to make peace with their adversaries quickly, lest they be handed over to a judge, who will then hand them over to a guard (ὑπηρέτῃ "attendant"), a term appropriate to a synagogue official in Palestine, while in Luke 12:58, the same warning suggests that the judge might give them to an officer (πράκτορι "officer of the court"), an official functionary of a Roman court (Jeremias 1972, 27).

From this data it might be concluded that the form of much of the teaching of Jesus—aphorisms—lends itself to accurate transmission in an oral context. Aphorisms are remembered in verbatim memory. Long-term verbatim memory is formed through frequent rehearsal such as would have taken place as Jesus taught his disciples. By any analogy known from the ancient world, Jesus' teaching would have been passed on from Jesus to the disciples and from the disciples to those they instructed by a process of rehearsal and repetition. An examination of the Gospel materials reveals that, even given the fact that the current versions of the aphorisms of Jesus have been shaped by the circumstances and that there is some variation between the wording of the instances of the various aphorisms as they are recorded in the Synoptic Gospels, a strong case can be made that they have been reliably transmitted from Jesus through his disciples and into the traditions that make up the Gospel accounts. Aphorisms, after all, are remembered (nearly) verbatim or not at all!

Jesus as the Origin of the Teachings Traditions

In sum, then, what is known of the characteristics of human memory, the teaching methodology almost certainly adopted by Jesus and his disciples, and the evidence of the Synoptic parallels all support the contention that aphorisms and parables were likely to have been transmitted with great reliability in earliest Christianity. But though they may be reliably transmitted, can it be guaranteed that the aphorisms and parables of Jesus as recorded in the Synoptic Gospels are to be traced back to Jesus himself? Does this process of reliable transmission extend back as far as Jesus?

These questions can only be answered in terms of probabilities. C. H. Dodd, for example, argues in the following manner:

When all allowance has been made for these limiting factors—the chances of oral transmission, the effect of translation, the interest of teachers in making the sayings "contemporary", and simple human fallibility—it remains that the first three gospels offer a body of sayings on the whole so consistent, so coherent, and withal so distinctive in manner, style and content, that no reasonable critic should doubt, whatever reservations he may have about individual sayings, that we find reflected here the thought of a single, unique teacher. (1971, 33)

Dodd also observed, "the reported sayings of Jesus bear the stamp of an individual mind" (1971, 49).

Dodd's evaluation that the teachings attributed to Jesus in the Gospels have the stamp of an individual mind, while subjective, has a certain intrinsic credibility. After all, the teachings attributed to Jesus are an incisive, brilliantly formulated, quite revolutionary expression of a new reality. They convey a unique understanding of God and his interaction with humankind and the world. A very sophisticated understanding of the kingdom of God, for example, is expressed with concrete images and apparently simple stories. The teachings attributed to Jesus could come from no ordinary mind, and if they do not go back to Jesus himself, it is hard to find a suitable origin for them. Even in the last quarter of the first century, Christian numbers were small indeed. Rodney Stark estimates this number to be around 7,500 by the year 100 and smaller before this (Stark 1997, 7; cf. Hopkins 1998, 212). These numbers may underrepresent the actual number of Christians at this time period, but perhaps not by much.[13] Of those who left written records, Paul stands out as a creative

---

13. Successes such as those reported in Acts 2 would be tempered by the persecutions reported in Acts 7 and 8. The many thousands of Christian zealous for the law mentioned by James in Acts 21:20 apparently avoided the destruction of Jerusalem following the revolt later in the first century by escaping to Pella, but while one can trace their influence in some later Christian groups, they had become marginalized. Nor can one discount the possibility of many deaths among Palestinian Christians associated with the ruthless suppression of the revolt by the Romans. That Christianity experienced many setbacks as it moved into the wider Roman world is illustrated by Pliny's suppression of Christianity, which he describes matter-of-factly to Trajan in book 10.96 of his letters. He reported that his policy of allowing suspected Christians to prove their innocence by worshiping an image of the emperor and cursing Christ and executing those who did not was effective in suppressing Christianity. "For this contagious superstition is not confined to the cities only, but has spread through the villages and rural districts; it seems possible, however, to check and cure it. 'Tis certain

and impressive thinker, but one who thinks quite differently from the one who formulated the parables and aphorisms found in the Gospels. Martin Dibelius and Rudolf Bultmann, on the other hand, would suggest that many of these traditions originated in the time period of the early church. But how likely is it that such original material arose "naturally" in group contexts? Indeed, that such teaching grew organically seems unlikely.[14]

Thus, the probability is that the aphorisms and parables attributed to Jesus in the Synoptic Gospels can be traced back to Jesus himself. The mechanism by which they ended up in the Synoptic Gospels is likely to have been complex. It must have involved the collective memories of the early Christian communities in some ways. In particular, it is likely to have involved the teaching activities of Jesus and the disciples as they deliberately formed memories of a body of Jesus' teaching that was formally handed down from teacher to disciple by a process of memorization via repetition. These processes eventually would have led to the formation of a relatively well-defined body of oral tradition about Jesus and his teachings from which the Evangelists could draw as they shaped the available traditions into the Gospels. The forms in which the teachings attributed to Jesus are found in the Gospels—parables and short aphoristic-like sayings rich in imagery and parallelism—make a relatively reliable transmission highly likely. With this observation, the main elements of the model being developed to account for the various inputs available to the Evangelists are now in place. They will be drawn together in the next chapter.

---

at least that the temples, which had been almost deserted, begin now to be frequented; and the sacred festivals, after a long intermission, are again revived" (the translation is that of Melmoth 1915, 403). While the sporadic persecution to which Christianity was subjected had the ultimate effect of increasing the numbers of Christians, persecutions like that which took place in Bithyinia under the leadership of Pliny would cause considerable reversion back to paganism in the short term.

14. As Harald Riesenfeld has already been quoted as saying: "I cannot enter here into a detailed critique of these theories [the methodology of *Formgeschichte*]. The very existence of such an anonymous creative generation in primitive Christianity presupposes, in view of what we know from the New Testament about the apostles and the other members of the early Christian community, a truly miraculous and incredible factor in the history of the Gospel tradition" (Riesenfeld 1957, 9). See also Rodríguez 2010, 50–64.

10
Conclusions: Memory, Jesus, and the Gospels

Personal event memories, forgetting curves, suggestibility, hindsight bias, eyewitness memory, collective memory, and the teaching methodologies employed in the Greco-Roman world are but some of the kaleidoscope of topics that have appeared in the preceding pages. The task of investigating the various aspects of human memory relevant to assessing the characteristics of the traditions found in the Synoptic Gospels has proved to be fascinatingly complex. This chapter attempts to draw together the various threads that have been explored and to use them to form a final assessment of the authenticity of the Gospel traditions.

At the heart of this investigation is a simple observation. Between the death and resurrection of Jesus and the writing of the Gospels, the teachings and deeds of Jesus were preserved in human memory—with all its frailties—for a period of many years, possibly as long as thirty to sixty years. Memory is transient. One might even describe it as reliably transient, in that it has proved possible to represent the process of forgetting with a smooth curve on a graph. Many, if not most, types of memory exhibit a similar forgetting curve (described in chapter 2 as an Ebbinghausian forgetting curve). Although some types of memory decay at a slower rate than other types, most of them follow a similar pattern. Much is forgotten very quickly, although the rate of forgetting slows over time.

Does this mean that scholars such as Rudolf Bultmann are correct in saying that almost nothing would remain of the memories of the real Jesus by the time the Gospels were written? Not necessarily. It turns out that memories of events and verbal material that have persisted for as long as three to five years are thereafter relatively stable;[1] that is, of course, until memory functions begin to decline in some aged individuals. Conse-

---

1. Evidence for this statement may be found in chapter 2.

quently, the first three to five years would have been the most significant period for the formation of stable long-term memories about Jesus in eyewitnesses. Evidence is presented in appendix A that suggests that, while surviving eyewitnesses would not have been numerous, some of them who were particularly lucky and hardy would still have been alive in the period that the Gospels were likely to have been written. It is safe to conclude that the memories of most eyewitnesses thirty to sixty years after the crucifixion would have been as reliable and complete as their memories three to five years after it. Not that this automatically guarantees that such memories are free from error. Human memory is capable of extraordinary feats. It works well in extracting meaning and significance from the cascade of sensory events that continuously impinge on humans. Yet this very ability to extract meaning and significance leaves human memory susceptible to transience, suggestibility, hindsight bias, and (innocent) confabulation (see chs. 2–4 and 6).

Human memory serves well in preserving the meaning and trend of events; however, it is less reliable at the level of details. In general terms, then, this is likely to have been true of the memories that were incorporated into the traditions from which the Gospel materials were derived. But further considerations relating to (1) collective memories and (2) the teaching methods likely to have been used by Jesus significantly nuance this general finding. Let us consider these one after the other. (1) While susceptible to being molded to present circumstances, the essential elements of collective memories resist change, something highly likely to have been true also of the collective memories of early Christian groups that, perforce, contributed to the traditions now found in the Synoptic Gospels (see ch. 6). (2) Jesus, like other first-century teachers, would have used repetition and memorization as one of his key pedagogical methods of instructing his disciples (see ch. 9). His teachings preserved in the Synoptic Gospels appear to be expressed in the type of memorable forms that had a high probability of being successfully transmitted from teacher to disciple.

Given these and other observations that have been made throughout this book concerning memory and its contribution to the preservation of the Gospel materials, it is now possible to form a description of their qualities. The Gospel materials were formed and preserved in an oral context. They remained in an oral context for an unknown period that could have been as short as a few years but is likely to have been decades. Previous chapters of this book (e.g., ch. 9) have argued that the teachings and doings of Jesus were preserved by mechanisms that tended to accurately transmit and preserve them, insofar as orally preserved materials can be accurately transmitted and preserved. The reliability of the written documents that eventually grew out of these oral traditions stems from the intersection of the collective memory of the earliest followers of Jesus, eyewitness memories, and the process of repetition and rehearsal that constituted the teaching methodology almost certainly adopted by the surviving disciples and other early Christian teachers. I would go so far as to describe the teaching traditions as carefully controlled oral tradition.

That a carefully controlled oral tradition lies behind much of what is found in the Synoptic Gospels is not of itself a guarantee of its authenticity. Errors might have been introduced at every stage of the formation, transmission, and preservation of the tradition. Eyewitnesses and the processes of the formation of collective memory are critical at the earliest stages of the formation of these traditions. The best research available suggests that eyewitnesses, though generally reliable, report up to 20 percent incorrect details about what they have seen (see ch. 1). They are susceptible to errors of suggestibility and hindsight bias, and over time eyewitnesses can become more confident about their errors than what they report correctly. Their memories decline rapidly over time, and even though some personal event memories are formed, this is no guarantee that such memories are better than other memories of events. In fact, characteristic of the subclass of personal event memories known as flashbulb memories is an overconfidence in the accuracy of the memory (see ch. 3). Some of this error rate declines when collective memories are formed from the accounts of several eyewitnesses, but a significant level of error remains, and almost everyone in the group comes to believe the resultant compromise. Furthermore, if there is any validity in the kind of reconstruction suggested in earlier chapters in part 2, some of the key elements of the collective memories out of which the traditions grew were largely formed after the crucial and disturbing events of Easter, which would introduce a strong element of hindsight bias. As traditions were translated into Greek, further changes would have been introduced, with yet further changes introduced as individual members of the small groups of Palestinian believers moved between the key centers of Christianity scattered around the Roman Empire. Nor should one ignore the fact that a considerable time period elapsed between the events described in the Gospels and their writing down. Finally, one cannot but observe that the Evangelists each presented a unique view of Jesus as he selected traditions to incorporate into his Gospel. Human memory has frailties that make the tradition vulnerable to error at each of the stages of its formation, and the evidence of the Synoptic Gospels reveals that the traditions were not exempt from the normal frailties of human memory.

Does this mean, then, that the general approach advocated by Bultmann is right and that one should approach all of the Synoptic traditions with doubt and accept only those that can be indisputably attributed to Jesus? Not at all! Such an approach is not only unnecessarily pessimistic; it misrepresents what is known about human memory. To be sure, eyewitness testimony may contain 20 percent error of detail. But it must be remembered that eyewitnesses have been shown to report 80 percent of details correctly, and they also almost always correctly indicate the correct general course of events (see ch. 1). In other words, even the details that are wrong are consistent with the general course of events. One would wish that accuracy of individual details might be 100 percent, but the beneficial ability of human observation and memory to make sense out of complex data means that 100 percent accuracy is just not available. It would also be comforting to be able to work out which of the 20 percent of details are incorrect in eyewitness testimony. In a law court, this is attempted by taking the evidence of multiple witnesses. With the Gospel traditions, this was done during the process of forming the collective memory of the early Christian groups. The nature of the evidence makes it impossible to check whether or not their decisions on what was accurate testimony would be the same as a modern group might make. Nor did the process of the preservation of the tradition leave many alternate records that are available to modern scrutiny. Just about all that remains is the selection of evidence preserved in the Gospels. Yet even given these careful qualifications, it must not be overlooked that eyewitness memory is generally reliable, and the eyewitness memories that lie behind the Gospel accounts should therefore be approached with an attitude that expects them to be a generally reliable record of Jesus' sayings and doings. It should further be noted that collective memory only very rarely contains information that is unrelated to actual events. There are strict limits to innovations that can be introduced into the collective memory that any group has for its founder. Any newly introduced materials must be consistent with what is remembered of the founder's doings and sayings (see chs. 6 and 9). This has to be true also of the collective memories from which the Gospel materials grew. While the collective memories of Jesus would be shaped by such things as the present circumstances of the groups of early Christians in which they flourished, they could not have been changed into something that was inconsistent with who Jesus was, what he said, and what he did. Radical change that is inconsistent with reality is almost never found in collective memories. Nor should one expect to find such change in the narrative parts of the Gospel materials.

The teachings of Jesus form a significant component of the Gospel materials, and the form in which they are expressed, combined with the known teaching activities of Jesus and his earliest followers, allow an even more positive evaluation to be placed on the aphorisms and parables attributed to Jesus. Jesus, his disciples, and several significant early Christians are depicted as teaching in the New Testament. By any teaching practices known from the ancient world, these Christian teachers would have used a pedagogy that consisted of a series of interchanges whereby the teacher invited the pupil to repeat back what had just been taught. The aphoristic-like structure, rich imagery, and parallelism of much of the teachings attributed to Jesus in the Gospels would mean that these aphorisms would have been remembered with near verbatim accuracy. They would then have been transmitted through Christian teachers to be available within the wider collective memories of early Christian groups and to these who were formulating the Gospels (see ch. 9). Parables by their very nature—coherent stories that culminate in a punch-line—were also ideal for accurate transmission.

So it can be concluded that, like most products of human memory and despite all the frailties of such memory, the Gospels should be considered to be generally reliable. If the evidence presented thus far may be relied on, then—at least for the apophthegmata, the parables, and the aphorisms—the burden of proof should lie with those who wish to claim that a saying found in the Gospels is not from Jesus or that an incident reported about him did not happen, not with those who assume its authenticity. Human memory is a remarkable facility, and the traditions found in the Synoptic Gospels may be considered to be a product of its effectiveness.

Appendix A
The Potential Pool of Eyewitnesses at the Time the Gospels Were Written

Two issues grow out of the length of time that the teachings and activities of Jesus were preserved in the memory of eyewitnesses. The first—the quality of their individual memories—has been the topic of much of this book. The second—their likely survival rates given the life expectancy of individuals living in the Roman Empire—is equally important and is the issue considered in this appendix.

First-Century Life Expectancy

As has already been observed, Jesus was crucified within a few years of 31 C.E. (Riesner 1998, 35–58), while the appearances of the Gospels of Matthew, Mark, and Luke are usually dated somewhere between 60 and 90 C.E.[1] These dates presuppose a period of at least thirty to sixty years

---

1. While it is impossible to determine the date of the writing of any of the Gospels with any certainty, at least with Luke-Acts one can give a reasonably reliable estimate of the *earliest* date that it could have been composed. Acts cannot have been written earlier than the events it describes. The last chapter of Acts places Paul in Rome awaiting an opportunity to place his case before Caesar, and Acts 28:30 states "He lived there two whole years at his own expense." So Acts must have been written at least two years after the arrival of Paul in Rome. In *Paul's Early Period*, Rainer Riesner argues that Paul arrived in Rome in the spring of 60 C.E., which if one adds the two years mentioned in Acts 28:30, gives the earliest possible date for the writing of Acts to be 62 C.E. (Riesner 1998, 225–227, 322). Udo Schnelle gives 59 C.E. as the date for Paul's arrival in Rome (2002, 45), and other possible dates are canvassed in Riesner 1998, 3–28. Indeed, there is a general consensus that Paul arrived in Rome within a few years (plus or minus) of 60 C.E. Luke—the companion volume of Acts—is highly likely to have been written at the same time as Acts, or sometime after 62, but how much after? On the basis of the separation of the eschatological discourse found in Mark

between events in the life of Jesus and the time at which they were recorded in the Gospels.[2] Modern Westerners have a reasonable expectation of living well into their seventies. Thus, in a modern context the thirty to sixty years between crucifixion and the writing of the Synoptic Gospels would be expected to fall within the lifetimes of many of the generation that witnessed the original events. But the evidence of tomb inscriptions, skeletal remains and "life-tables" that represent the demographics of the Roman Empire show that things were quite different in the ancient world.

There are considerable difficulties in determining the life expectancy and demographic profiles of the various geographic regions that made up

---

13 and Matt 24 into two segments, one particularly appropriate to the destruction of Jerusalem in 70 C.E. (Luke 21:5–36), and one particularly appropriate to the end of the world (Luke 17:20–37), most academics specializing in Luke would date it to the decade after the destruction of Jerusalem in 70 C.E., although this suggestion is based on very ill-defined evidence. Much less can be said with any confidence concerning the date of composition of the other Gospels. For example, the phrase "to this day" in Matt 27:8; 28:15 gives the impression of the passage of some time since the events described but no idea of how much. John 21:23 is usually considered evidence that the Fourth Gospel was written after the death of the Beloved Disciple, but again, without further information about when this happened, little can be said with any certainty about the dating of John. In his monograph, *Redating the New Testament* John A. T. Robinson proposed dates as early as 40–60+ for Matthew, 45–60 for Mark, 57–60+ for the Gospel of Luke (Robinson 1976, 352), and similar dates have been suggested by John Wenham (1991, xxv, 223–44) and Bo Reicke (1986, 174–80). Reicke explicitly dates Luke to around 60 (1986, 180). See also the range of dates, including one scholar who argued that Matthew was written between 40 and 50, in Davies and Allison 1988, 27–28. Robertson, Wenham, and Reicke represent some of the earliest dating that has been seriously proposed, but nevertheless, even by their dating, there is a period of ten to thirty-five years between the events of the life of Jesus and the writing of the Gospels. Most who work with the Synoptic Gospels would, however, tend to use dates closer to those suggested by Werner Georg Kümmel of 64–70 for Mark, 80–100 for Matthew, 70–90 for Luke, and 90–100 for John (1975, 98, 120, 151, 246), or those suggested by Schnelle, of shortly before or after 70 for Mark, about 90 for Matthew and Luke, and 100–110 for John (2002, 244, 266, 288).

2. See comments in chapter 8 on the possible importance of written sources earlier than the extant Gospels. It is argued there that, while it is possible that the Gospels writers may have drawn upon earlier written sources (see Luke 1:1–3), these sources are unlikely to have been written within the critical memory period of three to five years after Easter. Eyewitness memories that remain stable for this length of time are likely to be preserved for the thirty to sixty years between Easter and the writing of the Gospels.

the first-century Roman Empire.³ For example, while many epitaphs have been found on Roman-period gravestones, they do not produce reliable data about age profiles at death. One reason for this is that most babies were not given a gravestone, so reliable figures on infant mortality is hard to determine. Furthermore, some ages on the surviving gravestones are unrealistic, either because they are usually recorded only in terms of numbers ending in 5 or 0 (Parkin 1992, 6–7; see also Scheidel 1996, 53–91, especially the graphs on 78–82, 87–88)⁴ or they report ages of 160 or 170 years. Many tombs do not give an indication of the age at death, nor should it be expected that the entire population is represented by those burials that have survived. Even so, the average age on Jewish tombs (which did not report anyone older than 102 years of age) is twenty-eight years of age, which Pieter van der Horst suggests appears to be a relatively good estimate of adult life expectancy (van der Horst 1991, 73–84).⁵

On the basis of early Neolithic to Imperial Roman skeletal remains, Ian Morris gives 38.8 for males and 34.2 for females as the average age at death of adult skeletal remains for Imperial Rome (Morris 1992, 76). Note that these are average ages of *adult* skeletal remains, not that of the whole population of skeletal finds, and because of high infant mortality, life expectancy at birth is likely to have been lower.⁶ For some time peri-

---

3. As Walter Scheidel so cogently says, "The age structure of a population is a function of three variables: mortality, fertility and migration. There is no ancient evidence that permits direct measurement of any of these factors" (Scheidel 2001, 13). Both Scheidel's article (2001, 1–81) and the book *Demography and Roman Society* by Tim Parkin (1992) provide excellent introductions to the challenges of forming an accurate idea of demography in the Roman Empire.

4. See also the graph at Scheidel 1996, 99, which shows the marked preference for ages in multiples of five in the age-of-death records of the Roman army.

5. On the basis of his life table (discussed in the main text in the following paragraphs) and the analysis of skeletal remains, Bruce Frier notes two tendencies in the grave inscriptions: the very old are more likely to have an age recorded, and this age is likely to be overestimated; there is an overreporting of those who are considered to have died young. He concludes that "it does not appear that *any* of these mortality patterns [derived from tomb inscriptions in various parts of the ancient Roman world] can be correct" (Frier 1983, 343). J. Lawrence Angel also reports that, compared to the skeletal evidence, there as an overreporting of the deaths in subadult and early adult ages (Angel 1947, 18–24, esp. 22).

6. Both John Dominic Crossan and Edwin M. Yamauchi estimate that male life expectancy in the first century was between thirty-nine and forty years of age, and Crossan also states that the life expectancy of a woman was thirty-four years of age

ods skeletal remains of small children are nonexistent; at others, plentiful. Data from skeletal remains in Israel give similar results. Nagar and Torgeé report Hellenistic and Roman period skeletal remains from eight caves from the Shephelah and Samaria regions, which represent a population with a life expectancy of twenty-six years at age ten, with a mean age at death of thirty-eight for adults (Nagar and Torgeé 2003, 170), while Christian burials in the Negev from the Byzantine period reveal a population with a life expectancy of thirty years at age ten (Nagar and Sonntag 2008, 90).

For the purposes of this investigation, though, perhaps the most useful evidence of Roman-era life expectancies are found in life tables, which show, among other things, the number of survivors at various ages of an original cohort of 100,000 live births. Several lines of evidence can be cited as the basis for developing life tables for the first-century Roman Empire. For example, Bruce Frier developed an approximate life table for the population of the Roman Empire using, among other evidence, what has come to be known as Ulpian's life table (Frier 1982, 213–51; see also Bagnall and Frier 1994, 175–80; Scheidel 1996, 93–138).

Ulpian's life table is found in the third-century jurist Aemilius Macer's (fl. 230 C.E.) commentary on a law of Augustus from 6 C.E. that established a 5 percent tax on inheritances, *lex Julia de vicesima hereditatium*.[7] The text from Aemilus concerns itself with annual annuities that an heir might be ordered to pay to various legatees under the terms of the will.[8] There were several reasons that an estimate needed to be made of the total liability of the bequest. For example, another law—the *lex Falcidia* of 40 B.C.E.—decreed that the total legacies should not exceed three quarters of the entire inheritance. There were also some circumstances in which the government tax office would also need to estimate the entire worth of the life annuity. Crucial to such a calculation is some estimate of the life expectancy of the legatee, which is done on the basis of a life table. To do so, Macer cites a schedule presented by Ulpian, a jurist murdered in 223

(Crossan 1998, 181; Yamauchi 2000, 1). These appear to be estimates of the life expectancy of those who survived childhood.

7. Aemilius Macer's commentary itself survives as an edited excerpt in Justinian's *Digest*.

8. There are two basic categories of annuity: the first, a support annuity for life, called an *alimenta*; the second, an usufruct for life on the income generated from property. An usufruct is the use and profit but not the ownership of property.

APPENDIX A: THE POTENTIAL POOL OF EYEWITNESSES   193

C.E., which Ulpian presented as providing an estimate of life expectancy in calculating tax for annuities.[9] Ulpian contrasts his table with the customary way of working out life expectancy, which was to assume that legatees aged between birth and thirty years of age would live another thirty years and that the life expectancy of older legatees could be worked out by subtracting their age from the number sixty. For example, if calculated in the customary manner, a thirty-five-year-old would then be expected to live a further twenty-five years (sixty minus thirty-five). Ulpian's life table, though, adjusts these figures in a direction closer to what is claimed to be actual life expectancies of the time. Thus, according to Ulpian's table, the thirty-five-year-old would be expected to live a further twenty years. So for Ulpian, the calculation of the total value of a life annuity for a thirty-five-year-old is then done by multiplying how much it is worth in any one year by twenty (not 60–35 = 25, as had previously been done), the expected number of years for which the annuity would be collected. This, then, is the use to which Ulpian's table would have been put in its original context.

Having established the purpose of the life table, Frier next uses Ulpian's table to discover the demographic profile it gives for the population of the second-century Roman Empire, then compares it with known demographic profiles of various populations that are derived from reliable statistics. The figures in Ulpian's table are very low when compared to just about all known modern populations,[10] although they correspond closely to the demographic profile of Mauritius from 1942 to 1946, when

---

9. Frier 1982 argues that Ulpian was citing not something he had worked out but something in current use by the taxation office, although he, along with others working on the text, continues to call the table Ulpian's life table.

10. The dramatic differences between the life tables of Ulpian (as well as those cited later in this chapter) and those derived from modern populations are illustrated by the comparison between Ulpian's life table with demographic statistics for the United States and Australia. In the United States in 2006, of 100,000 live births, 99,329 will be alive one year later (compared to Frier's estimate of 64,178 for the Roman Empire), 99,147 would be alive ten years later (compared to 45,828); 98,747 alive twenty years later (cf. 40,385); 96,495 alive forty years later (cf. 26,401), and 88,057 alive sixty years later (cf. 11,096). The equivalent Australian figures for 2006–2008 for men are 99,494; 99,348; 99,055; 97,183; and 91,053; those for women are 99,558; 99,444; 99,283; 98,455; and 94,681. These were the latest figures available on 8 November 2010 at http://www.cdc.gov/nchs/data/nvsr/nvsr58/nvsr58_21.pdf and http://www.abs.gov.au/AUSSTATS/abs@.nsf/DetailsPage/3302.0.55.0012006-2008. See also Moore 1993:17–21.

the island was under British rule. Statistical analysis shows that the Mauritian figures match those of Ulpian's table very well indeed.[11] Frier further demonstrates the suitability of using the demographic profile of Mauritius by comparing it with grave inscriptions from Quattuor Coloniae around Cirta in North Africa. This comparison shows that the match between the demographic profile derived from these inscriptions is statistically very close to those of Mauritius for males between the ages of four and forty-five, and females between the ages of five and fifty-five.[12] Frier considers that the difference for those over age fifty between both Ulpian's life table and the inscriptions from Quattuor Coloniae should be explained by the notorious tendency for the elderly in antiquity to overestimate their ages.

That the demographic profile of Mauritius in the 1940s is such a close match, not only with Ulpian's table but also the profile discernable in the grave inscriptions, suggests to Frier that it is highly likely that Mauritius between 1942 and 1946 may provide a very good model for the demographics of the population of the Roman Empire. In the rest of the article he uses it, together with Ulpian's life table, to form such a model. Some of the statistics in his model are provided in table A1 below, although perhaps a further explanation is needed for the various columns. Statistics are presented for the following populations: the population that is reflected by Ulpian's life table (labeled "Ulpian"); the population statistics for Mauritius 1942–1946; and the demographic profile of the Roman Empire suggested by Frier. The label "Survivors l(x)" on a column means that the figures in

---

11. Frier 1982, 233, notes that for Mauritian males the coefficient of determination (r^2) of the standard linear regression between the actual figures from Mauritius and the interpolated figures for Ulpian is a very high 0.980, while r^2 for females is an even higher .992.

12. Frier 1982, 236, notes an r^2 of 0.969 for males between ages five and forty-five, and an r^2 of 0.995 for females between ages five and fifty-five between the calculated population demographics of Quattuor Coloniae and those of Mauritius. The demographic profile of Quattuor Coloniae was calculated on the number of graves in each age group and adding these together cumulatively from the oldest to the youngest. In his later article, which compares the age-at-death analysis of a group of 120 skeletons from Roman Pannonia with that of grave inscriptions of 813 Egyptian tombs, 2,345 tombs from Asia, Greece, and Illyricum, and 1,111 tombs of males in Iberia, Frier discovers that tomb inscriptions from Roman times found elsewhere in the territory of the former Roman Empire do not correspond as closely to his life table as he would like. He outlines several factors, similar to those noted by Peter van der Horst above, that would explain the differences. See Frier 1983, 328–44.

that column represent the number of survivors from a cohort of 100,000 live births who would still be alive in the age band indicated (0/364 days; 1–4 years; 5–9 years; 10–14 years, etc.). Thus, according to Frier's estimate, only 48,968 of the 100,000 babies would live to age five (49 percent, or just less than half), and only 671 would make it to age eighty (less than 1 percent).[13] The columns labeled "Av. Life Exp. e(x)" means the average remaining life expectancy of somebody who has already reached a certain age. Thus, according to Frier, the average remaining life expectancy once somebody has reached age fifteen is thirty-one years of age (or a total age of forty-six at death). The column labeled "% of the tot. pop. c(x)" [percentage of total population] should be self-explanatory. The column labeled "Prob. of Death q(x)" represents the probability of a person alive at age x living to the next age cohort. Thus a fifteen-year-old has a .0741 (or about 7 percent) chance of dying before reaching the age of twenty.

Others, however, are less sanguine than Frier that Ulpian's table can be used to estimate the demographic profile of the first-century Roman Empire. Tim Parkin, for example, has made several substantial criticisms of Frier's use of Ulpian, many of which relate to the interpretation of the Latin evidence and the reconstruction that Frier puts upon it (Parkin 1992, 27–31). His most cogent argument, though, is that the figures given for the over sixty-year-olds by Ulpian's table is "demographically implausible" (1992, 31). Parkin's criticism of the use of Ulpian's life table follows his previous analysis of the problems of using grave epitaphs and surviving skeletal remains. He concludes that "the various sources that have too often been supposed to be useful in producing data for demographic studies of the ancient world are in fact so plagued with biases and produce such potentially misleading or improbably information that they cannot be considered usable" (1992, 58). What should be considered instead, Parkin suggests, are a set of life tables developed by Ansley Coale and Paul Demeny, first published in 1966 and revised in 1983 (Coale and

---

13. These figures allow some observations on the nature of the population of the Roman Empire, e.g.: "The average age of the population would be very young, about 25.4 years; the average age of adults (those aged 15 and over) would be 35.7 years. ... About 35.7 percent of the population would be under 15 years of age, while 7.87 percent would be 50 years or older" (Frier 1982, 247–48). Frier also notes that in a population with this demographic makeup, every woman in the population who reached the age of fifteen would need to have about five children just to maintain population levels (1982, 248).

Table A1. Frier's Life Table for the Roman Empire

	Ulpian	Mauritius 1942–46		Frier – Demographics of Roman Empire			
Age	Survivors l(x)	Survivors l(x)	Av. Life Exp e(x)	Survivors l(x)	Av. Life Exp e(x)	% of tot. pop. c(x)	Prob. of Death q(x)
0		100,000	33	100,000	21	4	.3585
1		81,614	39	64,178	32	10	.2374
5	50459	72,193	40	48,968	37	11	.0641
10	46072	69,952	37	45,828	35	11	.0482
15	42258	68,205	32	43,618	31	10	.0741
20	38301	64,452	29	40,385	28	9	.0827
25	34328	58,939	27	37,047	26	8	.0929
30	30623	53,356	24	33,604	23	8	.1056
35	27233	48,025	22	30,055	21	7	.1216

APPENDIX A: THE POTENTIAL POOL OF EYEWITNESSES

40	24160	42,836	19	26,401	18	6	.1424
45	21392	37,289	16	22,642	16	5	.1707
50	18343	31,476	14	18,777	13	4	.2114
55	14800	25,443	11	14,807	11	3	.2506
60	9498	19,171	9	11,096	9	2	.3278
65	5986	13,041	8	7,459	7	1	.4132
70	2987	7,801	6	4,377	6	1	.5278
75	1160	4,079	5	2,067	5	0	.6753
80	426	1,803	4	671	4	0	1.0000

Demeny 1983). Coale and Demeny provide no fewer than twenty-five life tables for each gender. These tables are derived from a collection of 326 actual life tables for both genders[14] and give results for a range of values of life expectancy, as well as age-related mortality patterns. The mortality patterns are classified by Coale and Demeny according to the points of the compass: east represents high infant mortality and increasing mortality over fifty years of age; north represents low mortality for both infants and aged. The two sets of tables of most potential use for estimating the demographics of the Roman Empire, though, are those labeled south and west. South life tables are derived from actual life tables from Portugal, Spain, southern Italy, and Sicily. They feature high infant and early childhood mortality and high mortality from age sixty-five onwards (Coale and Demeny 1983, 12). West tables are "standard" or "average" pattern and based on tables from places as geographically diverse as Australia, Belgium, Canada, England, Israel, Japan, New Zealand, Sweden, and Taiwan.

As Parkin considers that the evidence from the Roman Empire is so problematical, he suggests that it is advisable to use the "west" life tables, as these are the more generic tables. Parkin then provides a range of tables for life expectancies ranging from twenty to thirty years at birth (1992, 145). This makes sense, in the light of his best estimates of actual life expectancy in the Roman Empire. As he says in another place, "There is every reason to believe that the average life expectancy at birth of the population of the Roman Empire as a whole was in the range of 20 to 30 years" (2003, 49). Although Parkin himself does not say so, given the vagaries of war and plague in the ancient world, the actual life expectancy could well have varied between twenty and thirty years of age at different time periods.

In his review of the likely demographics of Galilee in the first century, archaeologist Jonathan Reed notes the Coale and Demeny tables and cites as most pertinent that which represents a population for which the life expectancy is twenty-five years at birth (Coale-Demeny model west level 3 [female]). He also notes that medieval Tuscany and parish registers in Tudor/Stuart England show a very similar pattern (Reed 2010, 347).

---

14. Some twenty-three of these tables are for European locations that date before 1870, and every continent bar Africa is represented among the ninety life tables from 1871 to 1918. A total of 213 further tables, including those from Africa, date from the years after 1919. See Coale and Demeny 1983, 5 table 1.

APPENDIX A: THE POTENTIAL POOL OF EYEWITNESSES   199

He further points out that the population of Galilee more than doubled between 50 B.C.E. and 50 C.E. (2010, 351), despite the widespread occurrence of such diseases as dysentery, typhus, typhoid, tuberculosis, plague, and (especially) malaria. Because of the resultant high levels of infant mortality, to achieve a growing population, women who survived to adulthood would have had to give birth to between six and nine children each (2010, 350). Reed suggests that the "particular evidence relevant to first-century Galilee matches this general picture" (i.e., the Coale-Demeny model west level 3 [female]; 2010, 349).

Table A2 lists four life tables. They represent data relating to the numbers of survivors from 100,000 live births [l(x)] for the Coale-Demeny level 3 life table from the south and west group. They also include information on the average number of years remaining to be lived (expectation of life) at each age [e(x)]. For west level 3 female, additional data is provided that gives the likelihood of a person at one age level to die before the next age level [q(x)]. For three sets of data, the life expectancy at birth is twenty-five years, although those children who survive to ten years of age can expect between thirty-six and forty-one further years of life, on average.

As may be observed, the differences are not that great between the survival rates for the south and west patterns for both men and women. In west level 3, the life expectancy at birth of men is less than that of women (22.85 versus 25.00), and more women survived to old age than men (e.g., 7,934 versus 5,432 at age seventy). But these differences lie well within the error range of any estimates possible, given the general uncertainty provided by the archeological and other data from the Roman period. There seems no reason to differ from the practice of Parkin (1983) and Reed (2010) to use the life table west level 3 female as a possible estimate of the demographic profile of the Roman Empire in general and first-century Galilee and Judea in particular, provided that it is realized that the life table is a general representation rather than an exact model.

What is perhaps worthy of note, though, is an observation made in several places by Parkin. For example, as he comments on the very great differences between modern and ancient life expectancies, he says, "it must be stressed … that this does not mean that people are living significantly longer lives today than they did some 2,000 years ago, only that *more* are surviving into old age because of a lowered risk of mortality in early years, and that the proportion of older people is also growing because of lower fertility rates" (Parkin 2003, 47–48). Thus, while life

Table A2: Coale-Demeny South and West Models Level 3

	South Level 3						West Level 3					
	Women		Men				Women			Men		
Age	Survivors l(x)	Av. Life Exp e(x)	Survivors l(x)	Av. Life Exp e(x)	Survivors l(x)	Av. Life Exp e(x)	Prob. of Death q(x)	Survivors l(x)	Av. Life Exp e(x)
0	100000	25	100000	25	100000	25	.30556	100000	23
1	73567	33	71056	34	69444	35	.21582	64826	34
5	51304	43	50567	43	54456	40	.06061	50906	39
10	47505	41	47212	41	51156	38	.04738	48041	36
15	45613	37	45701	37	48732	34	.06153	46099	33
20	43123	34	43507	34	45734	31	.07660	43579	29
25	40192	32	40368	31	42231	29	.08565	40201	27
30	37257	29	37455	28	38614	26	.09654	36713	24

APPENDIX A: THE POTENTIAL POOL OF EYEWITNESSES 201

35	34421	26	34768	25	34886	24	.10541	33035	21
40	31662	23	32034	22	31208	21	.11227	29177	19
45	29074	20	29058	19	27705	18	.11967	25101	16
50	26555	17	25911	16	24389	16	.15285	21092	14
55	23575	14	22383	13	20661	13	.19116	16915	12
60	20003	10	18412	10	16712	10	.27149	12932	10
65	15193	8	13746	8	12175	8	.34835	8936	8
70	9858	6	8889	6	7934	6	.47131	5432	6
75	4829	4	4450	4	4194	5	.60808	2694	5
80	1510	3	1480	3	1644	4	.73485	944	3
85	317	2	333	2	436	3	.86502	225	2
90	31	2	37	2	59	2	.95126	27	2
95	1	1	1	1	3	1	1.00000	1	1

expectancy at birth in the ancient world was quite low, there were still significant numbers of individuals who survived into their sixties and seventies.[15]

The Potential Pool of Eyewitnesses to the Life and Ministry of Jesus

Any of the potential demographic profiles of the population of the Roman Empire cited so far may be used as the basis of a statistical model by which one can estimate the number of eyewitnesses to the life and ministry of Jesus who might still be alive at the time of the writing of the Gospels. Naturally, such a model must assume that the demographics of first-century Palestine would not be that different from those of the wider empire. On the basis of the kind of evidence noted above and also cited by Jonathan Reed (2010), this might be considered to be a fair assumption. In any event, the actual demographics of Palestine are not likely to be dramatically different from the rest of the first-century Mediterranean.

Which particular life table should be used to estimate the number of surviving eyewitnesses could be debated. Of those reported so far, Frier's life table has larger mortality rates for both infants and the aged than any of the level 3 Coale-Demeny tables. For example, Frier estimates that approximately 671 individuals out of 100,000 live births would survive to age eighty, while the Coale-Demeny life table west level 3 female has it that 1,644 individuals will survive to that age. If anything, then, the Frier life table is likely to underrepresent the number of potential eyewitnesses surviving at the time the Gospels were actually written. It may, in fact, be useful to compare the results that can be obtained by the two life tables, given that they are based on different types of evidence. Table A3 gives the results of using the life tables of both Frier and Coale-Demeny level 3 female to estimate the number of eyewitnesses of Jesus' ministry who would be still alive at different periods after the crucifixion. They are given

---

15. One might note that all the minimum ages set for the offices of quaestor, praetor, and consul (approximately thirty, thirty-nine, forty-two, respectively) are greater than the estimated life expectancy at birth of between twenty and thirty years. A population life expectancy of less than thirty did not mean that there were significant numbers of thirty- to fifty-year-olds who did not survive. One might consult with profit the list of known ages of Magistracies prior to the Sullan Reforms in Harlow and Laurence 2002, 105 table 8.1 and the further data found on 104–10.

for three separate groups of potential eyewitnesses: the inhabitants of Capernaum, a very rough estimate that represents the potential crowds from the villages around the northern shores of Lake Galilee (labeled "Large Crowds"), and those who were in Jerusalem during the week that ended with the crucifixion of Jesus.

Capernaum was chosen because Jesus used it as the base for his public ministry, and several of the Gospel accounts are located there (Matt 4:13; 8:5; 17:24; Mark 1:21; 2:1; 9:33; Luke 4:31; 7:1). The figures are derived from two datum points. The first is the estimate of the population of first-century Capernaum provided by archaeologists, who give estimates of population ranging from 1,000 to 1,700.[16] Thus an approximation of 1,500 individuals is unlikely to underestimate the total population of first-century Capernaum. But how many of this group would be able to act as eyewitnesses to the life of Jesus, especially after the period of thirty to sixty years? The life tables provide the second datum point with which to answer this question. Young children would have very uncertain memories, thus it might be best to consider only those above the age of fifteen years at the time of Jesus as candidates for eyewitnesses. According to Frier's table, those above fifteen years of age would form approximately 64 percent[17] of the total population, or 964 individuals.[18] The equivalent figure from the Coale-Demeny life table west level 3 female is 1,005. The

---

16. Jonathan Reed concludes the population of first-century Capernaum to be 1,700 (1992, 15), although this has been revised downward to 1,000 in Crossan & Reed 2001, 81, and to between 600 and 1,500 in Reed 2000, 152. Stanislao Loffreda notes that the town grew to its greatest extend during the Byzantine period, where the population might have been as high as 1,500 people (Loffreda 1986, 18). An estimate of 1,500 is perhaps a little generous but has to be within one order of magnitude of the correct number.

17. The spreadsheet on which this calculation is based, like that of Frier's original statistics, carried an accuracy of 2 decimal places. To make it easier to read, the table reports these to the nearest whole number. Any difference between 52 percent and adding the whole numbers listed in the tables for the relevant age groups may be attributed to the greater "accuracy" of the underlying figures.

18. Of course, to derive exactly 964 individuals from the very approximate starting number of "about 1,500" is to add much greater accuracy than the figures warrant. It might be better to say "about 1,000." On the other hand, if each age-step was rounded in this manner, the final estimates would contain a considerable rounding error. Thus it was decided to keep these exact figures, although the reader should keep in mind that they are at best only accurate to one significant figure and probably only accurate to one order of magnitude.

actual number may differ a little from these two estimates but appears more than likely to fall within the range 950 to 1,050 individuals. In a village as small as Capernaum, Jesus and his doings would have to be well known to everyone in the village, including this group of potential eyewitnesses.

That those living at Capernaum would form part of the group of potential eyewitnesses is a given, and it is possible to gain some estimate of the number of individuals concerned. It is quite a different matter trying to estimate how many were in the large crowds that are said to have listened to and observed the miracles of Jesus at various times in his ministry (e.g., Matt 4:25; 8:1; 13:2; 19:2). Just how many people might be in a "large crowd," and would there be more of them in the plural grouping, "large crowds" (e.g., Matt 4:25)? There are two estimates of crowd numbers in the Gospel accounts, the largest being found in Matt 14:13–21; Mark 6:30–44; Luke 9:10–17; and John 6:14, which all relate a miracle of Jesus where five thousand men were fed, as well as women and children. Is this a typical number of the kind of crowds that listened to Jesus, or is it exceptional that such a large number would gather? Would the elderly be underrepresented at this event? Were there more men than women present? Did anybody actually make a head count, or is five thousand but a rough estimate? These questions are impossible to answer, but if a large number of older children and women were present but not included in the count of "five thousand men," an upper limit might be ten thousand potential eyewitnesses. This would be a large number indeed, considering the sizes of the villages around the northern parts of Galilee and also the logistical problems associated with the gathering and the movement of such a large number of people across the undulating countryside. Naturally, the potential number of eyewitnesses in Galilee extend beyond the crowds present at the feeding of the five thousand, but as a very rough guide, a case could be made for using ten thousand as a possible estimate of all those from the small villages in the region who may have had eyewitness memories of Jesus.[19]

---

19. Jesus is never recorded as entering Sepphoris and Tiberius, the two large cities in the district. That some from these cities were among the crowds that heard him is likely, but it is impossible to say how many. Indeed, it is not unlikely that Jesus had a much smaller impact on Tiberius and Sepphoris than on the smaller villages (see McIver 1997c, 221–32).

APPENDIX A: THE POTENTIAL POOL OF EYEWITNESSES

The estimate of the population of Jerusalem is derived from that of Magan Broshi, who primarily uses population densities and the known area of Jerusalem to form his estimates of its population at different time periods, though he also takes into consideration the water supply and whether it would have been adequate to support the population suggested by a consideration of area and population density. He concludes that, at the time of Herod the Great, Jerusalem had a population of forty thousand and just before its destruction a population of eighty thousand (Broshi 1978, 12; Shanks 1995, 130). At the time of Jesus, the population would have fallen somewhere between these two numbers. As the population of Jerusalem during the week that culminated with the crucifixion of Jesus was swelled by those who had come to celebrate Passover, it is probably reasonable to take the higher number as the basis for an estimate of the number of eyewitnesses.[20] Again, one should probably only consider those over the age of fifteen at the time, which gives a very rough estimate of the possible number of eyewitnesses to be 51,432 (from Frier's life table) or 51,750 (from Coale-Demeney), or somewhere between 51,000 and 52,000 in round numbers. Whereas it was possible to be very confident that everyone in Capernaum knew Jesus, such confidence is not possible in the case of Jerusalem. The triumphal entry and the cleansing of the temple would have made him notorious, and the fact that the Romans paraded him through the city on the way to the crucifixion would mean that there would be few in the city who did not know of his existence. Furthermore, a good many would have personally witnessed at least some of the activity that took place during the last week of his life. Even so, the figure of about 52,000 seems to be an upper estimate of the actual number of potential eyewitnesses.

Given these starting numbers, table A3 records how many eyewitnesses the two life tables suggest would survive for various time intervals between the crucifixion and the writing of the Gospels?

The three columns of table A3 give as a rough estimate a pool of 62,000 to 63,000 potential adult eyewitnesses immediately after the life and ministry of Jesus. Given these starting numbers and the life tables, it is possible

---

20. It is impossible to give a reliable estimate of how much the population of Jerusalem expanded during the larger religious festivals, although the already-crowded living conditions and the absolute upper limit on the availability of water would tend to limit the total number of additional bodies that could be added to the city for even short periods.

Table A3: Surviving Eyewitnesses of Jesus at Later Time Periods

	According to Life Table of Frier				According to Coale-Demeny West Level 3 Females			
	Capernaum	Large Crowds	Jerusalem	Subtotals	Capernaum	Large Crowds	Jerusalem	Subtotals
Yr 0	964	10,000	51,432	62,396	1,005	10,000	51,750	62,755
Yr +5	826	8,570	44,075	53,471	847	8,636	44,692	54,175
Yr +10	697	7,225	37,159	45,081	701	7,356	38,069	46,126
Yr +15	576	5,974	30,723	37,273	573	6,174	31,952	38,700
Yr +20	465	4,826	24,819	30,110	466	5,094	26,360	31,919
Yr +25	365	3,790	19,493	23,648	374	4,117	21,307	25,799
Yr +30	277	2,874	14,782	17,933	294	3,244	16,787	20,326
Yr +35	201	2,084	10,721	13,006	224	2,469	12,775	15,467
Yr +40	138	1,427	7,338	8,902	162	1,786	9,243	11,191

Yr + 45	87	906	4,662	5,655	110	1,208	6,250	7,568
Yr + 50	50	515	2,650	3,215	67	740	3,830	4,637
Yr + 55	24	252	1,296	1,572	36	399	2,067	2,502
Yr + 60	9	97	499	606	16	177	918	1,111

to estimate how many might be alive thirty or even sixty years after the events of Jesus' life and ministry.[21] Of the 60,000 or so potential eyewitnesses, between 18,000 and 20,000 would be still alive after thirty years, and between 600 and 1,100 after sixty years. Of course, the population profile is based on the assumption that the population is static. Periods of war and natural disasters could and did make significant reductions in survival rates. Such events were common in the ancient world. Rodney Stark gives a catalogue of the natural and social disasters that happened to Syrian Antioch, which might serve as a case study. During its six hundred years of intermittent Roman rule, the city was taken by force eleven times and plundered and sacked on five of those occasions. It was burned in whole or in major part four times, not including the substantial fires that were associated with the six times that major riots wracked the whole city. It was destroyed by earthquake eight times; there were three killer epidemics in which the death rate was higher than 25 percent and five serious famines. "That comes to forty-one natural and social catastrophes, or an average of one every fifteen years" (Stark 1991, 197–98). That these types of natural and social catastrophes would also be present in Palestine is a given. No doubt many of the potential eyewitnesses felt the severity of the famine that took place under the reign of Claudius according to Acts 11:28–29 and for which Paul collected money for the relief of the believers in Judea (Acts 11:29; see also Rom 15:25–28; 2 Cor 9:1–5). Nor would they have escaped the general disasters attendant on the revolt against Rome that ended with the destruction of the temple in 70 C.E., and many would have perished at that time.

Not only this, most ancient populations were relatively settled. Thus, if we take one of the later dates that have been suggested for the writing of the Gospels (e.g., 90 C.E.), and if indeed, as the life table might predict, there were as few as nine surviving eyewitnesses from Capernaum to the life and ministry of Jesus, we must ask whether or not most of them would still have been living in Capernaum, and not where the Gospel materials

---

21. The spreadsheet calculations were derived by using the following procedure for each of the three groups: an initial demographic profile of the group for Year 0 was determined for each group using the percentages provided by the life tables. Then, at iterations of five years, the numbers to survive from each age group were determined from the "Probability of Death q(x)" column of the life tables. The number of survivors from all the age groups were then totaled, and these totals were consolidated into table A3.

were gathered into their final form. On the other hand, if one or more of the Gospels was written at the earlier date of, say, 60 C.E., or at about the thirty-plus year mark, there could have been approximately 277 surviving eyewitnesses from Capernaum. But how many of them would have moved away from Capernaum and been available to the Evangelists writing their Gospels? Peter and some of the other disciples who were located at Capernaum at the time of Jesus' ministry clearly traveled nationally and internationally, but how many of the other potential eyewitnesses did? There is no reason to suppose that Luke 1:2 is incorrect in stating that eyewitnesses had significant input into the Gospel accounts. But this input is much more likely to have been made in the early years after the resurrection as the tradition was forming, and only a very few of the most hardy and lucky eyewitnesses would have been available for consultation in the latter half of the first century. Bauckham, then, appears to be correct in his assessment that "living eyewitnesses were becoming scarce" (2006, 7) when Matthew, Luke, and John were composed. There were scarce indeed! Indeed, if the usual dating of Mark is correct, they were probably also scarce when Mark was produced. Nevertheless, as is evident from the life tables, some surviving eyewitness would have been available to the Evangelists to consult had they so wished.

WORKS CITED

Aguilar, Paloma, and Carsten Humlebaek. 2002. Collective Memory and National Identity in the Spanish Democracy: The Legacies of Francoism and the Civil War. *History and Memory* 14:121–64.

Allan, Diana. 2005. Mythologising *al-Nakba*: Narratives, Collective Identity and Cultural Practice among Palestinian Refugees in Lebanon. *Oral History* 33:47–56.

Angel, J. Lawrence. 1947. The Length of Life in Ancient Greece. *Journal of Gerontology* 2:18–24.

Asselen, Marieke van, Rob H. J. Van der Lubbe and Albert Postma. 2006. Are Space and Time Automatically Integrated in Episodic Memory? *Memory* 14:232–40.

Atherton, Catherine 1998. Children, Animals, Slaves and Grammar. Pages 214–44 in *Pedagogy and Power: Rhetorics of Classical Learning*. Edited by Yun Lee Too and Niall Livingstone. Cambridge: Cambridge University Press.

Bagnall, Roger S., and Bruce W. Frier. 1994. *The Demography of Roman Egypt*. Cambridge: Cambridge University Press.

Bahrick, Harry P. 1984. Semantic Memory Content in Permastore: Fifty Years of Memory for Spanish Learned in School. *Journal of Experimental Psychology: General* 113:1–29.

———. 2000. Long Term Maintenance of Knowledge. Pages 247–362 in *The Oxford Handbook of Memory*. Edited by Endel Tulving and Furgus I. M. Craik. Oxford: Oxford University Press.

Bahrick, Harry P., P. O. Bahrick, and R. P. Wittlinger. 1975. Fifty Years of Memory for Names and Faces: A Cross-Sectional Approach. *Journal of Experimental Psychology: General* 104:54–75.

Bailey, Kenneth E. 1991. Informal Controlled Oral Tradition and the Synoptic Gospels. *Asia Journal of Theology* 5:34–54.

———. 1995. Middle Eastern Oral Tradition and the Synoptic Gospels. *Expository Times* 106:363–67.

Bartlett, Frederic C. 1961. *Remembering: A Study in Experimental and Social Psychology*. Cambridge: Cambridge University Press.

Basden, Barbara H., Matthew B. Reysen, and David R. Basden. 2002. Transmitting False Memories in Social Groups. *American Journal of Psychology* 115:211–31.

Basden, Barbara H., David R. Basden, Susan Bryner, and Robert L. Thomas III. 1997. A Comparison of Group and Individual Remembering: Does Collaboration Disrupt Retrieval Strategies. *Journal of Experimental Psychology: Learning, Memory, and Cognition* 23:1176-89.

Bauckham, Richard. 2006. *Jesus and the Eyewitnesses: The Gospels as Eyewitness Testimony.* Grand Rapids: Eerdmans.

Bauer, Patricia J., Jennifer A. Wenner, Patricia L. Dropick, and Sandi S. Wewerka. 2000. *Parameters of Remembering and Forgetting in the Transition from Infancy to Early Childhood.* Oxford: Society for Research in Child Development.

Baum, Armin D. 2008a. *Der mündliche Faktor und seine Bedeutung für die synoptische Frage.* Tübingen: Francke.

———. 2008b. Matthew's Sources—Written or Oral? A Rabbinic Analogy and Empirical Insights. Pages 1-23 in *Built opon the Rock: Studies in the Gospel of Matthew.* Edited by Daniel M. Gurtner and John Nolland. Grand Rapids, Eerdmans.

Baumeister, Roy F., and Stephen Hastings. 1997. Distortions of Collective Memory: How Groups Flatter and Deceive Themselves. Pages 277-93 in *Collective Memory of Political Events: Social Psychological Perspectives.* Edited by James W. Pennebaker, Dario Paez, and Bernand Rimé. Mahwah, N.J.: Erlbaum.

Baym, Carol L., and Brian De Gonsalves. 2010. Comparison of Neural Activity That Leads to True Memories, False Memories and Forgetting: An fMRI Study of the Misinformation Effect. *Cognitive, Affective and Behavioral Neuroscience* 10:339-48.

Ben-Yehuda, Nachman. 1996. *The Masada Myth: Collective Memory and Mythmaking in Israel.* Madison: University of Wisconsin Press.

Berntsen, Dorthe, and Dorthe K. Thomsen. 2005. Personal Memories for Remote Historical Events: Accuracy and Clarity of Flashbulb Memories Related to World War II. *Journal of Experimental Psychology: General* 134:245.

Betz, Andrew L., John J. Skowronski, and Thomas M. Ostrom. 1996. Shared Realities: Social Influence and Stimulus Memory. *Social Cognition* 14:113-40.

Blomberg, Craig L. 1990. *Interpreting the Parables.* Leicester, U.K.: Apollos.

———. 1991. Interpreting the Parables of Jesus: Where Are We and Where Do We Go from Here? *Catholic Biblical Quarterly* 53:50-78.

Bockmuehl, Markus. 2007. New Testament *Wirkungsgeschichte* and the Early Christian Appeal to Living Memory. Pages 341-68 in *Memory in the Bible and Antiquity.* Edited by Loren T. Stuckenbruck, Stephen C. Barton, and Benjamin G. Wold. WUNT 212. Tübingen: Mohr Siebeck.

Bodnar, John. 1992. *Remaking America: Public Memory, Commemoration, and Patriotism in the Twentieth Century.* Princeton: Princeton University Press.

Bonds-Raacke, Jennifer M., Lakeysha S. Freyer, Sandra D. Nicks, and Rena T. Durr. 2001. Hindsight Bias Demonstrated in the Prediction of a Sporting Event. *The Journal of Social Psychology* 141:349-52.

Bradfield, Amy, and Gary L. Wells. 2005. Not the Same Old Hindsight Bias: Outcome Information Distorts a Broad Range of Retrospective Judgments. *Memory and Cognition* 33:120-30.

Brainerd, C. J. 2005. Fuzzy-Trace Theory: Memory. Pages 219-38 in Izawa and Ohta 2005.

Brainerd, C. J., D. G. Payne, Ron Wright, and V. F. Reyna. 2003. Phantom Recall. *Journal of Memory and Language* 48:445–67.
Brainerd, C. J., and V. F. Reyna. 1998. When Things That Were Never Experienced Are Easier to "Remember" Than Things That Were. *Psychological Science* 9:484–89.
———. 2004. Fuzzy-Trace Theory and Memory Development. *Developmental Review* 24:396–439.
Brainerd, C. J., Y. Yang, V. F. Reyna, M. L. Howe, and B. A. Mills. 2008. Semantic Processing in "Associative" False Memory. *Psychonomic Bulletin and Review* 15:1035–53.
Brewer, William F. 1988. Memory for Randomly Sampled Autobiographical Events. Pages 23–90 in *Remembering Reconsidered: Ecological and Traditional Approaches to the Study of Memory*. Edited by Ulric Neisser and Eugene Winograd. Cambridge: Cambridge University Press.
Brueckner, Katja, and Steffen Moritz. 2009. Emotional Valence and Semantic Relatedness Differentially Influence False Recognition in Mild Cognitive Impairment, Alzheimer's Disease, and Healthy Elderly. *Journal of the International Neuropsychological Society* 15:268–76.
Brog, Mooli. 2003. Victims and Victors: Holocaust and Military Commemoration in Israel Collective Memory. *Israel Studies* 8:65–99.
Broshi, Magan. June 1978. Estimating the Population of Ancient Jerusalem. *Biblical Archaeological Review* 4.2:10–15.
Brown, Robert, and James Kulik. 1977. Flashbulb Memories. *Cognition* 5:73–99.
Bruce, Darryl, L. Amber Wilcox-O'Hearn, John A. Robinson, Kimberly Phillips-Grant, Lori Francis, and Marilyn C. Smith. 2005. Fragment Memories Mark the End of Childhood Amnesia. *Memory and Cognition* 33:567–76.
Budge, Ernest A. Wallis. 1934. *The Wit and Wisdom of the Christian Fathers of Egypt: The Syrian Version of the* Apophthegmata Patrum. London: Oxford University Press.
Bultmann, Rudolf. 1935. *Jesus and the Word*. London: Ivor Nicholson & Watson.
———. 1952. *Theology of the New Testament*. 2 vols. London: SCM.
———. 1968. *The History of the Synoptic Tradition*. Oxford: Blackwell.
Burke, Peter. 1997. *Varieties of Cultural History*. Ithaca, N.Y.: Cornell University Press.
Byrskog, Samuel. 2002. *Story as History—History as Story: The Gospel Tradition in the Context of Ancient Oral History*. Boston: Brill.
———. 2004. A New Perspective on the Jesus Tradition: Reflections on James D. G. Dunn's *Jesus Remembered*. *Journal for the Study of the New Testament* 26:457–71.
———. 2006. A New Quest for the *Sitz im Leben*: Social Memory, the Jesus Tradition and the Gospel of Matthew. *New Testament Studies* 52:321–22.
Cabeza, Roberto, and E. Robert Lennartson. 2005. False Memory across Languages: Implicit Associative Response vs Fuzzy Trace Views. *Memory* 13:1–5.
Carruthers, Mary J. 1990. *The Book of Memory: A Study of Memory in Medieval Culture*. Cambridge: Cambridge University Press.
Ceci, Stephen J. 1995. False Beliefs: Some Developmental and Clinical Considerations. Pages 91–125 in *Memory Distortion: How Minds, Brains, and Societies Reconstruct the Past*. Edited by Daniel L. Schacter. Cambridge: Harvard University Press.

Christianson, Sven-Åke. 1992. Do Flashbulb Memories Differ from Other Types of Emotional Memories? Pages 191–211 in *Affect and Accuracy in Recall: Studies of Flashbulb Memories*. Edited by Eugene Winograd and Ulric Neisser. Cambridge: Cambridge University Press.

Chrobac, Quin M., and Maria S. Zaragoza. 2008. Inventing Stories: Forcing Witnesses to Fabricate Entire Fictitious Events Leads to Freely Reported False Memories. *Psychonomic Bulletin and Review* 15:1990–95.

Coale, Ansley J., and Paul Demeny. 1983. *Regional Model Life Tables and Stable Populations*. 2nd ed. New York: Academic Press.

Coluccia, Emanuele, Carmela Bianco, and Marie A. Brandimonte. 2006. Dissociating Veridicality, Consistency, and Confidence in Autobiographical and Event Memories of the *Columbia* Shuttle Disaster. *Memory* 14:452–70.

Confino, Alon. 1997. Collective Memory and Cultural History: Problems of Method. *American Historical Review* 102:1386–1403.

Conway, Martin A. 1995. *Flashbulb Memories*. Hove: Elrbaum.

———. 1997. The Inventory of Experience: Memory and Identity. Pages 21–45 in *Collective Memory of Political Events: Social Psychological Perspectives*. Edited by James W. Pennebaker, Dario Paez, and Bernand Rimé. Mahwah, N.J.: Erlbaum.

Conway, Martin A., Gillian Cohen, and Nicola Stanhope. 1991. On the Very Long-Term Retention of Knowledge Acquired through Formal Education: Twelve Years of Cognitive Psychology. *Journal of Experimental Psychology: General* 120:395–409.

Cooper, Joel. 2007. *Cognitive Dissonance: Fifty Years of a Classic Theory*. Los Angeles: Sage.

Cranfield, C. E. B. 1959. *The Gospel according to Saint Mark*. Cambridge: Cambridge University Press.

Crawley, Ros A., and Madeline J. Eacott. 2006. Memories of Early Childhood: Qualities of the Experience of Recollection. *Memory and Cognition* 34:287–94.

Cribiore, Raffaella. 1996. *Writing, Teachers, and Students in Graeco-Roman Egypt*. Atlanta: Scholars Press.

Crombag, Hans F. M., Willem A. Wagenaar, and Peter J. van Koppen. 1996. Crashing Memories and the Problem of "Source Monitoring." *Applied Cognitive Psychology* 10:95–104.

Crossan, John Dominic. 1983. *In Fragments: The Aphorisms of Jesus*. San Francisco: Harper & Row.

———. 1998. *The Birth of Christianity: Discovering What Happened in the Years Immediately after the Execution of Jesus*. San Fancisco: HarperSanFrancisco.

Crossan, John Dominic, and Jonathan L. Reed. 2001. *Excavating Jesus: Beneath the Stones, Behind the Texts*. San Francisco: HarperSanFrancisco.

Cunningham, David, Colleen Nugent, and Caitlin Sloddin. 2010. The Durability of Collective Memory: Reconciling the "Greensboro Massacre." *Social Forces* 88:1517–42.

Curci, Antonietta, and Olivier Luminet. 2006. Follow-Up of a Cross-National Comparison on Flashbulb and Event Memory for the September 11th Attacks. *Memory* 14:329–44.

Dalton, Andrea L., and Meredyth Daneman. 2006. Social Suggestibility to Central and Peripheral Misinformation. *Memory* 14:486–501.
Davies, W. D., and Dale C. Allison. 1988. *A Critical and Exegetical Commentary on the Gospel according to Saint Matthew*. Vol. 1. Edinburgh: Clark.
DeConick, April D. 2008. Human Memory and the Sayings of Jesus: Contemporary Experimental Exercises in the Transmission of Jesus Traditions. Pages 135–79 in *Jesus, the Voice and the Text*. Edited by Tom Thatcher. Waco, Tex.: Baylor University Press.
Deese, J. 1959. On the Prediction of Occurrence of Particular Verbal Intrusions in Immediate Recall. *Journal of Experimental Psychology* 58:17–22.
Dibelius, Martin. 1971. *From Tradition to Gospel*. Cambridge: Clarke.
Dodd, C. H. 1971. *The Founder of Christianity*. London: Collins.
Dundes, Alan. 1999. *Holy Writ as Oral Lit: The Bible as Folklore*. Lanham: Rowman & Littlefield.
Dunn, James D. G. 1987. *The Living Word*. London: SCM.
———. 1998. *The Theology of Paul the Apostle*. Grand Rapids: Eerdmans.
———. 2000. Jesus in Oral Memory: The Initial Stages of the Jesus Tradition. *Society of Biblical Literature Seminar Papers* 39:287–326.
———. 2003a. Altering the Default Setting: Re-envisaging the Early Transmission of the Jesus Tradition. *New Testament Studies* 49:139–75.
———. 2003b. *Jesus Remembered*. Grand Rapids: Eerdmans.
———. 2004. On History, Memory and Eyewitnesses: In Response to Bengt Holmberg and Samuel Byrskog. *Journal for the Study of the New Testament* 26:473–87.
———. 2005. *A New Perspective on Jesus: What the Quest for the Historical Jesus Missed*. Grand Rapids: Baker Academic.
———. 2007. Social Memory and the Oral Jesus Tradition. Pages 179–94 in *Memory in the Bible and Antiquity*. Edited by Stephen C. Barton, Loren T. Stuckenbruck, and Benjamin G. Wold. WUNT 212. Tübingen: Mohr Siebeck.
Ebbinghaus, Herman. 1964. *Memory: A Contribution to Experimental Psychology*. New York: Dover.
Eddy, Paul Rhodes, and Gregory A. Boyd. 2007. *The Jesus Legend: A Case for the Historical Reliability of the Synoptic Jesus Tradition*. Grand Rapids: Baker Academic.
Edwards, Derek, and Jonathon Potter 1992. The Chancellor's Memory: Rhetoric and Truth in Discursive Remembering. *Applied Cognitive Psychology* 6:187–215.
Epstein, I., ed. 1959. *The Babylonian Talmud: Seder Mo'ed 'Erubin*. New York: Rebecca Bennet.
Feldman-Sevelsberg, Pamela, Flavien T. Ndonko, and Song Yang. 2005. Remembering "The Troubles": Reproductive Insecurity and the Management of Memory in Cameroon. *Africa* 75:10–28.
Fentress, James, and Chris Wickham. 1992. *Social Memory*. Oxford: Blackwell.
Festinger, Leon. 1957. *A Theory of Cognitive Dissonance*. Stanford, Calif.: Stanford University Press.
Festinger, Leon, Henry W. Riecken, and Stanley Schachter. 1956. *When Prophecy Fails*. New York: Harper & Row.

Fields, R. Douglas. Feb. 2005. Making Memories Stick. *Scientific American* 292.2:59–65.
Fischhoff, Baruch. 1975. Hindsight ≠ Foresight: The Effect of Outcome Knowledge on Judgment Under Uncertainty. *Journal of Experimental Psychology: Human Perception and Performance* 1:288–99.
———. 2007. An Early History of Hindsight Research. *Social Cognition* 25:10–13.
Fiske, Kate E., and David B. Pillemer. 2006. Adult Recollections of Earliest Childhood Dreams: A Cross-Cultural Study. *Memory* 14:57–67.
Fodor, Jerry. 2000. *The Mind Doesn't Work That Way: The Scope and Limits of Computational Psychology.* Cambridge: MIT Press.
Frier, Bruce. 1982. Roman Life Expectancy: Ulpian's Evidence. *Harvard Studies in Classical Philology* 86:213–51.
———. 1983. Roman Life Expectancy: The Pannonian Evidence. *Phoenix* 37:328–44.
Gedi, Noa, and Yigal Elam. 1996. Collective Memory—What Is It? *History and Memory* 8:30–50.
Gerhardsson, Birger. 1986. *The Gospel Tradition.* Malmö: Gleerup.
———. 1998. *Memory and Manuscript.* Grand Rapids: Eerdmans.
———. 2005. The Secret of the Transmission of the Unwritten Jesus Tradition. *New Testament Studies* 51:1–18.
Goodacre, Mark. 2001. *The Synoptic Problem: A Way through the Maze.* London: Sheffield Academic Press.
———. 2002. *The Case against Q.* Harrisburg, Pa.: Trinity Press International.
Goody, Jack, and Ian Watt. 1968. The Consequences of Literacy. Pages 27–68 in *Literacy in Traditional Societies.* Edited by Jack Goody. Cambridge: Cambridge University Press.
Griffin, Larry J. 2004. "Generations and Collective Memory" Revisited: Race, Region, and Memory of Civil Rights. *American Sociological Review* 69:544–57.
Halbwachs, Maurice. 1992. *On Collective Memory.* Chicago: University of Chicago.
Halford, W. Kim, Emma Keefer, and Susan M. Osgarby. 2002. "How Has the Week Been for You Two?" Relationship Satisfaction and Hindsight Memory Biases in Couples' Reports of Relationship Events. *Cognitive Therapy and Research* 26:759–73.
Harley, Erin M., Keri A. Carlsen, and Geoffrey R. Loftus. 2004. The "Saw-It-All-Along" Effect: Demonstrations of Visual Hindsight Bias. *Journal of Experimental Psychology: Learning, Memory, and Cognition* 30:960–68.
Harlow, Mary, and Ray Laurence. 2002. *Growing Up and Growing Old in Ancient Rome.* London: Routledge.
Harvey, John H., Shelly K. Stein, and Paul K. Scott. 1995. Fifty Years of Grief: Accounts and Reported Psychological Reactions of Normandy Invasion Veterans. *Journal of Narrative and Life History* 5:315–32.
Hasian, Marouf, Jr. 2004. Collective Amnesias: The *Rudolph Kastner* Trial and Holocaust Consciousness in Israel, 1948–1955. *The Southern Communication Journal* 69:136–56.
Hill, Nicole M., and Walter Schneider. 2006. Brain Changes in the Development of Expertise: Neuroanatomical and Neurophysiological Evidence about Skill-Based

Adaptations. Pages in 653–82 *The Cambridge Handbook of Expertise and Expert Performance*. Edited by K. Anders Ericsson, Neil Charness, Paul J. Feltovich, and Robert R. Hoffman. Cambridge: Cambridge University Press.

Hirst, William, and David Gluck. 1999. Revisiting John Dean's Memory. Pages 253–81 in *Ecological Approaches to Cognition: Essays in Honor of Ulric Neisser*. Edited by Eugene Winograd, Robyn Fivush, and William Hirst. Mahwah, N.J.: Erlbaum.

Hock, Ronald F., and Edward N. O'Neil. 1986. *The Progymnasmata*. Vol. 1 of *The Chreia in Ancient Rhetoric*. Society of Biblical Literature Texts and Translations 27. Atlanta: Scholars Press.

Hoffrage, Ulrich, Ralph Hertwig, and Gerd Gigerenzer. 2000. Hindsight Bias: A By-Product of Knowledge Updating? *Journal of Experimental Psychology: Learning, Memory, and Cognition* 26:566–81.

Holmberg, Bengt. 2004. Questions of Method in James Dunn's *Jesus Remembered*. *Journal for the Study of the New Testament* 26:445–57.

Hölzl, Erik, Erich Kirchler, and Christa Rodler. 2002. Hindsight Bias in Economic Expectations: I Knew All Along What I Want to Hear. *Journal of Applied Psychology* 87:437–43.

Hopkins, Keith. 1998. Christian Number and Its Implications. *Journal of Early Christian Studies* 6:185–226.

Horst, Pieter van der. 1991. *Ancient Jewish Epitaphs*. Kampen: Kok Pharos.

Hulse, Lynn M., Kevin Allan, Amina Memon, and J. Don Read. 2007. Emotional Arousal and Memory: A Test of the Poststimulus Processing Hypothesis. *American Journal of Psychology* 120:73–90.

Hunter, Ian M. L. 1985. Lengthy Verbatim Recall: The Role of Text. Pages 207–35 in *Progress in the Psychology of Language*. Edited by Andrew W. Ellis. London: Erlbaum.

Hutton, Patrick H. 1993. *History as an Art of Memory*. Hanover, Vt.: University Press of New England.

Hyman, Ira E., Jr. 1999. Creating False Autobiographical Memories: Why People Believe Their Memory Errors. Pages 229–52 in *Ecological Approaches to Cognition: Essays in Honor of Ulric Neisser*. Edited by Eugene Winograd, Robyn Fivush, and William Hirst. Mahwah, N.J.: Erlbaum.

Irwin-Zarecka, Iwona. 1994. *Frames of Remembrance: The Dynamics of Collective Memory*. New Brunswick, N.J.: Transaction.

Izawa, Chizuko, and Nobuo Ohta, eds. 2005. *Human Learning and Memory: Advances in Theory and Application. The 4th Tsukuba International Conference on Memory*. Mahwah, N.J.: Erlbaum.

Jeremias, Joachim. 1972. *The Parables of Jesus*. London: SCM.

Jones, Stephen D. 1997. *Rabbi Jesus: Learning from the Master Teacher*. Macon, Ga.: Peake Road.

Jordan, Jennifer A. 2010. Landscapes of European Memory: Biodiversity and Collective Remembrance. *History and Memory* 22:5–34.

Kammen, Michael. 1991. *Mystic Chord of Memory: The Transformation of Tradition in American Culture*. New York: Knopf.

———. 1995. Some Patterns and Meanings of Memory Distortion in American History. Pages 329–45 in *Memory Distortion: How Minds, Brains, and Societies Reconstruct the Past*. Edited by Daniel L. Schacter. Cambridge: Harvard University Press.

Kansteiner, Wulf. 2002. Finding Meaning in Memory: A Methodological Critique of Collective Memory Studies. *History and Theory* 41:179–97.

Karney, Benjamin R., and Robert H. Coombs. 2000. Memory Bias in Long-Term Close Relationships: Consistency or Improvement? *Personality and Social Psychology Bulletin* 26:959–70.

Kassin, Saul M., V. Anne Tubb, Harmon M. Hosch, and Amina Memon. 2001. On the "General Acceptance" of Eyewitness Testimony Research: A New Survey of the Experts. *American Psychologist* 56:405–16.

Kelber, Werner H. 2002. The Case of the Gospels: Memory's Desire and the Limits of Historical Criticism. *Oral Tradition* 17:55–86.

———. 2005. The Works of Memory: Christian Origins as MnemoHistory—A Response. Pages 221–48 in *Memory, Tradition and Text: Uses of the Past in Early Christianity*. Edited by Alan Kirk and Tom Thatcher. Semeia Studies 52. Atlanta: Society of Biblical Literature.

Kennedy, George A. 2003. *Progymnasmata: Greek Textbooks of Prose Composition and Rhetoric*. Society of Biblical Literature Writings from the Greco-Roman World 10. Atlanta: Society of Biblical Literature.

Knapp, Mark L., Cynthia Stohl, and Kathleen K. Reardon. 1981. "Memorable" Messages. *Journal of Communication (pre-1986)* 31:4–31.

Krystal, John H., Steven M. Southwick, and Dennis S. Charney. 1995. Post Traumatic Stress Disorder: Psychobiological Mechanisms of Traumatic Remembrance. Pages 150–72 in *Memory Distortion: How Minds, Brains, and Societies Reconstruct the Past*. Edited by Daniel Schacter. Cambridge: Harvard University Press.

Kümmel, Werner Georg. 1973. *The Theology of the New Testament*. Nashville: Abingdon.

———. 1975. *Introduction to the New Testament*. London: SCM.

Kvavilashvili, Lia, Jennifer Mirani, Simone Schlagman, and Diana E. Kornbrot. 2003. Comparing Flashbulb Memories of September 11 and the Death of Princess Diana: Effects of Time Delays and Nationality. *Applied Cognitive Psychology* 17:1017–31.

Lampinen, James Michael, and Timothy N. Odegard. 2006. Memory Editing Mechanisms. *Memory* 14:649–54.

Laqueur, Thomas W. 1994. Memory and Naming in the Great War. Pages 150–67 in *Commemorations: The Politics of National Identity*. Edited by John R. Gillis. Princeton: Princeton University Press.

Larsen, Steen F. 1992. Potential Flashbulbs: Memories of Ordinary News as the Baseline. Pages 32–64 in *Affect and Accuracy in Recall: Studies of "Flashbulb" Memories*. Edited by Eugene Winograd and Ulric Neisser. Cambridge: Cambridge University Press.

Lebovics, Herman. 1994. Creating the Authentic France: Struggles over French Identity in the First Half of the Twentieth Century. Pages 239–57 in *Commemorations:*

The Politics of National Identity. Edited by John R. Gillis. Princeton: Princeton University Press.

Lentz, Tony M. 1989. *Orality and Literacy in Hellenic Greece.* Carbondale: Southern Illinois University Press.

Levine, Linda J., and Martin A. Safer. 2002. Sources of Bias in Memory for Emotions. *Current Directions in Psychological Science* 11:169-73.

Linton, Marigold. 1975. Memory for Real World Events. Pages 376-404 in *Explorations in Cognition.* Edited by Donald A. Norman and David E. Rumelhart. San Francisco: Freeman.

———. 1978. Real World Memory after Six Years: An *in vivo* Study of Very Long Term Memory. Pages 69-76 in *Practical Aspects of Memory.* Edited by M. M. Gruneberg, P. E. Morris, and R. N. Sykes. London: Academic Press.

Lira, Elizabeth. 1997. Remembering: Passing Back through the Heart. Pages 223-35 in *Collective Memory of Political Events: Social Psychological Perspectives.* Edited by James W. Pennebaker, Dario Paez, and Bernand Rimé. Mahwah, N.J.: Erlbaum.

Loffreda, Stanislao. 1986. *Recovering Capharnaum.* Gerusalemme: Edizioni Custodia Terra Santa.

Loftus, Elizabeth F. 2002. Memory Faults and Fixes. *Issues in Science and Technology* 18:41-50.

Loftus, Elizabeth F. Julie Feldman, and Richard Dashiell. 1995. The Reality of Illusory Memories. Pages 47-68 in *Memory Distortions: How Minds, Brains, and Societies Reconstruct the Past.* Edited by Daniel L. Schacter. Cambridge: Harvard University Press.

Loftus, Elizabeth F., and Jacqueline E. Pickrell. 1995. The Formation of False Memories. *Psychiatric Annals* 25:720-25.

Louie, Theresa A., Mahesh N. Rajan, and Robert E. Sibley. 2007. Tackling the Monday-Morning Quarterback: Applications of Hindsight Bias in Decision-Making Settings. *Social Cognition* 25:32 47.

Lowe, D. Jordan, and Philip M. J. Reckers. 1994. The Effect of Hindsight Bias on Juror's Evaluations of Auditor Decisions. *Decision Sciences* 25:401-26.

Luz, Ulrich. 2005. *Studies in Matthew.* Grand Rapids: Eerdmans.

Mack, Burton L. 1993. *The Lost Gospel: The Book of Q and Christian Origins.* San Francisco: HarperSanFrancisco.

Maki, Ruth, Arne Weigold, and Abigail Arellano. 2008. False Memory for Associated Word Lists in Individuals and Collaborative Groups. *Memory and Cognition* 36:598-603.

Malina, Bruce J. 1981. *The New Testament World: Insights from Cultural Anthropology.* Atlanta: Knox.

Mannheim, Karl. 1970. The Problem of Generations. *Psychoanalytic Review* 57:378-404.

Markowitsch, Hans J. 2000. Neuroanatomy of Memory. Pages 465-84 in *The Oxford Handbook of Memory.* Edited by Endel Tulving and Fergus I. M. Craik. Oxford: Oxford University Press.

Mazzoni, Guiliana, and Manila Vannucci. 2007. Hindsight Bias, the Misinformation Effect, and False Autobiographical Memories. *Social Cognition* 25:203-20.

McDermott, Kathleen B. 1996. The Persistence of False Memories in List Recall. *Journal of Memory and Language* 35:212–30.
McIver, Robert K. 1989. The Problem of Synoptic Relationships in the Development and Testing of a Methodology for the Reconstruction of the Matthean Community. PhD dissertation, Andrews University.
———. 1995. The Sabbath in the Gospel of Matthew: A Paradigm for Understanding the Law in Matthew? *Andrews University Seminary Studies* 33:231–43.
———. 1997a. Implications of New Data Pertaining to the Problem of Synoptic Relationships. *Australian Biblical Review* 45:20–39.
———. 1997b. The Place of the Matthean Community in the Stream of Early Christian History. Pages 110–20 in *Ancient History in a Modern University*. Edited by T. Hillard, R. Kearsley, C. E. V. Nixon, and A. Nobbs. Grand Rapids: Eerdmans.
———. 1997c."Sepphoris and Jesus: Missing Link or Negative Evidence?" Pages 221–32 in *To Understand the Scriptures: Essays in Honor of William H. Shae*. Edited by David Merling. Berrien Springs, Mich.: Institute of Archaeology, Andrews University.
———. 1999. Twentieth-Century Approaches to the Matthew Community. *Andrews University Seminary Studies* 37:23–38.
McIver, Robert K., and Marie Carroll. 2002. Experiments to Develop Criteria for Determining the Existence of Written Sources, and Their Potential Implications for the Synoptic Problem. *Journal of Biblical Literature* 121:667–87.
———. 2004. Distinguishing Characteristics of Orally Transmitted Material Compared to Material Transmitted by Literary Means. *Applied Cognitive Psychology* 18:1251–69.
Meade, Michelle L., and Henry L. Roediger III. 2002. Explorations in the Social Contagion of Memory. *Memory and Cognition* 30:995–1009.
Meeter, M., J. M. J. Murre, and S. M. J. Janssen. 2005. Remembering the News: Modeling Retention Data from a Study with 14,000 Participants. *Memory and Cognition* 33:793–810.
Melmoth, William, trans. 1915. *Pliny: Letters*. Vol. 2. Loeb Classical Library. London: Heinemann.
Millard, Alan. 2000. *Reading and Writing in the Time of Jesus*. Sheffield: Sheffield Academic Press.
Moore, Thomas J. 1993. *Lifespan: Who Lives Longer—and Why*. New York: Simon & Schuster.
Morgan, Tessa. 1998. *Literate Education in the Hellenistic and Roman World*. Cambridge: Cambridge University Press.
Morris, Ian. 1992. *Death Ritual and Social Structure in Classical Antiquity*. Cambridge: Cambridge University Press.
Moscovitch, Morris. 1995. Confabulation. Pages 226–51 in *Memory Distortion: How Minds, Brains, and Societies Reconstruct the Past*. Edited by Daniel E. Schacter. Cambridge: Harvard University Press.
Mournet, Terence C. 2005. *Oral Tradition and Literary Dependency*. WUNT 195. Tübingen: Mohr Siebeck.

Münsterberg, Hugo 1908. *On the Witness Stand: Essays on Psychology and Crime.* New York: Doubleday.
Nagar, Yossi, and Flavia Sonntag. 2008. Byzantine Period Burials in the Negev: Anthropological Description and Summary. *Israel Exploration Journal* 58:79–93.
Nagar, Yossi, and Hagit Torgeé. 2003. Biological Characteristics of Jewish Burial in the Hellenistic and Early Roman Periods. *Israel Exploration Journal* 53:164–71.
Neisser, Ulric. 1981. John Dean's Memory: A Case Study. *Cognition* 9:1–22.
Neisser, Ulric, and Nicole Harsch. 1992. Phantom Flashbulbs: False Recollections of Hearing the News about *Challenger*. Pages 9–31 in *Affect and Accuracy in Recall: Studies of "Flashbulb" Memories.* Edited by Eugene Winograd and Ulric Neisser. Cambridge: Cambridge University Press.
Newell, Allan, and Paul S. Rosenbloom. 1981. Mechanisms of Skill Acquisition and the Law of Practice. Pages 1–55 in *Cognitive Skills and Their Acquisition.* Edited by John R. Anderson. Hillsdale, N.J.: Erlbaum.
Nineham, D. E. 1958, 1960. Eye-Witness Testimony and the Gospel Tradition. *Journal of Theological Studies* 9:13–25, 243–52; 11:253–64.
Offer, Daniel, Marjorie Kaiz, Kenneth I. Howard, and Emily S. Bennett. 2000. The Altering of Reported Experiences. *Journal of the American Academic of Child and Adolescent Psychiatry* 39:735–42.
Olick, Jeffrey K., and Joyce Robbins. 1998. Social Memory Studies: From "Collective Memory" to the Historical Sociology of Mnemonic Practices. *Annual Review of Sociology* 24:105–40.
Ong, Walter J. 1982. *Orality and Literacy: The Technologizing of the Word.* London: Routledge.
Orr, Julian E. 1990. Sharing Knowledge, Celebrating Identity: Community Memory in a Service Culture. Pages 169–89 in *Collective Remembering.* Edited by David Middleton and Derek Edwards. London: Sage.
Otani, Hajime, Terry M. Libkuman, Robert I. Widner Jr., and Emily I. Graves. 2007. Memory for Emotionally Arousing Stimuli: A Comparison of Younger and Older Adults. *Journal of General Psychology* 134:23–42.
Padden, Carol A. 1990. Folk Explanation in Language Survival. Pages 190–202 in *Collective Remembering.* Edited by David Middleton and Derek Edwards. London: Sage.
Parkin, Tim G. 1992. *Demography and Roman Society.* Baltimore: John Hopkins University Press.
———. 2003. *Old Age in the Roman World: A Cultural and Social History.* Ancient Society and History. Baltimore: Johns Hopkins University Press.
Payne, David G., Claude J. Elie, Jason M. Blackwell, and Jeffrey S. Neuschatz. 1996. Memory Illusions: Recalling, Recognizing, and Recollecting Events That Never Occurred. *Journal of Memory and Language* 35:261–85.
Pease, Meridith E., Amy E. McCabe, Laura A. Brannon, and Michael J. Tagler. 2003. Memory Distortions for Pre-Y2K Expectancies: A Demonstration of the Hindsight Bias. *Journal of Psychology* 137:397–98.
Petersen, S. E., P. T. Fox, M. I. Posner, M. Mintun, and M. E. Raichle. 2000. Positron Emission Tomographic Studies of the Cortical Anatomy of Single-Word Process-

ing. Pages 397–404 in *Minds, Brains, and Computers: The Foundations of Cognitive Science*. Edited by Robert Cummins and Denise Dellarosa Cummins. Oxford: Blackwell.

Piehler, G. Kurt. 1994. The War Dead and the Gold Star: American Commemoration of the First World War. Pages 168–85 in *Commemorations: The Politics of National Identity*. Edited by John R. Gillis. Princeton: Princeton University Press.

Pillemer, David B. 1998. *Momentous Events, Vivid Memories*. Cambridge: Harvard University Press.

Pohl, Rüdiger F., Stefan Schwarz, Sabine Sczesny, and Dagmar Stahlberg. 2003. Hindsight Bias in Gustatory Judgments. *Experimental Psychology* 50:107–15.

Porter, Stephen, Sabrina Bellhouse, Ainslie McDougal, Leanne ten Brinke, and Kevin Wilson. 2010. Prospective Investigation of the Vulnerability of Memory for Positive and Negative Emotional Scenes to the Misinformation Effect. *Canadian Journal of Behavioural Science* 42:56–61.

Pressley, Michael, and Wolfgang Schneider. 1997. *Introduction to Memory Development during Childhood and Adolescence*. Mahwah, N.J.: Erlbaum.

Redman, Judith C. S. 2010. How Accurate Are Eyewitnesses? Bauckham and the Eyewitnesses in the Light of Psychological Research. *Journal of Biblical Literature* 129:177–97.

Reed, Jonathan L. 1992. The Population of Capernaum. The Institute for Antiquity and Christianity, The Claremont Graduate School, Occasional Papers 24.

———. 2000. *Archaeology and the Galilean Jesus*. Harrisburg, Pa.: Trinity.

———. 2010. Instability in Jesus' Galilee: A Demographic Perspective. *Journal of Biblical Literature* 129:343–65.

Reicke, Bo. 1986. *The Roots of the Synoptic Gospels*. Philadelphia: Fortress.

Reisberg, Daniel, and Friederike Heuer. 1992. Remembering the Details of Emotional Events. Pages 162–90 in *Affect and Accuracy in Recall: Studies of "Flashbulb" Memories*. Edited by Eugene Winograd and Ulric Neisser. New York: Academic Press.

Reyna, Valerie F. 2005. Fuzzy-Trace Theory (FTT), Judgment, and Decision-Making: A Dual-Processes Approach. Pages 241–56 in Izawa and Ohta 2005.

Reysen, Matthew B. 2007. The Effects of Social Pressure on False Memories. *Memory and Cognition* 35:59–65.

Riesenfeld, Harald. 1957. *The Gospel Tradition and Its Beginnings: A Study in the Limits of "Formgeschichte."* London: Mowbray.

Riesner, Rainer. 1981. *Jesus als Lehrer: Eine Untersuchung zum Ursprung der Evangelien-Überlieferung*. Tübingen: Mohr Siebeck.

———. 1984. *Jesus als Lehrer: Eine Untersuchung zum Ursprung der Evangelien-Überlieferung*. 2nd ed. Tübingen: Mohr Siebeck.

———. 1988. *Jesus als Lehrer: Eine Untersuchung zum Ursprung der Evangelien-Überlieferung*. 3rd ed. Tübingen: Mohr Siebeck.

———. 1991. Jesus as Preacher and Teacher. Pages 185–210 in *Jesus and the Oral Gospel Tradition*. Edited by Henry Wansbrough. Sheffield: JSOT Press.

———. 1998. *Paul's Early Period: Chronology, Mission Strategy, Theology*. Grand Rapids: Eerdmans.

———. 2002. *Der Ursprung der Jesus-Überlieferung*. 2nd ed. Bad Liebenzell: VLM.

———. 2008. Teacher, Teaching Forms, and Styles. Pages 624–30 in *Encyclopedia of the Historical Jesus*. Edited by Craig A. Evans. New York: Routledge.
Riniolo, Todd C., Myriah Koledin, Gregory M. Drakulic, and Robin A. Payne. 2003. An Archival Study of Eyewitness Memory of the *Titanic's* Final Plunge. *The Journal of General Psychology* 130:89–95.
Robinson, John A. T. 1976. *Redating the New Testament*. London: SCM.
Rodríguez, Rafael. 2010. *Structuring Early Christian Memory: Jesus in Tradition, Performance, and Text*. London: T&T Clark.
Roediger, Henry L., III, and Kathleen B. McDermott. 1995. Creating False Memories: Remembering Words Not Presented in Lists. *Journal of Experimental Psychology: Learning, Memory and Cognition* 21:803–14.
Roediger, Henry L., III, David A. Balota, and Jason M. Watson. 2001. Spreading Activation and Arousal of False Memories. Pages 95–115 in *The Nature of Remembering: Essays in Honor of Robert G. Crowder*. Edited by Henry L. Roediger III. Washington, D.C.: American Psychological Association.
Roediger, Henry L., III, Jason M. Watson, Kathleen B. McDermott, and David Gallo. 2001. Factors That Determine False Recall: A Multiple Regression Analysis. *Psychonomic Bulletin and Review* 8:385–407.
Roediger, Henry L., III, Michelle L. Meade, and Erik T. Bergman. 2001. Social Contagion of Memory. *Psychonomic Bulletin and Review* 8:365–71.
Roediger, Henry L., III, J. Derek Jacoby, and Kathleen B. McDermott. 1996. Misinformation Effects in Recall: Creating False Memories through Repeated Retrieval. *Journal of Memory and Language* 35:300–318.
Roese, N. J., and S. D. Maniar. 1997. Perceptions of Purple: Counterfactual and Hindsight Judgments at Northwestern Wildcats Football Games. *Personality and Social Psychology Bulletin* 23:1245–53.
Rolls, Edmund T. 2000. Memory Systems in the Brain. *Annual Review of Psychology* 51:599–630.
Rose, Steven. 2003. *The Making of Memory: From Molecules to Mind*. 2nd ed. London: Vintage.
———. 2005. *The Future of the Brain: The Promise and Perils of Tomorrow's Neuroscience*. Oxford: Oxford University Press.
Ross, David Frank, J. Don Read, and Michael P. Toglia, eds. 1994. *Adult Eyewitness Testimony: Current Trends and Developments*. Cambridge: Cambridge University Press.
Rovee-Collier, Carolyn, and Peter Gerhardstein. 1997. The Development of Infant Memory. Pages 5–39 in *The Development of Memory in Childhood*. Edited by Nelson Cowan. Hove: Psychology Press.
Rovee-Collier, Carolyn, and Harlene Hayne. 2000. Memory in Infancy and Early Childhood. Pages 267–82 in *The Oxford Handbook of Memory*. Edited by Endel Tulving and Fergus I. M. Craik. Oxford: Oxford University Press.
Rubin, David C. 1995. *Memory in Oral Traditions: The Cognitive Psychology of Epic, Ballads, and Counting-Out Rhymes*. New York: Oxford University Press.
Sachs, Jacqueline Strunk. 1967. Recognition Memory for Syntactic and Semantic Aspects of Connected Discourse. *Perception and Psychophysics* 2:437–42.

———. 1974. Memory in Reading and Listening to Discourse. *Memory and Cognition* 2 95–100.
Schacter, Daniel L. 1995. Memory Distortions, History and Current Status. Pages 1–43 in *Memory Distortion: How Minds, Brains, and Societies Reconstruct the Past.* Edited by Daniel Schacter. Cambridge: Harvard University Press.
———. 2001. *The Seven Sins of Memory: How the Mind Forgets and Remembers.* Boston: Houghton Mifflin.
Schacter, Daniel L., Anthony D. Wagner, and Randy L. Buckner. 2000. Memory Systems of 1999. Pages 627–43 in *The Oxford Handbook of Memory.* Edited by Endel Tulving and Fergus I. M. Craik. Oxford: Oxford University Press.
Scheidel, Walter. 1996. *Measuring Sex, Age and Death in the Roman Empire: Explorations in Ancient Demography.* Ann Arbor, Mich.: Journal of Roman Archaeology.
———. 2001. Progress and Problems in Roman Demography. Pages 1–81 in *Debating Roman Demography.* Edited by Walter Scheidel. Brill: Leiden.
Schlagman, Simone, Joerg Schulz, and Lia Kvavilashvili. 2006. A Content Analysis of Involuntary Autobiographical Memories: Examining the Positivity Effect in Old Age. *Memory* 14:161–75.
Schmolck, H., E. A. Buffalo, and L. R. Squire. 2000. Memory Distortions Develop over Time: Recollections of the O. J. Simpson Trial Verdict after 15 and 32 Months. *Psychological Science* 11:39–45.
Schnelle, Udo. 2002. *Einleitung in das Neue Testament.* 4th ed. Göttingen: Vandenhoeck & Ruprecht.
Schooler, Jonathan W., and Eric Eich. 2000. Memory for Emotional Events. Pages 379–92 in *The Oxford Handbook of Memory.* Edited by Endel Tulving and Fergus I. M. Craik. Oxford: Oxford University Press.
Schröter, Jens. 1997. *Erinnerung an Jesu Worte.* Nuekirchen-Vluyn: Nuekerchen.
Schubotz, Ricarda I., and Christian J. Fiebach. 2006. Integrative Models of Broca's Area and the Ventral Premotor Cortex. *Cortex* 42:461–63.
Schudson, Michael. 1995. Dynamics of Distortion in Collective Memory. Pages 346–64 in *Memory Distortion: How Minds, Brains, and Societies Reconstruct the Past.* Edited by Daniel E. Schacter. Cambridge: Harvard University Press.
Schuman, Howard, and Jacqueline Scott. 1989. Generations and Collective Memories. *American Sociological Review* 54:359–81.
Schuman, Howard, Robert F. Belli, and Katherine Bischoping. 1997. The Generational Basis of Historical Knowledge. Pages 47–77 in *Collective Memory of Political Events: Social Psychological Perspectives.* Edited by James W. Pennebaker, Dario Paez, and Bernand Rimé. Mahwah, N.J.: Erlbaum.
Schürmann, Heinz. 1960. Die vorösterlichen Anfänge der Logienttradition. Pages 361–69 in *Die historische Jesus und der kerygmatische Christus.* Edited by Helmut Ristow and Karl Matthiae. Berlin: Evangelische.
Schwartz, Barry. 1990. The Reconstruction of Abraham Lincoln. Pages 81–107 in *Collective Remembering.* Edited by David Middleton and Derek Edwards. London: Sage.
———. 1991. Social Change and Collective Memory: The Democratization of George Washington. *American Sociological Review* 56:221–36.

———. 1996. Memory as a Cultural System: Abraham Lincoln in World War II. *American Sociological Review* 61:908–27.

———. 2000. *Abraham Lincoln and the Forge of National Memory*. Chicago: University of Chicago Press.

———. 2008. *Abraham Lincoln in the Post-heroic Era: History and Memory in Late Twentieth-Century America*. Chicago: University of Chicago Press.

Scott, Jacqueline, and Lilian Zac. 1993. Collective Memories in Britain and the United States. *Public Opinion Quarterly* 57:315–31.

Seamon, John G., Madeleine S. Goodkind, Adam D. Dumey, Ester Dick, Marla S. Aufseeser, Sarah E. Strickland, Jeffrey R. Woulfin, and Nicholas S. Fung. 2003. "If I Didn't Write It, Why Would I Remember It?" Effects of Encoding, Attention, and Practice on Accurate and False Memory. *Memory and Cognition* 31:445–57.

Semb, George B., and John A. Ellis. 1994. Knowledge Taught in School: What Is Remembered? *Review of Educational Research* 64:253–86.

Shanks, Hershel. 1995. *Jerusalem: An Archaeological Biography*. New York: Random House.

Shapiro, Lauren R. 2006. Remembering September 11th: The Role of Retention Interval and Rehearsal on Flashbulb and Event Memory. *Memory* 14:129–47.

Sligo, Frank, and Nicole Stirton. 1998. Does Hindsight Bias Change Perceptions of Business Ethics? *Journal of Business Ethics* 17:111–24.

Smith, Alison C., and Edith Greene. 2005. Conduct and Its Consequences: Attempts at Dibiasing Jury Judgments. *Law and Human Behaviour* 29:505–26.

Smith, Mark S. 2002. Remembering God: Collective Memory in Israelite Religion. *Catholic Biblical Quarterly* 64:631–51.

Stark, Rodney. 1991. Antioch as the Social Situation of Matthew's Gospel. Pages 189–210 in *Social History of the Matthean Community*. Edited by David L. Balch. Minneapolis: Fortress.

———. 1997. *The Rise of Christianity*. San Francisco: HarperSanFrancisco.

Suroweicki, James. 2004. *The Wisdom of Crowds*. London: Abacus.

Takahashi, Masanobu. 2007. Does Collaborative Remembering Reduce False Memories? *British Journal of Psychology* 98:1–13.

Talarico, Jennifer M., and David C. Rubin. 2003. Confidence, Not Consistency, Characterizes Flashbulb Memories. *Psychological Science* 14:455–61.

Tannehill, Robert C. 1984. Types and Functions of Apophthegms in the Synoptic Gospels. Pages 1792–1829 in vol. 2.25.2 of *Aufstieg und Niedergang der Römischen Welt*. Edited by Hildegard Temporin and Wolfgang Haase. Berlin: de Gruyter.

Thomas, Ayanna K., and Elizabeth F. Loftus. 2002. Creating Bizarre False Memories through Imagination. *Memory and Cognition* 30:423–31.

Tree, Jean E. Fox, and Mary Susan Weldon. 2007. Retelling Urban Legends. *American Journal of Psychology* 120:459–76.

Trevor-Roper, Hugh. 1983. The Invention of Tradition: The Highland Tradition of Scotland. Pages 15–41 in *The Invention of Tradition*. Edited by Eric Hobsbawm and Terence Ranger. Cambridge: Cambridge University Press.

Tulving, E. 1972. Episodic and Semantic Memory. Pages 381–403 in *Organization of Memory*. Edited by E. Tulving and W. Donaldson. New York: Academic Press.

———. 1983. *Elements of Episodic Memory.* London: Oxford University Press.

———. 2001. Origin of Autonoesis in Episodic Memory. Pages 17–34 in *The Nature of Remembering.* Edited by Henry Roediger III, James S. Nairne, Ian Neath, and Aimée M. Surprenant. Washington, D.C.: American Psychological Association.

Wade, Kimberly A., Maryanne Garry, J. Don Read, and D. Stephen Lindsay. 1992. A Picture Is Worth a Thousand Lies: Using False Photographs to Create False Childhood Memories. *Psychonomic Bulletin and Review* 9:597–603.

Wagenaar, Willem A. 1986. My Memory: A Study of Autobiographic Memory over Six Years. *Cognitive Psychology* 18:225–52.

Wagenaar, Willem A., and Jop Groeneweg. 1990. The Memory of Concentration Camp Survivors. *Applied Cognitive Psychology* 4:77–87.

Ward, Benedicta. 1975. *The Sayings of the Desert Fathers: The Alphabetical Collection.* Kalamazoo, Mich.: Cistercian Publications.

Weldon, Mary Susan, and Krystal D. Bellinger. 1997. Collective Memory: Collaborative and Individual Processing in Remembering. *Journal of Experimental Psychology: Learning, Memory, and Cognition* 23:1160–75.

Wells, Gary L., Roy S. Malpass, R. C. L. Lindsay, Ronald P. Fisher, John W. Turtle, and Solomon M. Fulero. 2000. From the Lab to the Police Station: A Successful Application of Eyewitness Research. *American Psychologist* 55:581–98.

Wenham, John. 1991. *Redating Matthew, Mark and Luke: A Fresh Assault on the Synoptic Problem.* London: Hodder & Stoughton.

Werth, Lioba, and Fritz Strack. 2003. An Inferential Approach to the Knew-It-All-Along Phenomenon. *Memory* 11:411–19.

White, Richard T. 1982. Memory for Personal Events. *Human Learning* 1:171–83.

Wickelgren, Wayne A. 1974. Single-Trace Fragility Theory of Memory Dynamics. *Memory and Cognition* 2:775–80.

Wilkinson, James. 1996. A Choice of Fictions: Historians, Memory, and Evidence. *Publications of the Modern Language Association of America* 111:80–92.

Winger, Michael. 2000. Word and Deed. *Catholic Biblical Quarterly* 62:679–92.

Winningham, Robert G., Ira E. Hyman Jr., and Dale L. Dinnel. 2000. Flashbulb Memories? The Effects of When the Initial Memory Report Was Obtained. *Memory* 8:209–216.

Wixted, John T. 2004. The Psychology and Neuroscience of Forgetting. *Annual Review of Psychology* 55:235–69.

Wixted, John T., and Ebbe B. Ebbesen. 1991. On the Form of Forgetting. *Psychological Science* 2:409–15.

———. 1997. Genuine Power Curves in Forgetting: A Quantitative Analysis of Individual Subject Forgetting Functions. *Memory and Cognition* 25:731–39.

Yamauchi, Edwin M. 2000. Attitude toward the Aged in Antiquity. *Near East Archaeological Society Bulletin* 45:1–9.

Yuille, John C., and Judith L. Cutshall 1986. A Case Study of Eyewitness Memory of a Crime. *Journal of Applied Psychology* 71:291–301.

Zaragoza, Maria S., and Karen J. Mitchell. 1996. Repeated Exposure to Suggestion and the Creation of False Memories. *Psychological Science* 7:294–300.

Zerubavel, Yael. 1994. The Historic, the Legendary, and the Incredible: Invented Tradition and Collective Memory in Israel. Pages 105–23 in *Commemorations: The Politics of National Identity.* Edited by John R. Gillis. Princeton: Princeton University Press.

Zimmermann, Ruben. 2008. Gleichnisse als Medien der Jesuserinnerung: Die Historizität der Jesusparabeln im Horizont der Gedächtnisforschung. Pages 87–121 in *Hermeneutik der Gleichnisse Jesus.* Edited by Ruben Zimmermann and Gabi Kern. Tübingen: Mohr Siebeck.

Index of Ancient Texts and Authors

New Testament

Matthew	1, 9, 118, 126, 148, 151, 158, 189
1–26	157 n. 14
1:6–11	156
3:1	126
3:1–12	152 n. 10
3:13	126
3:14–15	159
4:1	126
4:1–11	102
4:13	203
4:18–22	146
4:25	204
5:1	156, 168
5:3–11	156
5:4–5	159
5:7–10	159
5:13–16	178–79
5:14	159
5:16–17	159
5:19–20	159
5:21–24	159
5:27–28	159
5:33–37	159
5:41	159
6:1–4	159
6:5–8	159
6:7–15	118
6:10b	159
6:15	159
6:16–18	159
6:22–23	178–79
6:24	178
7:7–11	177–78
7:7–12	152 n. 10
7:15	159
7:21–23	159
8:1	204
8:5	203
8:5–13	152 n. 10
8:18–22	134, 134 n. 12, 135, 138, 138 n. 13, 139–40
8:18–24	152 n. 10
8:23–27	118
8:28–34	155
9:9	146, 150, 155
9:14–17	140
9:16–17	171 n. 8
9:27–31	159
9:37	126
9:37–38	178
10:3	150, 155
10:5–15	168
10:5b-6	159
10:16–25	138
10:23	159
10:41	159
11:1–19	152 n. 10
11:20	126
11:25	126
11:25–30	152 n. 10
12:1	126
12:1–14	125 n. 1
12:5–7	159
12:11	159
12:36–37	159
12:38–42	152 n. 10
13:1	126

Matthew (cont.)		22:15	137
13:1–9	171–74	22:15–22	134, 134 n. 12, 135, 138 n. 13
13:2	204		
13:10–17	174	22:23	126
13:10–23	168	23:1–3	159
13:18–23	174	23:5	159
13:21–32	171, 174	23:8–10	159
13:24–30	159	23:15–22	159
13:36	168	23:27–28	159
13:36–52	159	23:32–33	159
13:57	164	24	190 n. 1
14:1	126	24:10–12	159
14:13–21	204	24:14	159
14:28–31	159	24:32–35	171
15:12–13	159	24:45–51	152 n. 10, 171
15:23–24	159	25:1–13	159
15:41	159	25:14–30	175
16:3	159	25:31–46	159
16:12	159	27:8	190 n. 1
16:14	164	27:55	129
16:17–19	159	28:1–10	129
16:24–28	178	28:15	190 n. 1
16:27	159	28:16–20	159
16:28–17:1	155		
17:1	126	Mark	1, 9, 126, 148, 159, 189
17:14–18	118	1:9–11	102
17:24	203	1:14–20	146
17:24–27	159	1:21	203
18:1	126	1:38	168
18:1–4	134	1:40–45	101
18:1–5	118	2:1	203
18:3–4	159	2:1–12	101
18:10	159	2:14	155
18:14–35	159	2:15–17	134
18:21–22	134	2:18–22	140
18:23–35	159	2:21–22	171 n. 8
19:2	204	2:23–28	134
19:12	159	3:1–6	101
19:28b	159	3:18	155
20:1–16	159	3:31–35	134
21:14–17	159	4:1–9	171–73
21:28–32	159	4:2	168
21:33–46	171, 174	4:10–12	174
21:43	159	4:13–20	174
22:1–14	171	4:30–32	171, 174

INDEX OF ANCIENT TEXTS AND AUTHORS 231

4:35–41	101, 118	5:3	168
5:1–20	155	5:27	155
6:4	164	5:36–39	171 n. 9
6:7–13	168	5:33–39	140
6:12	168	6:1–5	125
6:15	164	6:1–11	125
6:30–44	204	6:6–11	125
6:45–52	101	6:12	126
7:17–23	134	6:15	155
8:34–9:1	178	6:17	156
9:1–2	155	6:20–26	156
9:2	126	7:1	203
9:2–8	102	7:1–10	152 n. 10
9:9–10	169	7:11	125
9:14–27	118	7:18–35	152 n. 10
9:31–32	169	8:1	125
9:33	203	8:1–3	129
9:33–37	118	8:4–8	171–73
9:38–41	140	8:9–10	174
10:1	168	8:11–15	174
10:10–12	134	8:22–25	118
10:46–52	101	8:26–39	155
11:12	126	9:1–6	168
11:27	137	9:6	168
12:1–12	171, 174	9:10–17	204
12:13–17	101, 134, 134 n. 12, 135–38, 138 n. 13	9:18	125
		9:28	155
13	190 n. 1	9:37	126
13:3–13	138	9:37–43	118
13:28–31	171	9:44–45	169
14:3–9	134	9:46–48	118
15:40–41	129	9:57–62	134, 134 n. 12, 135, 138, 138 n. 13, 139–40, 152 n. 10
Luke	1, 9, 118, 126, 148, 151, 189	10:2	178
1:1	169	10:21	126
1:1–3	190 n. 2	10:21–24	152 n. 10
1:2	5, 7, 7 n. 1, 209	10:30–37	159
1:39	126	11:1–4	118
1:69	164	11:5–13	159 n. 16
2:1	125–26	11:9–13	152 n. 10, 177–78
2:11	164	11:14	125
2:31–52	101	11:29–32	152 n. 10
3:1–20	152 n. 10	11:33–36	178–79
3:29–30	156	12:41–48	152 n. 10, 171
4:31	203	13:18–19	171, 174

Luke (cont.)	
13:31	126
14:15–24	171
14:17	126
14:34–35	178–79
15:11–32	159
16:13	178
17:5–6	134
17:20–37	190 n. 1
18:1–14	159 n. 16
18:31–34	169
19:1–10	134
19:11–27	175
20:9–19	171, 174
20:19	137
20:20–26	134, 134 n. 12, 135–38, 138 n. 13
21:5–36	190 n. 1
21:29–32	171
24:13	126

John	
1:45–51	101
4:42	164
6:14	204
12:16	169
13:7	169
21:23	190 n. 1
21:25	144

Acts	
1:13	155
1:21–22	7, 168
2:42	169
4:2	169
11:28–29	208
12:12–17	145 n. 1
13:1–3	128
28:30	189
28:31	169

Romans	
12:7	169
13:11–12	151 n. 9
15:25–28	208

1 Corinthians	
7:29–31	151 n. 9
14:6	169

2 Corinthians	
9:1–5	208

Galatians	
2:11–12	128

Philippians	
4:5	151 n. 9

1 Thessalonians	
4:17	151 n. 9

1 Timothy	
5:17	169

2 Peter	
1:16	5

ANCIENT AUTHORS

Akiba, Rabbi	166, 166 n. 5
Irenaeus	169
Justinian	192 n. 7
Papias	6, 134 n. 10, 169, 169 n. 7
Theon, Aelius,	132, 132 n. 6
Ulpian	192–197

Index of Modern Authors

Aguilar, Paloma	83	Bockmuehl, Markus	148 n. 3
Allan, Kevin	33 n. 11	Bodnar, John	83, 108 n. 6
Allen, Diana	117 n. 14	Bonds-Raacke, Jennifer M.	73
Allison, Dale C.	190 n. 1	Boyd, Gregory A.	150 n. 7
Angel, J. Lawrence	191 n. 5	Bradfield, Amy	73
Arellano, Abigail	70, 70 n. 10	Brainerd, C. J.	61, 62, 167
Asselen, Marieke van	34 n. 13	Brandimonte, Marie A.	48
Atherton, Catherine	165 n. 2	Brannon, Laura A.	73
Aufseeser, Marla S.	61 n. 2, 63	Brewer, William F.	47 n. 5
Bagnall, Roger S.	192	Brinke, Leanne ten	66
Bahrick, Harry P.	28 n. 6, 35–38	Brueckner, Katja	61 n. 1
Bahrick, P. O.	37–38	Brog, Mooli	83
Bailey, Kenneth E.	99, 115–17, 120	Broshi, Magan	205
Bartlett, Frederic C.	23	Brown, Robert	41–46, 48–49, 54, 145, 145–46 n. 1
Basden, Barbara H.	70, 70 n. 9		
Basden, David R.	70, 70 n. 9	Bruce, Darryl	50 n. 8
Bauckham, Richard	5–9, 20, 134 n. 10, 153	Bryner, Susan	70
		Buckner, Randy L.	76
Bauer, Patricia J.	51 n. 9	Budge, Ernest A. Wallis	133
Baum, Armin D.	114	Buffalo, E. A.	47–48 n. 6
Baumeister, Roy F.	105–106	Bultmann, Rudolf	99, 99–100 n. 1, 100 n. 2, 100–103, 105, 109–10, 115, 120, 134, 134 nn. 10–11, 134–35 n. 12, 157, 174, 182–83, 186
Baym, Carol L.	67		
Beck, Frederick	165 n. 3		
Bellhouse, Sabrina	66		
Belli, Robert F.	86	Burke, Peter	108
Bellinger, Krystal D.	70	Byrskog, Samuel	5, 83 n. 3, 128, 128 n. 4, 129 n. 5
Bennett, Emily S.	39		
Ben-Yehuda, Nachman	88, 88–89 n. 10	Cabeza, Roberto	62–63, 63 n. 4
Bergman, Erik T.	69, 70, 78	Carlsen, Keri A.	73
Berntsen, Dorthe	52 n. 12, 53, 54 n. 14	Carroll, Marie	149 n. 6, 167, 169, 171
Betz, Andrew L.	70 n. 9	Carruthers, Mary J.	165 n. 4
Bianco, Carmela	48	Ceci, Stephen J.	51 n. 11
Bischoping, Katherine	86	Charney, Dennis S.	52 n. 12, 57 n. 15
Blackwell, Jason M.	62 n. 3	Christianson, Sven-Åke	58 n. 17
Blomberg, Craig L.	174	Chrobac, Quin M.	66

Coale, Ansley J.   195, 198, 198 n. 14, 199, 202–3, 205–7
Cohen, Gillian   37
Coluccia, Emanuele   48
Confino, Alon   83–84
Conway, Martin A.   37, 58 n. 16, 78
Coombs, Robert H.   74–75
Cooper, Joel.   108 n. 7
Cranfield, C. E. B.   148 n. 4
Crawley, Ros A.   50 n. 8
Cribiore, Raffaella   151
Crombag, Hans F. M.   65–66
Crossan, John Dominic   8–9, 20, 149, 176 n. 11, 191–92 n. 6, 203 n. 16
Cunningham, David   83
Curci, Antonietta   44–45 n. 2, 45–46 n. 4
Cutshall, Judith L.   12, 13 n. 4, 14–15, 15 n. 6, 22
Dalton, Andrea L.   70
Daneman, Meredyth   70
Davies, W. D.   190 n. 1
DeConick, April D.   153 n. 11
Deese, J.   60
Demeny, Paul   195, 198, 198 n. 14, 199, 202–3, 205–7
Dibelius, Martin   99, 101 n. 3, 101–3, 105, 109–10, 115, 120, 134–35 n. 12, 157, 182
Dick, Ester   61 n. 2, 63
Dinnel, Dale L.   48
Dodd, C. H.   180–81
Drakulic, Gregory M.   14 n. 5
Dropick, Patricia L.   51 n. 9
Dumey, Adam D.   61 n. 2, 63
Dundes, Alan   155 n. 13, 176–77 n. 12
Dunn, James D. G.   22, 99, 115, 117, 117 n. 15, 118, 118 nn. 16–17, 119, 119 nn. 18–19, 120–21, 151–52 n. 9
Durr, Rena T.   73
Eacott, Madeline J.   50 n. 8
Ebbesen, Ebbe B.   25–30
Ebbinghaus, Herman   23–28
Eddy, Paul Rhodes   150 n. 7
Edwards, Derek   18–19
Eich, Eric   50 n. 7, 146 n. 2

Elam, Yigal   82 n. 2, 83
Elie, Claude J.   62 n. 3
Ellis, John A.   40 n. 20
Epstein, I.   166 n. 6
Feldman-Sevelsberg, Pamela   83
Fentress, James   79 n. 19, 83, 94 n. 14
Festinger, Leon   108, 108 n. 7, 109 n. 8
Fiebach, Christian J.   77 n. 16
Fields, R. Douglas   68 n. 7
Fischhoff, Baruch   71–73
Fisher, Ronald P.   11–12, 12 n. 3
Fiske, Kate E.   50 n. 8
Fodor, Jerry   77
Fox, P. T.   77 n. 15
Francis, Lori   50 n. 8
Freyer, Lakeysha S.   73
Frier, Bruce W.   191 n. 5, 192–93, 193 nn. 9–10, 194, 194 nn. 11–12, 195, 195 n. 13, 196–97, 202–3, 203 n. 17, 205–7
Fulero, Solomon M.   11–12, 12 n. 3
Fung, Nicholas S.   61 n. 2, 63
Gallo, David   61, 61 n. 1, 63
Garry, Maryanne   64–65, 78, 78 n. 18
Gedi, Noa   82 n. 2, 83
Gerhardsson, Birger   99, 111, 111 n. 9, 112, 112 n. 10, 113–14, 120–21, 166 n. 5, 170, 176
Gerhardstein, Peter   51 n. 9
Gigerenzer, Gerd   75
Gluck, David   16 n. 7
Gonsalves, Brian De   67
Goodacre, Mark   152 n. 10
Goodkind, Madeleine S.   61 n. 2, 63
Goody, Jack   91–92
Graves, Emily I.   33 n. 11
Greene, Edith   74
Griffin, Larry J.   85 nn. 4–5
Groeneweg, Jop   55–56
Halbwachs, Maurice   82 n. 2, 93, 94 n. 14, 117 n. 15
Halford, W. Kim   73
Harley, Erin M.   73
Harlow, Mary   202 n. 15
Harsch, Nicole   46–47
Harvey, John H.   56

INDEX OF MODERN AUTHORS 235

Hasian, Marouf, Jr. 83
Hastings, Stephen 105–6
Hayne, Harlene 51 n. 9
Hertwig, Ralph 75
Heuer, Friederike 58
Hill, Nicole M. 76, 76 n. 13
Hirst, William 16 n. 7
Hock, Ronald F. 132 n. 6
Hoffrage, Ulrich 75
Holmberg, Bengt 119
Hölzl, Erik 74
Hopkins, Keith 181
Horst, Pieter van der 191, 194 n. 12
Hosch, Harmon M. 11
Howe, M. L. 62
Howard, Kenneth I. 39
Hulse, Lynn M. 33 n. 11
Humlebaek, Carsten 83
Hunter, Ian M. L. 120
Hutton, Patrick H. 82 n. 2
Hyman Jr., Ira E. 47 n. 5, 48, 65 n. 5, 78
Irwin-Zarecka, Iwona 83
Jacoby, J. Derek 67
Janssen, S. M. J. 34 n. 14
Jeremias, Joachim 174, 180
Jones, Stephen D. 164
Jordan, Jennifer A. 83
Kaiz, Marjorie 39
Kammen, Michael 83, 107
Kansteiner, Wulf 84, 120
Karney, Benjamin R. 74–75
Kassin, Saul M. 11
Keefer, Emma 73
Kelber, Werner H. 8–9
Kennedy, George A. 132, 132 n. 6
Kirchler, Erich 74
Knapp, Mark L. 52–53 n. 13
Koledin, Myriah 14 n. 5
Koppen, Peter J. van 65–66
Kornbrot, Diana E. 44 n. 2
Krystal, John H. 52 n. 12, 57 n. 15
Kulik, James 41–46, 48–49, 54, 145, 145–46 n. 1
Kümmel, Werner Georg 1, 151 n. 9, 190 n. 1

Kvavilashvili, Lia 34 n. 12, 44 n. 2
Lampinen, James Michael 79–80
Laqueur, Thomas W. 83
Larsen, Steen F. 43 n. 1
Laurence, Ray 202 n. 15
Lebovics, Herman 83
Lennartson, E. Robert 62–63, 63 n. 4
Lentz, Tony M. 165, 165 n. 3
Levine, Linda J. 73
Libkuman, Terry M. 33 n. 11
Lindsay, D. Stephen 64–65, 78, 78 n. 18
Lindsay, R. C. L. 11–12, 12 n. 3
Linton, Marigold 30 n. 8
Lira, Elizabeth 83
Loffreda, Stanislao 203 n. 16
Loftus, Elizabeth F. 12 n. 2, 63–65
Loftus, Geoffrey R. 73
Louie, Theresa A. 74
Lowe, D. Jordan 74
Luminet, Olivier 44–45 n. 2, 45–46 n. 4
Luz, Ulrich 157 n. 14
Mack, Burton L. 148 n. 5, 152 n. 10
Maki, Ruth 70, 70 n. 10
Malina, Bruce J. 81, 81 n. 1
Malpass, Roy S. 11–12, 12 n. 3
Mannheim, Karl 86 n. 6, 87 n. 8
Markowitsch, Hans J. 77 n. 15
Mazzoni, Guiliana 78–79
McCabe, Amy E. 73
McDermott, Kathleen B. 60–61, 61 n. 1, 62, n. 3, 63, 67
McDougal, Ainslie 66
McIver, Robert K. 125 n. 1, 149 n. 6, 159 n. 17, 167, 169, 171, 204 n. 19
Meade, Michelle L. 69, 69 n. 8, 70, 78
Meeter, M. 34 n. 14
Melmoth, William 182 n. 13
Memon, Amina 11, 33 n. 11
Millard, Alan 149–51
Mills, B. A. 62
Mintun, M. 77 n. 15
Mirani, Jennifer 44 n. 2
Mitchell, Karen J. 66–67
Moore, Thomas J. 193 n. 10
Morgan, Tessa 165 n. 2

Moritz, Steffen 61 n. 1
Morris, Ian 191
Moscovitch, Morris 104
Mournet, Terence C. 118 n. 17
Münsterberg, Hugo 10–11, 14
Murre, J. M. J. 34 n. 14
Nagar, Yossi 192
Ndonko, Flavien T. 83
Neisser, Ulric 16, 16 n. 7, 17–18, 46–47
Neuschatz, Jeffrey S. 62 n. 3
Newell, Allan 29
Nicks, Sandra D. 73
Nineham, D. E. 126, 126 n. 2, 127, 127 n. 3, 130
Nugent, Colleen 83
Odegard, Timothy N. 79–80
Offer, Daniel 39
Olick, Jeffrey K. 82 n. 2
O'Neill, Edward N. 132 n. 6
Ong, Walter J. 92–93
Orr, Julian E. 83
Osgarby, Susan M. 73
Ostrom, Thomas M. 70 n. 9
Otani, Hajime 33 n. 11
Padden, Carol A. 94 n. 14
Parkin, Tim G. 191 n. 3, 195, 198–99
Payne, David G. 62, 62 n. 3
Payne, Robin A. 14 n. 5
Pease, Meridith E. 73
Petersen, S. E. 77 n. 15
Phillips-Grant, Kimberly 50 n. 8
Pickrell, Jacqueline E. 64–65
Piehler, G. Kurt. 83
Pillemer, David B. 49–53, 145,
Pohl, Rüdiger F. 73
Porter, Stephen 66
Posner, M. I. 77 n. 15
Postma, Albert 34 n. 13
Potter, Jonathon 18–19
Pressley, Michael 50 n. 8
Raichle, M. E. 77 n. 15
Rajan, Mahesh N. 74
Read, J. Don 33 n. 11, 64–65, 78, 78 n. 18
Reardon, Kathleen K. 52–53 n. 13

Reckers, Philip M. J. 74
Redman, Judith C. S. 153
Reed, Jonathan L. 199, 203 n. 16
Reicke, Bo 190 n. 1
Reisberg, Daniel 58
Reyna, V. F. 61, 62, 167
Reysen, Matthew B. 70 n. 9, 154 n. 12
Riecken, Henry W. 108, 109 n. 8
Riesenfeld, Harald 110–11, 114, 120, 182, n. 14
Riesner, Rainer 1, 98–99, 113, 113 n. 11, 114, 114 nn. 12–13, 120, 168, 189, 189 n. 1
Riniolo, Todd C. 14 n. 5
Robbins, Joyce 82 n. 2
Robinson, John A. 50 n. 8
Robinson, John A. T. 190 n. 1
Rodler, Christa 74
Rodríguez, Rafael 108, 157 n. 14, 182 n. 14
Roediger III, Henry L. 60–61, 61 n. 1, 63, 67, 69, 69 n. 8, 70, 78
Rolls, Edmund T. 77
Rose, Steven 67–68, 68 n. 6, 77, 77 n. 15, 79 n. 20
Rosenbloom, Paul S. 29
Rovee-Collier, Carolyn 51 n. 9
Rubin, David C. 7, 45, 167
Sachs, Jacqueline Strunk 167
Safer, Martin A. 73
Schachter, Stanley 108, 109 n. 8
Schacter, Daniel L. 21, 22 n. 1, 71, 76–78, 78 n. 17
Scheidel, Walter 191, 191 nn. 3–4, 192
Schlagman, Simone 34 n. 12, 44 n. 2
Schmolck, H. 47–48 n. 6
Schneider, Walter 76, 76 n. 13
Schneider, Wolfgang 50 n. 8
Schnelle, Udo 1, 189–90 n. 1
Schröter, Jens 150 n. 8
Schooler, Jonathan W. 50 n. 7, 146 n. 2
Schubotz, Ricarda I. 77 n. 16
Schudson, Michael 88 n. 9, 108
Schulz, Joerg 34 n. 12
Schuman, Howard 84–86

INDEX OF MODERN AUTHORS

Schürmann, Heinz 168
Schwartz, Barry 87 n. 8, 89, 89 n. 11, 90–91, 91 n. 13, 160
Schwarz, Stefan 73
Scott, Jacqueline 84, 85 n. 4, 86
Scott, Paul K. 56
Sczesny, Sabine 73
Seamon, John G. 61 n. 2, 63
Semb, George B. 40 n. 20
Shanks, Hershel 205
Shapiro, Lauren R. 46 n. 4
Sibley, Robert E. 74
Skowronski, John J. 70 n. 9
Sligo, Frank 74
Sloddin, Caitlin 83
Slotki, Israel W. 166 n. 6
Smith, Alison C. 74
Smith, Marilyn C. 50 n. 8
Smith, Mark S. 83
Sonntag, Flavia 192
Southwick, Steven M. 52 n. 12, 57 n. 15
Squire, L. R. 47–48 n. 6
Stahlberg, Dagmar 73
Stanhope, Nicola 37
Stark, Rodney 181, 208
Stein, Shelly K. 56
Stirton, Nicole 74
Stohl, Cynthia 52, 53 n. 13
Strack, Fritz 75 n. 12
Strickland, Sarah E. 61 n. 2, 63
Suroweicki, James 70 n. 10
Tagler, Michael J. 73
Takahashi, Masanobu 70 n. 10
Talarico, Jennifer M. 45
Tannehill, Robert C. 132, 134–35 n. 12
Thomas, Ayanna K. 63
Thomas III, Robert L. 70
Thomsen, Dorthe K. 52 n. 12, 53, 54 n. 14
Torgeé, Hagit 192
Tree, Jean E. Fox 104, 104 n. 4
Trevor-Roper, Hugh 105, 105 n. 5
Tubb, V. Anne 11
Tulving, E. 76, 76 n. 14
Turtle, John W. 11–12, 12 n. 3

Van der Lubbe, Rob H. J. 34 n. 13
Vannucci, Manila 79
Wade, Kimberly A. 64–65, 78, 78 n. 18
Wagenaar, Willem A. 30–35, 55–56, 65–66
Wagner, Anthony D. 76
Ward, Benedicta 133, 133 nn. 7–8
Watson, Jason M. 61, 61 n. 1, 63
Watt, Ian 91–92
Weigold, Arne 70, 70 n. 10
Weldon, Mary Susan 70, 104, 104 n. 4
Wells, Gary L. 11–12, 12 n. 3, 73
Wenham, John. 190 n. 1
Wenner, Jennifer A. 51 n. 9
Werth, Lioba 75 n. 12
Wewerka, Sandi S. 51 n. 9
White, Richard T. 30, 33–34 n. 12
Wickelgren, Wayne A. 28 n. 6
Wickham, Chris 79 n. 19, 83, 94 n. 14
Widner Jr., Robert L. 33 n. 11
Wilcox-O'Hearn, L. Amber 50 n. 8
Wilkinson, James 94 n. 14
Wilson, Kevin 66
Winger, Michael 131
Winningham, Robert G. 48
Wittlinger, R. P. 37–38
Wixted, John T. 25–30
Woulfin, Jeffrey R. 61 n. 2, 63
Wright, Ron 62
Yamauchi, Edwin M. 191–92 n. 6
Yang, Song 83
Yang, Y. 62
Yuille, John C. 12, 13 n. 4, 14–15, 15 n. 6, 22
Zac, Lilian 85 n. 4
Zaragoza, Maria S. 66–67
Zerubavel, Yael 90 n. 12
Zimmermann, Ruben 174 n. 10

Subject Index

abstract canonical categories, 42, 46, 54, 145 n. 1
aphorisms, 176, 176 n. 11, 177–80, 182, 187
Akiba, Rabbi, 166, 166 n. 5
apophthegmata, 131–35, 137–38, 140–41, 170, 187
Bahrick, Harry P., 35–38, 40
Bailey, Kenneth 98–99, 115–17, 120
Bauckham, Richard, 5–9, 20, 134 n. 10, 153
Baum, Armin, 114
bias, 21–22, 59–60, 71, 74–75, 78, 97, 143, 158. *See also* hindsight bias *and* consistency and change bias
Brown, Robert, 41–46, 48–49, 54, 145, 145–46 n. 1
Bultmann, Rudolph, 98–99, 99–100 n. 1, 100 n. 2, 100–103, 105, 109–10, 115, 120, 134, 134 nn. 10–11, 134–35 n. 12, 157, 174, 182–83, 186
Burnaby, Vancouver, 12, 20, 124, 160
Challenger disaster, 46
chreiai. *See* apophthegmata
Coale, Ansley J. *See* life tables
collective memory. *See* memory, collective
confabulation, 99, 103–5, 108–9
consistency and change bias, 74–75
Crossan, John Dominic, 8–9, 20, 176 n. 11
Dean, John, 16–20, 71 n. 11, 124. *See also* testimony, John Dean's
Deese, Roediger, and McDermott false memory procedure (DRM), 60–63, 70 n. 10, 153–54, 156, 170. *See also* memory, false
Demeny, Paul. *See* life tables
demographics
    Capernaum, 203, 203 n. 16, 204–5, 208–9
    Jerusalem, 205, 208
    Roman Empire, 193–96, 198–99, 202
Dibelius, Martin, 98–99, 101 n. 3, 101–3, 105, 109–10, 115, 120, 134–35 n. 12, 157, 182
dual trace theory. *See* fuzzy-trace theory
Dunn, James D. G. 22, 98–99, 115, 117, 117 n. 15, 118, 118 nn. 16–17, 119, 119 nn. 18–19, 120–21, 151–52 n. 9
Ebbinghaus, Hermann, 23–28, 39
Ebbinghausian curve of forgetting, 34–35, 39–40, 144, 183
eyewitness memory, 6, 123–31, 143–44, 147, 155, 157, 160–61, 183, 190 n. 2. *See also* eyewitness testimony
eyewitness testimony, 5–12, 124, 126, 153, 160, 186. *See also* eyewitness memory
eyewitness traditions, characteristics of written texts derived from, 123–25
eyewitnesses to Jesus' life and ministry, 202–9
flashbulb memory. *See* memory, flashbulb
forgetting curves, 23, 34–35, 45 n. 3
Frier life table, 196–97, 205–7
fuzzy-trace theory, 61–63
Gadarene demoniac(s), 155
Gerasene demoniac(s). *See* Gadarene demoniac(s)

-239-

Gerhardsson, Birger, 98–99, 111, 111 n. 9, 112, 112 n. 10, 113–14, 120–21, 166 n. 5, 170, 176

gist. *See* memory, gist

Gospels, Date of, 1, 189 n.1

Gospels traditions
and hindsight bias, 158–60
and transience, 145–53
and suggestibility, 153–56

gun shop robbery. *See* Burnaby, Vancouver

Gurkas, war with British, 71–73

hindsight bias, 71–75, 77, 79–80, 160, 170, 183–85. *See also* bias

Jesus, as teacher, 110–11, 113–15, 163–64, 167–70, 184–85

Kelber, Werner, 8–9, 170–71

Kennedy, John F., assassination, 41–42, 44, 49, 85, 85 n. 4, 86

Kulik, James, 41–46, 48–49, 54, 145, 145–46 n. 1

leading questions, 154

life expectancy, 189–91, 191–92 n. 6, 192–93, 195, 198–99, 202

life tables, 192–209.
Coale-Demeny life tables, 195, 198, 198 n. 14, 199, 202–3, 205–7
Frier life table, 196–97, 202–3, 205–7
Ulpian life table, 192–97

Lincoln, Abraham, 89–91, 93, 107

Masada, 88, 93

Mauritius, demographics of, 193–94, 196

memories as reconstruction, 76–80

memory
collective, 82–84, 86–94, 97–99, 102–3, 105–10, 113, 120–21, 128, 130, 135, 137, 157–58, 160, 163, 168–69, 182–86
communal. *See* memory, collective
declarative. *See* declarative memory
directives, 52–53
episodic, 34, 76, 123–24, 144, 147
everyday, 45
false, 59, 153–54, 65, 65 n. 5, 66, 70, 78, 154–56, 170. *See also* Deese,
Roediger, and McDermott false memory procedure (DRM)
flashbulb, 41–50, 53–54, 57–58, 58 n. 16, 145, 145–46 n. 1, 146, 146 n. 2, 147, 185
frailties 21–22. *See also* transience, bias, suggestibility
functions, 77, 79
gist, 18 n. 8, 19, 58, 58 n. 17, 61–63, 105, 137, 141, 147, 152 n. 10, 160–61, 167, 171–75, 177–79
influence of the present on collective, 87
loss, rates of, 29–40
personal event. *See* personal event memories
procedural, 76
reliability, 44–57
semantic, 76
social contagion of. *See* social contagion of memory
stable after first five years, 39–40, 149
subsystems 76–77
verbatim, 61–63, 165, 167, 178, 180
very long-term, 36–40

Münsterberg, Hugo, 10–11

oral societies, 91–93. *See also* oral traditions

oral traditions, 115–120, 141, 185. *See also* oral societies

Parables, 170–76

Pentecost, 169

pericope form, 125, 127, 127 n. 3, 130, 147, 157

personal event memories, 41–58, 126, 144–47, 149, 183

photos used in memory experiments, 64, 67, 69, 78

Pillemer, David, 49–53, 145, 145–46 n. 1, 146

preaching, 102

Poemen, Abba 133, 133 n. 7

Reliability of long-term human memory 53–57

retention curves, 32–33

Riesenfeld, Harald, 110–111, 114, 120
Riesner, Rainer, 1, 98–99, 113, 113 n. 11, 114, 114 nn. 12–13, 120, 168, 189, 189 n. 1
September 11 attacks, 44–45
social contagion of memory, 68–70
source documents, 148–149, 152
Spanish language study, 35–37, 40
suggestibility, 21–22, 59–70, 80, 97, 130, 143, 157, 160, 183–85

tradition, streams of, 169
transience, 21–22, 59, 97, 143–45, 147–48, 153, 160, 183–84
testimony, John Dean's, 16–20, 124
Ulpian. *See* life tables
verbatim memorization. *See* memory, verbatim
Wagenaar, Willem, A., 30–35, 123

www.ingramcontent.com/pod-product-compliance
Lightning Source LLC
Chambersburg PA
CBHW021807220426
43662CB00006B/214